D1242336

TURIN SHROUD

Lynn Picknett and Clive Prince

TURIN SHROUD

IN WHOSE IMAGE?

THE TRUTH BEHIND THE CENTURIES-LONG

CONSPIRACY OF SILENCE

HarperCollins*Publishers*

For John

'Miserable mortals, open your eyes'
LEONARDO DA VINCI
(1452-1519)

Note: Anyone wishing to add to the information in this book, or to book us to give a lecture on the subjects raised in it, please write to Lynn Picknett and Clive Prince at: 84 Marylebone High Street, London W1M 3DE. If you want us to reply, please enclose a stamped addressed envelope and have patience!

Credits for illustrations appear on page vi.

This book was published in Great Britain in 1994 by Bloomsbury Publishing, Ltd.

HarperCollins books may be purchased for educational, business, or sales promotional use. For information please write: Special Markets Department, HarperCollins Publishers, Inc., 10 East 53rd Street, New York, NY 10022.

FIRST U.S. EDITION

ISBN 0-06-017224-X

94 95 96 97 98 HC 10 9 8 7 6 5 4 3 2 1

CONTENTS

———————

ILLUSTRATIONS

ACKNOWLEDGEMENTS

We would like to thank:

Keith Prince, for his commitment to the replication experiments, his unfailing support and often remarkable inspiration. We could not have done it without him.

Craig Oakley, for his unswerving loyalty, good humour and frequently unorthodox ideas.

Andy Haveland-Robinson, for his dedication to this book and his long and arduous hours in front of a computer on its behalf. The incisiveness of his analysis was essential to the development of our hypothesis.

Lavinia Trevor, our agent, who although she came to this book late in its career, has encouraged and cheered its progress enormously.

Abigail Nevill, whose original comment on 'Shroudman' put us on the right track. Out of the mouths of babes . . .

Graham Hancock, whose work proved such an invaluable background for this book.

Vida Adamoli, for energetically translating all that Italian for us – and incidentally giving many other diners something to talk about!

A. N. Wilson and Ysenda Maxtone Graham, for the *London Evening Standard* article that really got us noticed.

Amanda Nevill, of the Royal Photographic Society, for her spirited support and advice from the very earliest days, and for the original intuition that led her to have a replica of the Shroud in the exhibition 'The Unexplained' (and for being the mother of Abigail).

Michael Austin, past President of the RPS, for his extremely incisive comments that proved very fruitful in our work.

Ian Dickinson, who, although sceptical about our hypothesis, has always supported us against hostility, prejudice and corruption, often with great inconvenience to himself. His information proved invaluable.

Mark Bennett, for his professional help, comment and advice – and thanks too for the rare videos of the 1970s Italian *Leonardo* television series.

Lillian and Jack Schwartz, for their suggestions and their hospitality.

Bill Homer, H. Rodney Sharp Professor of Art History, University of Delaware, and his wife Christine, for their advice on Leonardo the artist and their interest in our work, which we value very highly.

Marcel Martineau, who taught us so much and was a model of understanding about our difficulties with French vowels – and for his spectacular hospitality in the shadow of Montségur at wine-tasting time.

Joe Nickell, for his swift reply to our letters and for his useful information.

Clive Bull and Michael van Straten at LBC, for giving us so much air-time on this subject over the last few years and to John Sugar at BBC World Service for the invitation that may well have really started something, albeit unintentionally.

Sarah Litvinoff, whose commonsense, friendship and food has got us through many a problematic patch. Thanks for being 'family'.

Mary Aver, who saw it coming.

Mary Saxe-Falstein, for her unusual skills and insights, and for her endless and elegant hospitality.

Simon Gluckman, James Dew and Barry Grayson – three men who, although they do not know each other and live in different parts of the world, have each contributed to this project with their unfailing good cheer and belief in it. Their conversation was always a sure tonic on days when problems seemed overwhelming, and their sense of the absurd got us back on the right track.

Tony Pritchett, for his practical help and support.

The staff at Westminster Reference Library, for their tireless help in chasing the elusive and the esoteric.

Kathy Rooney at Bloomsbury for snapping us up so quickly and keeping us up to the mark throughout. And to her colleagues Becky Shaw, Deirdre Brown and Kate Quarry for their patience in seeing this often difficult project through to the end.

Jane Lyle, for the amenities, spirited help and laughter, 'on the street where you live'.

Sally 'Morgana' Morgan, for her interesting energies.

And thanks are also due to the following for their help, support and encouragement:

Sue Prince; Charles and Annette Fowkes; Dr Chris French; Vicki Thomas; Steve Pear and Jacqueline McMullen; Alan Wills; Nicole Hartley; Joanne Dalton; Maria O'Donnell; Lesley Manuel; Jonathan Chernett; Barbara Cann; Steve Wilson and Caroline Wise; Tim Haigh; Roger Brown and Adrian Warren; Katie Boyd; Michael Carson; Peter Tilbury; Andrew Collins; Lionel Beer; Melvyn Willin; Guy Lyon Playfair; Bob Rickard and Paul Sieveking at *Fortean Times*; Alison Cochran; Anne Evans; Jane Garton; Penny Thornton; Kate Glass; Ken Seddington; Helen Scott; Trevor Poots; 'Giovanni'; Will Fowler; Lorna Giles; Sheila and Eric Taylor; Amanda Harman; Frank Smyth; Jim Cochrane; Derek Newton; Barry Johnstone; Oscar Tipton; Ian Dougan; Barbara Russell; Dr Carl Sargent; Henry Lincoln; Gareth Medway; Helen Moss; J. B.; Nix Picasso and Ronnie Paris.

And, of course, thanks are due to the *late* Leonardo da Vinci, the fruits of whose tormented genius can still provide modern sophisticates with a few surprises.

INTRODUCTION

We can remember the news quite clearly: it was revealed on 13 October 1988 that the Turin Shroud had been carbon dated and it was not, as had been widely believed, 2000 years old at all, but instead dated from between 1260 and 1390. The item even made it on to the BBC's evening news, at the end as a tail-piece. This indicated that it was a fake, but was it really all over for the Shroud?

To many believers it was certainly not the end of their fight to have that vexed piece of cloth given its due honour as the true winding sheet of Jesus. To us it was the beginning of a strange and fraught quest that was to lead us to the conclusions, odd and shocking though they may seem, which are set out in this book.

We have been shocked. It is not a cosy story, and its implications are so far-reaching that many things we all hold most dear are implicitly overturned by it. But, to us, by far the most shocking aspect of our research has been the astonishing fragility of the Shroud establishment's capacity for tolerance, decency and honesty. We have been pilloried, libelled and physically manhandled by men whose alleged byword was Christianity.

We have obviously ruffled more than a few feathers – something that we do not crow about, for we did not set out to do that, and see no intrinsic value in being iconoclastic for its own sake. But it is axiomatic that such outrage is usually in direct ratio to the fear that is felt; our opponents are terrified that we are right. We believe we are. Although our conclusions disagree with theirs, we cannot deny that our research would have been impossible without the sterling work of others interested in the Shroud, notably STURP (the Shroud of Turin Research Project Inc) and other scientists.

Inevitably there will be those who find some of our dealings, as described in this book, somewhat fanciful. We sympathize – to begin with we thought so too. Yet we are living proof that truth is stranger than fiction, and life has some very quirky little ways indeed.

Now that this book is finished we can look back upon the last four-and-a-half years with amazement, but the strange thing is that

the Turin Shroud itself almost fades into the background. The Shroud
was, for us, merely the way into something much, much wider in scope,
for we have discovered the real reason why some of the world's secret
societies have been quite so secret for so long. A branch of one such
group has indicated that the world may be ready for some of its most
cherished secrets; we hope they are right.[1]

Lynn Picknett and Clive Prince
London
17 January 1994

— 1 —

MORE QUESTIONS THAN ANSWERS

'The Shroud of Turin is either the most awesome and instructive relic of Jesus Christ in existence . . . or it is one of the most ingenious, most unbelievably clever, products of the human mind and hand on record; there is no middle ground.'

John Walsh, *The Shroud* (1963)

THE MODERN Italian city of Turin is a sprawling industrial conurbation, a concrete hymn to the internal combustion engine. Yet it also is a place of pilgrimage, as it has been for many years – for Turin houses what has long been regarded as the most precious, inspiring and awesome of all Christian relics: the Holy Shroud of Jesus, miraculously imprinted with his image.

Pilgrims go, as they have always gone, to Turin Cathedral – dedicated to St John the Baptist – wherein the sacred artefact lies, safely ensconced behind two locked iron grilles above the altar of the Royal Chapel. It is kept inside three locked containers: a wooden case, an asbestos-covered iron chest, and a silver-decorated wooden casket. There are three key-holders for the inner grille.[1]

These elaborate measures are undoubtedly primarily for reasons of security; there have been attempts to steal the Shroud, and the 'kidnapping' of relics for enormous ransoms is a common crime in Italy today. But beyond this practical purpose there is more than a hint of the obsessive secrecy with which the Shroud is customarily invested by the Church authorities; whether this is because the object is uniquely holy, or because of less laudable, more sinister reasons, must remain a matter of personal belief and conjecture.

Inside its casket, the Shroud is rolled around a velvet-covered staff and wrapped in red silk. It has a backing of Holland cloth, which was added in 1532 after it was damaged in a fire.

It has been kept in this way since 1694, when the black marble Royal Chapel was built for the ruling Savoy family who have owned it for most of its known history. They acquired it in the mid-fifteenth century, and kept possession until 1983, when the exiled King Umberto II died, bequeathing it to the Vatican.

Although you may visit exhibitions about the Shroud – both in the cathedral itself and elsewhere in Turin – you may not look at the real thing. It is hidden from sight except for the rare occasions when it is removed to be shown to a distinguished visitor (such as Pope John Paul II in April 1980). Public expositions are very rare, happening approximately once a generation. This century it has been exhibited just three times: in 1931, for the wedding of the future King Umberto II (then Prince of Piedmont); the Holy Year of 1933; and in 1978, to commemorate the 400th anniversary of its arrival in Turin. It was also shown on television in 1973. Last century it was shown five times.

Perhaps because of the rarity of its showing, expositions cause great excitement among the faithful. In 1978, it was shown for forty-two days, and well over 3 million pilgrims filed past its bullet-proof glass case. But just what is it that has such potent appeal? What did all those pilgrims see? What is the Turin Shroud?[2]

It is a length of pale biscuit-coloured linen, 4.4m by 1.9m with an additional 8cm strip on its left-hand side. It bears various folds and blemishes accrued throughout its long life. Most conspicuous are the marks of the 1532 fire, which burned through one corner of the cloth (which was then kept folded), damaging it in several places, notably through the shoulders of the image. The burn-holes (fourteen large ones and eight small ones) have been repaired with patches of altar cloth, blackened areas still clearly visible around them. There are other isolated burns from specks of molten silver from the same fire.

There are also four sets of three round burn-holes dating from before the 1532 fire – they can be seen in earlier copies – which are generally known as 'poker marks', because that is what they are widely thought to have been. The four sets line up when the cloth is folded, proving that they were made at the same time, possibly in an attempt to test the Shroud's authenticity by subjecting it to 'trial by fire'. One wonders what conclusion the poker-wielding vandals came to after the cloth burnt in the normal way. A less melodramatic explanation might be that the 'poker holes' were caused by a dripping torch.[3]

The burn marks, whatever their provenance, are, however, not the reason that the pilgrim looks upon the Shroud. It is to the image that all eyes are drawn, and upon which all devout hearts feast, for is it not truly the image of the Lord Jesus Christ?

Down the centre of the cloth, taking up nearly 4m of its total length are two images showing the front and back of a naked, well-proportioned man, 'hinged' at the head. The cloth is believed to be a winding sheet, which means the corpse would have been laid on one half, and his front covered over with the other.

The man is bearded, with very long hair hanging down past the shoulders at the back, and stopping at shoulder-length at the front. The hands are crossed modestly over the loins. The sole of one foot, dreadfully darkened with what appears to be blood, is clearly outlined on the image of the back.

The eye is drawn unmercifully to dark lines and splotches on the body; apparently blood from several atrocious wounds. There are small, pierced wounds on the head, and a round one on the only visible wrist – as if a nail had been driven through it. There is a wound as if from a large stab in the chest, blood from which also runs across the small of the back, and there are small flows of blood on the front of both feet and much more on the sole of one foot. The face appears to be swollen and contused, and over 100 scourge marks have been counted on the back, wounds that also curl around the front of the body and legs.

Obviously, judging by these horrific marks the man on the Shroud was – or was supposed to be – Jesus Christ.

There are millions in the world who still believe in the sanctity of the man on the Shroud. At the forefront of the faithful is the international Shroud community, or 'sindonologists' (from the Greek *sindon*, a shroud), but who are known with more or less affection as 'Shroudies'.

Of the many organizations formed to study the Shroud throughout the world, most are overtly religious and primarily concerned with the 'message' of the cloth, such as the Holy Shroud Guild of the USA. Others were founded with – supposedly – more objective and scientific principles in mind, such as the Shroud of Turin Research Project Inc (STURP) in the USA, the Centro Internazionale di Sindonologia in Turin itself, CIELT in France (Centre International d'Études sur le Linceul de Turin), and the British Society for the Turin Shroud (BSTS) in the UK.

Over the years there have been dozens of books, pamphlets and articles written about the Shroud, and the above groups regularly add to the literature with their own publications, the most important being *Sindon* (published by the Centro Internazionale di Sindinologia) and *Shroud Spectrum International*, edited and published by Dorothy Crispino of the Indiana Centre for Shroud Studies, USA.

Despite a characteristic reluctance on the part of the Savoys and the Church authorities to release part or all of the cloth for scientific research, it has nevertheless been subjected to such scrutiny several times. Experts from many different disciplines have been involved in studying the Shroud; historians, textile specialists, physicists, chemists, photographers, artists, art historians, anatomists, surgeons and forensic scientists – even botanists. It has been subjected to a whole host of tests, including x-ray photographs, infrared light and ultraviolet light, examination under a microscope, ultraviolet spectrophotometry, infrared spectroscopy and x-ray fluorescence. Samples have been taken and given a variety of chemical tests.

Despite all this, the Shroud has steadfastly refused to give up its secrets, although many clues have surfaced.

It must be remembered that serious interest in the cloth is less than a century old. It had previously been viewed as a curiosity because the image is too faint to make out clearly with the naked eye; the body seems impossibly tall and thin, and the eyes look positively owl-like as if the man were wearing dark glasses.

But in 1898 a lawyer from Turin was asked to take the first photographs of the Shroud. Secondo Pia was a keen amateur photographer and local councillor. The Shroud was being displayed as part of the festivities to mark the fiftieth anniversary of Italy at the time, and this seemed a fitting and unique addition to the celebrations.[4]

Pia took ten photographs altogether (although it was thought until recently that he only took two),[5] and they were undoubtedly the most significant of his career. For, seen in photographic negative for the first time the image suddenly shot into focus. Instead of a vague outline of a bearded man, there is a massively detailed photograph of a terribly wounded, terribly real body.

It is a horrific, graphic catalogue of the art of crucifixion; every nail-hole, every lash of the Roman scourge cries out for our compassion. We are looking at the brutal proof of man's inhumanity to man writ large – but perhaps, even given the evidence of our own eyes, we would be making too many assumptions by immediately supposing that the man were actually Jesus Christ.

Yet all eyes are drawn to the face of the man on the Shroud. Long, lean and bearded, with a prominent and long nose (which may even be broken), it is a face of rather gaunt dignity. More, to many it is a face of stunning and memorable beauty, its very serenity revealing a triumph over the worst of deaths.

Small wonder that Secondo Pia was one of many to look on the face of the man on the Shroud and become transfixed. Hitherto an unpersuaded churchgoer, the Turin worthy abruptly took to his religion with a passion. For surely this image, this torn and tortured man, could be no other than Jesus himself. The power of the Shroud is never to be underestimated.

Others also reacted quickly to the photographic image. It was now increasingly hard to dismiss the cloth as a crude medieval forgery, for several reasons.

No artist could have created what is known as the 'negative effect' (indeed, several abortive attempts have been made to replicate the image using standard artistic techniques).[6] And no known medieval artist had either the skill or the anatomical knowledge needed to create such an image; besides, realism was not part of their artistic canon.[7]

For much of the century between Pia's discovery and the present day, researchers have had to be content with those photographs plus a second set taken by Giuseppe Enrie in 1931.[8] It was not until 1969 that the Church allowed hands-on investigation of the cloth itself, so as a result they had to confine their studies to the physiology of the man on the Shroud and speculations about what kind of process might have caused the image, with its spectacular negative effect.

Enrie's photographs – generally deemed to be superior to Pia's – included several close-ups of different areas of the cloth, of good enough quality to be blown up. These were seized on for detailed study of the cloth, the image and the bloodstains.

Later landmark studies included those of Paul Vignon, a wealthy French biologist and friend of the future Pope Pius XI who attempted to replicate the image-forming process.[9] Another notable early Shroudie was the Parisian anatomist and surgeon Pierre Barbet, who in the 1930s devoted himself to studying the effects of crucifixion, using corpses.[10] Although both men's work has a lasting interest, neither actually cracked the code of the Turin Shroud.

Then in 1969, Cardinal Michele Pellegrino, Archbishop of Turin, assembled a team of experts from various disciplines, to report on the state of preservation of the Shroud; the team usually referred to as the Turin Commission.

The 1969 examinations were a preliminary investigation only; further tests were recommended, and were carried out four years later, the day after the Shroud was exhibited on live television on 23 November 1973. It was on this occasion that Swiss criminologist Dr Max Frei took his now famous pollen samples (see below), and when for the first time strips, approximately 40mm × 10mm, were taken from the main cloth and its side strip, plus fifteen individual threads from both image and non-image areas.[11]

Curiously – but characteristically – the work of the Turin Commission was carried out in strict secrecy. There seems to be no obvious reason why. When rumours of the 1973 tests leaked out, the authorities denied that anything more than a routine examination had taken place. Only in 1976 was it admitted that the cloth had been tested, and those who had carried out the tests were named. This information was even withheld from King Umberto, the Shroud's legal owner.

The 1970s saw a quickening of scientific interest in the Shroud, particularly in the USA. In 1977 two key bodies were founded: the BSTS in the UK, and in the USA, following a conference on the Shroud held in Albuquerque, New Mexico, STURP. This last organization went on to conduct the most extensive tests yet on the cloth, in 1978.

It was a major year for Shroud studies. The Shroud was exhibited to the public between 26 August and 8 October, which led to a wave of popular interest, prompting several books on the subject to be published. Most notably, Ian Wilson's masterly *The Turin Shroud* was hailed as a significant breakthrough in making the Shroud a household name, and became an international bestseller.[12] There was also the BAFTA-award-winning documentary film *The Silent Witness* by Henry Lincoln (later co-author of *The Holy Blood and the Holy Grail*, published in 1982), from an idea by Ian Wilson.[13] The book and film between them raised the profile of the Shroud among Catholics and non-Catholics alike; the cloth became a topical point of discussion among people everywhere in Christendom, and the face of the man on the Shroud looked out from thousands of bookshop windows, with the haunting appeal of its curious serenity, straight into millions of faces – and perhaps, secretly, into as many hearts.

Wilson's contribution to Shroud studies should never be underestimated. Driven by an inner certainty that the cloth was indeed the winding sheet of Jesus Christ, he rarely allows that view to show too obviously in *The Turin Shroud*, and argues with intelligence and style – if little conviction – that there may be other explanations for its origins. To this day, his public pronouncements on the Shroud are models of reason and balance, but perhaps it would be naive in the extreme to be too swayed by such an appearance of objectivity. His original script for *The Silent Witness* was entitled *He Is Risen: The Story of the Holy Shroud of Christ*.[14]

But for those of a strictly scientific bent, the most important event of 1978 was STURP's series of tests, undertaken in conjunction with a small team of Italian scientists and Max Frei. For five days immediately following the October exposition, STURP was allowed full access to the Shroud, and even to take samples for later analysis.[15]

STURP's primary objective was to discover what the image was made of, and whether or not it was of human manufacture. Despite all their efforts, however, they failed.

They examined it under x-rays, infrared light and ultraviolet light, as well as by more conventional methods such as microscopy. Samples were taken by the simple expedient of sticking adhesive tape to the cloth and testing the loose threads that came away with it. Most of these tests were designed to reveal the presence of artificial pigments. In all, they spent more than 100,000 hours analyzing the data, and the whole project cost around $5,000,000.

The conditions were far from ideal: STURP had effectively to take the laboratory to the Shroud and not vice versa, and there was a strict time limit which meant that something could have been missed – so by the very nature of its work, it could not be checked as the tests could not be repeated.

Only one of STURP's proposed tests was rejected by the Church authorities. STURP had wanted to radiocarbon date the cloth, the ultimate test of its authenticity. The Church feared that a large portion of cloth would be destroyed in the test, and permission was not granted. However, it was pointed out to the Church authorities that samples already taken by the Turin Commission in 1973 would do perfectly well for the purpose. On hearing this, they demanded that the samples be returned, whereupon they were locked up in Turin Cathedral. When they were loaned out to STURP in 1979 a legal document prevented the fragments from being carbon dated.[16]

Eventually, however, the Church ran out of excuses and had to give in to the pressure. In October 1986 Pope John Paul II, after a meeting of representatives of seven laboratories (later reduced to three to minimize danger to the cloth) with the Pontifical Academy of Sciences in Turin, gave his approval to the tests – if not exactly his blessing.[17]

The principle of carbon dating is this: carbon-14 is a radioactive form of carbon which is produced in the upper atmosphere by the action of cosmic rays. It is absorbed by all organisms and can be detected in them. The rate of absorption is constant during that organism's life, and when it dies, the carbon-14 decays over a great length of time and at a constant rate. The carbon dating process measures the amount of carbon-14 in a given sample; as the amount that would have been present in the living organism can be calculated, the difference between that and the existing amount shows the age of the sample.

It was only after intensive lobbying from several interested parties – including Ian Wilson – that the Vatican finally gave permission for the cloth to be carbon dated. Three laboratories were involved: the University of Arizona in Tucson, the Oxford Research Laboratory, and the Swiss Federal Institute of Technology in Zürich. Professor Teddy Hall of Oxford was appointed as spokesman.

Typical Church secrecy surrounded the taking of samples; although officially scheduled for 23 April 1988, the event was switched, with little warning, to 4 am, 21 April, when the Italian President was in Turin, diverting Press interest. Representatives from each of the laboratories, including Teddy Hall, were present, and the operation was overseen by Michael Tite of the British Museum Research Laboratory.

A 7cm piece was cut from one corner, and in turn three samples were cut from that. They were sealed in special containers, along with control samples, and one was given to each of the laboratory representatives. The whole process was videotaped.

The results of the carbon dating were released on 13 October 1988, although they had already been 'leaked' beforehand. (This was the tenth anniversary of the final day of STURP's examination). They were first announced by the Shroud's custodian, Cardinal Anastasio Ballestrero in Turin, and later that day by Dr Tite at a Press conference at the British Museum.[18]

The carbon dating showed that it was 99.9 per cent certain that it originated from the period 1000 to 1500, and 95 per cent certain that the cloth dated from between 1260 and 1390.

The Holy Shroud of Turin was a fake.

To say believers in the Shroud's authenticity were plunged into a state of shock is to put it mildly; their very world was being hammered by the iron fist of a too brutal reality. The Shroud was so much more than a mere relic to them; it was the perfect and unique reminder of their Lord, and absolute proof of his holy, redemptive death. The deathly hush of shock spread throughout the Shroud community, its fragility being reinforced by Professor Hall's insensitive comment to the Press: 'Somebody just got a piece of cloth, faked it and flogged it. I don't think the Shroud of Turin is of much interest any longer.'[19]

The Church did not pronounce officially on this result, but appeared to profit by its Jesuitical streak when Professor Luigi Gonella, scientific advisor to the Vatican, said: 'The tests were not commissioned by the Church and we are not bound by the results.'[20]

Almost immediately rumours began to circulate about conspiracies among the researchers, and the cream of the Shroudies, including Ian Wilson, began to issue statements that typically included such phrases as, 'While we have the greatest regard for scientific testing . . .' Their implication was that carbon dating could be wrong, terribly wrong, and that this had been the case where the Shroud was concerned.

Sceptics whooped with joy and more than a touch of 'I told you so', while the believers licked their wounds. Of course some merely left the Shroudie world without a backward glance, granite-faced with disappointment. Others were angry at being taken for a ride, at being duped at their most vulnerable level, that of religious faith – but who could they blame except the unknown medieval hoaxer? Those whose sole concern was to believe at all costs and damn-the-evidence began to regroup, although not without a huge loss of credibility.

The full significance of the test results was not lost on them; for the dates they had suggested pinpointed exactly the same period in history as that when a Holy Shroud first appeared, unannounced. To many Shroudies, this happy coincidence was deeply suspicious.

The post carbon dating world of the Shroudies was very different from that which preceded the announcement of 13 October 1988.

For the Shroudies, the worst thing about the carbon dating was the ridicule. Cartoons began to appear, and jokes about it crept into television programmes, such as the irreverent satirical show, *Spitting Image*. The full-length transparency of the Shroud was later to figure in the British Museum's exhibition 'Fake: the Act of Deception'. When Ian Wilson gave a talk to the Wrekin Trust on 5 November 1988, and was introduced as 'being best known for his book *The Turin Shroud*' the large audience of respectable, intelligent people laughed. He may have smiled back, but one does not have to try too hard to understand his feelings.

It is at this point that our own story really begins, for it was the carbon dating that proved an irresistible challenge to us. I (Lynn) had been fascinated by the Shroud since reading Wilson's book, taking the rather vague line that the cloth may have accidentally been imprinted with an image through some form of energy release that would remain unknown, but that this phenomenon did not in itself prove that the cloth was Jesus' winding-sheet.

Clive had also been interested in the Shroud, although again, from the point of view of its value as an anomalous phenomenon. To both of us (we had known each other for years), the carbon dating simply added to its fascination.

We found ourselves rather ironically going along with the believers. It seemed to us to be outrageous to dismiss the Shroud totally, overnight. There were an enormous number of questions to be answered – more, in fact, now it had been shown to be a fake. What about the negative effect? If it was a painting, as the carbon dating implied, then where was the paint? Had the man whose image it bore actually been crucified? And if he had been, who was the unhappy model? And what medieval faker had the skill, the brains – and the nerve – to have created such a shocking joke for posterity?

Above all else, there was a sense of shock involved, even for those like us, whose spiritual centre had not been violated. This was no crudely botched daub; this was no relic that would blend in seamlessly with the tons of fake splinters from the 'True Cross'. You could not even rightly call it a 'work of art', for whatever art was involved in its creation was totally unknown.

As a fake, the Shroud of Turin had become the ultimate heretical relic, something created with a kind of perverse love for the job, an incredible eye for detail and a skill that was matchless throughout history. If you could stomach the implications, it was nothing short of wonderful.

Clive and I were hooked.

Yet here I must add a personal note which, despite rumours to the contrary, I wish I did not have to. Unfortunately, however, it is more than a little germane to this story.

On the day that Ian Wilson was being laughed at for his gullibility about the Shroud, I was also part of the Wrekin Trust's audience. To cut a long story mercifully short, within three weeks of meeting there, we had begun a two-year on/off relationship. The only reason for mentioning this painful episode is to show why I became yet more interested in the Shroud in the year following the carbon dating.

However, it must be remembered that Wilson had been vociferous in his support of the carbon dating before the event, writing in his 1978 bestseller: '. . . there is one scientific test . . . that could at a stroke determine whether the Shroud dates from the fourteenth century, or is indeed much older.'[21] Two years before the tests he had reinforced this belief, writing: '. . . A consistent fourteenth-century date . . . should certainly be decisive enough to cause a massive rethink among those who, in common with this author, support the Shroud's authenticity.'[22]

Three years after the carbon dating, in *Holy Faces, Secret Places*, he quoted Deuteronomy 6:16, 'You must not put the Lord your God to the test', adding: '. . . In a very real sense they [the scientists involved in the carbon dating] were aiming to demonstrate whether God had shown himself in the form of the Turin Shroud. Is it too much to suggest that God might have pulled down the blinds?'[23]

When something beloved dies – be it either a person or a dream – there must be a time of bereavement, a period of adjustment. Where the Shroudies were concerned, they never admitted there was a death in the first place. Is there any wonder that in the years following the carbon dating their bitterness and fear grew, turning them into a veritable Mafia? It is only too significant that all the doubts about the technique of carbon dating have surfaced since, not before, the actual tests.

Take the words of Rodney Hoare, the BSTS Chairman. Before the tests he wrote: 'Carbon dating would enable an estimate to within an accuracy of 150 years in 2000 . . . the refusal of the Roman Catholic Church custodians to grant permission is difficult to understand.'[24] But in a personal letter to Clive in 1993 he wrote: 'The carbon dating is likely to be too late rather than too early, if contaminants were "pressure-cooked" into the fibres by the fire of 1532 . . .'[25] And in that same year he wound up an unusual AGM by appealing to members for suggestions on how the carbon dating might be wrong.

Nevertheless, it is instructive to review the Shroudies' objections to the tests. As we have seen, the believers immediately fell back on allegations of conspiracy. The right-wing luminary of La Contre-Reforme Catholique au XXe Siècle, Brother Bruno Bonnet-Eymard, claimed that Dr Michael

Tite switched the samples for parts of a late thirteenth-century cope (a ceremonial cloak).[26] He also hastened to point out that Tite got Professor Teddy Hall's job at Oxford when the latter retired. In fact, the cope was used, but only as a control sample.

What would be the motive of such a conspiracy? Bonnet-Eymard thinks it is an attempt by scientists to undermine the Christian religion. Leading sindonologist Professor Werner Bulst goes further, and has spoken on German television of a 'Masonic anti-Catholic plot'.[27] However, it is difficult to see what the conspirators would hope to gain. Discrediting the Shroud would do little to shake the faith of most Christians – especially in the last century, the Church has been careful to avoid endorsing it as genuine. On the other hand, proving the Shroud authentic might conceivably attract more followers into the fold. It is easy to imagine a conspiracy aimed at proving a first-century date, but not so easy to imagine the scientists risking their reputations and careers by plotting to brand it a fake.

Recently, however, German researchers Holger Kersten and Elmar R. Gruber, in their *The Jesus Conspiracy* (published in Germany in 1992 and in the UK in early 1994), have advanced a bold – and novel – variation on the conspiracy theme. They believe that the carbon dating was rigged by the scientists in collusion with the Vatican.

Kersten and Gruber believe that pieces of 14th-century fabric were switched for samples cut from the Shroud. This happened, they claim, when Michael Tite sealed the samples in their containers before handing them over to representatives of the three laboratories, as this was (suspiciously) the only part of the operation that was carried out in private and out of sight of the video cameras that were recording the event.

They base their belief on the apparent discrepancies in and vagueness of the scientists' reports regarding the size of the samples they received, and the apparent differences in the samples before and after they were sealed up.

Unfortunately, the samples themselves were destroyed by the testing process, and so Kersten and Gruber have had to rely on photographs taken in Turin cathedral when the samples were first cut from the cloth and on photographs taken at the laboratories. They claim that it is impossible to match the pieces of cloth as seen on the two sets of photographs, which should have been identical. However, such comparisons are not as easy to make as might be first thought: it was not simply a matter of the original piece being snipped into three equal bits. The samples were cut from the middle of the piece, leaving material to spare.

Gruber and Kersten's cynical reconstruction of the sample-cutting has been challenged – for example by sindonologist Eberhard Lindner[28] – who has tried to show that the samples can all be matched up. At the time of writing this debate is still raging, and it seems unlikely that conclusive evidence will ever emerge one way or the other.

The most unlikely part of this scenario is the alleged alliance between the scientists – some of whom, like Teddy Hall, are vehement atheists – and the Vatican. Kersten and Gruber realise that the conspiracy they suggest can only work on the assumption that such a collusion actually took place, since Tite was accompanied when the supposed switch took place.

Their suggested motive is ingenious and intriguing: they assert that the Church wanted to discredit the Shroud because it proves that Jesus was alive when laid in the tomb, and that the Resurrection – the cornerstone of the Christian creed – never took place. The Church, they argue, had long been keen to acquire the Shroud so they could discredit it, but until it was bequeathed to them by King Umberto in 1983, they were powerless to do so.

This idea is not a new one. It was first published in the 1960s by a curious individual called Hans Naber. He claimed that, in 1947, he had had a vision of Jesus, who told him that the Resurrection never happened and that a study of the Shroud would prove it, and thereafter Naber saw it as his mission to bring this message to the world. He first achieved international publicity in 1969, when he learned of the Turin Commission's secret investigations and claimed that the Church intended to use the Commission to destroy the cloth in order to hide its secret. Naber was subsequently convicted of fraud.[29]

Since then, BSTS Chairman Rodney Hoare has written a series of books promoting a similar thesis, most recently in *The Turin Shroud Is Genuine* (1994). His ideas are discussed later.

Kersten and Gruber, like Naber, point to the way that the blood appears to be still flowing from the wounds as proof that Jesus was still alive when the Shroud image was formed. However, the weaknesses in their theory are:

Firstly, although the Church did not, legally, own the Shroud until 1983, it was still in their power, so they could easily have arranged for it to be destroyed, say in a fire. In fact, there have been several attempts to steal or burn the Shroud, all of which have been foiled by the Church guardians. There was no need to go to such lengths to enter into a conspiracy with the scientists. Secondly, all the arguments against authenticity remain. Kersten and Gruber follow Ian Wilson's Mandylion theory – believing that the Shroud had been the Mandylion of Constantinople and the head idol of the Knights Templar. However, all the arguments that we have listed against this theory are agreed with by Kersten and Gruber. Finally those authors never consider the possibility that the image might have been created by someone who was *deliberately* aiming to show that Jesus did not die on the cross.

In the light of the carbon dating, we began our research, looking for the identity of the author of this extraordinary hoax in the evidence of the cloth itself, and in its complex and vexed history. It was perhaps rather like the little boy who saw through the emperor's new clothes setting out to write a history of fashion, but we certainly came to Shroud research with a new eye.

So what are the hard facts about the Shroud? What has all that meticulous scientific research actually established? We had to go back to the beginning.

The fabric is bleached pure linen. The cloth measures 4.4m by 1.9m and is 0.3mm thick, with an 8cm strip on its left-hand side. This strip is almost an exact match, but appears to have been added to centralize the image; it has therefore been assumed it was sewn on when the Shroud was put on display.

Under the microscope traces of Middle Eastern cotton have been found in the linen fibres, indicating that it was woven on a loom used for cotton. This, and a tell-tale absence of any trace of wool, suggests that it was not woven in Europe. The weave is known as 'three-to-one herringbone twill' (the same as that used in denim jeans), an unusually elaborate and costly weave for a cheap fabric like linen. There is no evidence either way for it being compatible with cloth produced in first century Palestine.

One of the details much quoted by believers is that of the evidence of the pollen. Dr Max Frei, a famous Swiss criminologist and the only non-Italian member of the original Turin Commission, took samples of pollen from the cloth in 1973 by the simple method of attaching sticky tape to the cloth and pulling it off. The particles were analyzed under the microscope.

Frei published his results in 1976,[30] claiming that he had found – besides the expected European pollen – samples from plants unique to Palestine, the Anatolian steppes and Turkey, leading him to conclude that the Shroud had at some time been in each of those areas. Despite the claims of some, Frei's work cannot be used to date the Shroud, and there are difficulties with his conclusions (see Chapter 2). We consider that his findings were remarkably selective, to put it mildly. And his expertise in quite another field was to have far-reaching effects: he was the man who authenticated the 'Hitler diaries'.[31]

The body image is very faint; many find it extremely difficult to make out at all. All photographs – not just negatives – effectively enhance the image, partly because they are reduced in size and there-fore focus the image, and partly because film emulsion enhances the contrast. Up close, or under a magnifying glass, the image seems to disappear.

All the tests have failed to establish what produced the image, although they have eliminated many possibilites. No substantial traces of pigment, ink or dyes have been found (except by Dr Walter McCrone, see Chapter 4) on the cloth, although minute traces of pigment have been detected. This is said to be because painted images are known to have been placed on it to 'sanctify' them.

Under the microscope the colour of the image shows no sign of soaking along the threads (capillary action), as would most paints. There is no foreign matter adhering to the threads. The parts of the image next to the 1532 burn marks do not change in colour, neither do the parts where the tidemarks (where water was used to put out the fire) cross it.

Rather than being caused by something being added to the cloth, the image seems to have been created by something being taken away, some degradation of the structure of the linen. STURP scientists observed that the parts of the cloth that bear the image are structurally weaker than the non-image areas, and under high magnification the fibres can be seen to be damaged, and have a corroded appearance. Some have likened the damage to that caused by a weak acid.[32]

The image does not penetrate the cloth. It is hard to imagine any artistic technique that would not allow the paint to soak through something that is just 0.3 mm thick. Even individual threads can be seen, under the microscope, to be coloured on one side only.

The image is completely uniform in colour. The impression of contrasting areas is an illusion due to the variation in the number of coloured threads per square centimetre. (It is hard to equate this with the artistic forgery so beloved of the dismissive sceptic.)

The negative effect is still the most puzzling, and the most fascinating, characteristic of the Turin Shroud. It is a concept that would have been completely alien to a medieval forger, besides being totally pointless when it could never have been appreciated in photographic negative.

There have been suggestions that the image might have been painted in positive and the effect of ageing turned it negative – something which happened to a fresco in the church at Assisi – but in the case of the Shroud the dark background of the negative is the cloth itself. For an Assisi-like effect the cloth would have had to have been dark at first and then changed colour, and the image would have had to be lighter than the cloth to start with.

In fact, sceptics have a hard time trying to explain the negative effect, and can only really do so by denying that it exists. They claim that it was merely a by-product of the artist's efforts to reproduce the contact points – the areas where the body met the cloth. Walter McCrone wrote: 'I feel the negative character of the image is a coincidence resulting from the artist's conception of his commission.'[33]

Equally intriguing, or so we once thought, is the fact that the image apparently exhibits '3-D information'. This means, STURP told us, that there is a direct, measurable relationship between the intensity of the image and the distance of the cloth from the body.

This was first noticed by Paul Vignon at the turn of the century, and was demonstrated by two USA Air Force physicists who were later instrumental in setting up STURP, devout Catholics John Jackson and Eric Jumper. Their most dramatic demonstration of this effect was when they used the VP-8 Image Analyzer, originally developed for NASA, which produced 3-D images. This effect is impossible to create with ordinary paintings as the unequal density of the colour fails to give the Image Analyzer anything to work on.[34]

This 3-D effect was believed to be a highly significant characteristic of the Shroud image, although what it actually meant was acknowledged to be unclear. To believers, it is taken as proof of some form of radiation emitting from the body of Christ. Our own research, however, was to reveal something quite unexpected about this '3-D information'.

From the earliest studies it was realized that, if authentic, the image was caused by a process more complex than simple contact between body and cloth. For example, Paul Vignon proved that if the cloth had been draped over a body which had been covered in paint, the image would be grotesque and bloated-looking when the cloth was straightened out.

Parts of the image show that the body could not have even touched the cloth. If it had, the nose would have formed a 'tent' from its tip to the cheek, yet the image shows the nostrils and part of the cheek distinctly. In The Shroud of Christ (1902), Paul Vignon tells us that the image is 'the result of action at a distance', or 'a projection'.

There are a number of small flows of blood – or dark patches that appear to be blood – from the scalp, both back and front, that appear to be consistent with wounds caused by the Crown of Thorns. Blood also runs down the arms, and seeps from an apparent nail-wound in the sole visible wrist. There is a large patch of blood on the chest, which matches the centurion's spear-thrust in the Biblical account. Blood has gathered in the small of the back, perhaps pooling when the body was laid flat on the Shroud. Blood also leaks from wounds in the feet, and seems particularly concentrated on the sole of one foot.

However, there are significant differences between the image of the body and the image of the blood. Although the bloodstains appear to be similar in colour to the body image in indoor lighting, in natural light the blood is seen to be distinctly different – a vivid red, or carmine colour. The bloodstains themselves do not exhibit the negative effect.

Under the microscope the fibres are matted together by, and encrusted with the 'blood' which can be seen clearly to have been added. The 'bloodstains' do penetrate the cloth, and there are signs of capillary action along the fibres (although not as distinct as they should be with liquid blood).

The conclusion is crucial: since the two images – that of the body and that of the blood – are so different, then they must have been created by separate processes. Indeed, to the (unbiased) naked eye, the blood does seem to have been rather crudely added, as if overlaid somehow on the body image.[35]

But is it blood? Real blood dries brown, not red – in fact, tests by STURP concluded that it was not blood. However, when Italian scientists claimed to have proved that it was, and had also isolated the blood group (AB), STURP changed their minds and agreed that it was blood after all. The current consensus is that the stains are, or at least contain, human blood, although there is still room for doubt – and no one can tell how old it is.[36]

The image has been studied by many anatomists and forensic scientists who agree that the physique is consistent with a real human body. Some have gone so far as to say that it is too flawless to be the work of an artist.

The man on the Shroud is generally taken to be around 180cm, but there are estimates as low as 162cm, depending on assumptions made about the lie of the cloth. And there is at least one serious attempt to describe the man as being 203cm tall.

The physique is usually taken to be that of a healthy, well-developed male, who was not given to manual labour. Harvard ethnologist Carleton S. Coon pronounced the features to be ethnically those of a Sephardic Jew or an Arab, but it is impossible to be dogmatic on this issue. This assumption has been added to by the 'evidence' of the long hair on the back image, which is often described as being the 'unbound pigtail' of the young Jewish male of the first century.

The man appears to be between forty and fifty years old; it is possible, according to one school of thought, to make a case for Jesus having been older than the accepted thirty-three years at the time of his crucifixion.

Pierre Barbet, working with freshly-amputated arms, demonstrated that the only way that the weight of a nailed body can be supported is by nailing it through the *wrists* (the 'space of Destot'), as here. He also discovered that the nail hit the median nerve, which causes the thumb to contract into the palm. The thumbs of the man on the Shroud are invisible.[37]

However, it would be untrue to say that this somewhat specialist knowledge is modern; the nailing of the wrists was actually mentioned in the first work specifically devoted to the Shroud, by Cardinal Gabrielle Paleotti, Archbishop of Bologna, in 1598. He says that this was 'proved by the experiments carried out by talented sculptors on corpses with a view to making a picture'.[38] Van Dyck (1599–1641) and Rubens (1577–1640) also depicted Jesus as being crucified in this way. It was not, however, known in the pre-Renaissance period in which the Shroud is assumed to have been faked.

Analysis of the angles at which the blood flowed on the arms shows that it is consistent with that of a man being crucified with his arms held above his head, forming a 'Y' shape rather than the usual 'T' shape of artistic depiction. The blood flows along the arms, with occasional downward drips due to gravity. These run at two slightly different angles from the line of the arms and there have been claims that this fits exactly what would have happened in crucifixion.

There are two main theories as to how crucifixion kills. Pierre Barbet believed that death is caused by asphyxiation, as it would be impossible to breathe with the arms in that position unless there is support for the legs. The victim could only raise his chest by pressing down on the nails in his feet, which in turn would be agonizing, causing a sort of see-saw motion: rising to draw breath, falling from the pain, rising from pain to yet more pain. Barbet claimed that the two angles of the blood flow are consistent with the two positions. It does, however, require that the only lower support for the body is the nail or nails in the feet, there being no crotch support (sedile).[39]

Another school of thought, supported by BSTS Chairman Rodney Hoare,[40] is that there was a sedile, and that death was caused by some other factor. The arms would be kept in one position while the victim was alive, changing as he lost consciousness and slumped to one side. This school also claims that the angles of the blood flow support their view.

The course the blood has taken does seem to be realistic. The most noticeable of all the flows, which forms the shape of a figure '3' on the forehead, for example, behaves exactly the way blood wells up from a puncture-wound, and even shows changes of direction over the furrows of the brow. Some have even seen signs of the separation of serum from the blood – although it could equally well be the separating out of the components of artificial 'blood'.

Some have seen the clearer patches in the middle of the chest wound as indications of the 'blood and water' that is said to have issued from Jesus (John 19:34), and have even worked out medical explanations for just how it happened. However, any forger working from the Biblical account would have been careful to have included this detail.

The spear wound is curved on one side, apparently corresponding to examples of the Roman *lancea*, the weapon specifically referred to in John's gospel. Although frequently cited as evidence for the Shroud's authenticity, it is inadmissible evidence as no one has ever shown that the wound does not match those caused by weapons of any other place or period, such as Renaissance Italy. No one had ever thought to look. (However, even a cursory glance through an encyclopaedia of weaponry shows that similar lances were used in almost every period – there are, after all, limited possibilities for the design of such an object.)

The facial wounds are a contentious area. Most researchers agree that the man shows signs of violence here, but they disagree as to how much his face suffered.

Secondo Pia's original photographs seem to show a far greater degree of bruising and swelling than those since. Giuseppe Enrie found that this was because Pia had failed to lie the cloth flat, so the image was distorted. His own view, interestingly, was that the face shows no marks of violence at all.[41] At the other extreme are those such as Dr David Willis (a British doctor, and devout Catholic, who made a special study of the wounds), who lists a horrific catalogue of facial injuries, such as swollen eyebrows, and a torn eyelid – an injury virtually impossible to sustain, even in the most severe beatings.[42]

Over 100 marks, as of scourging, can be detected, mainly on the back of the image. Forensic scientists have been able to calculate the number, height and position of the scourgers. The claim has been made that the shape of the wounds matches that of the Roman flagrum, a whip with dumbbell-shaped metal tips. However, no comparable studies of scourges used in other times and places have been made, although it is known that the Flagellants during the Black Death in the fourteenth century used similar whips, and from the mid-fifteenth century onwards the 'Florentinian Flagellants' provided rich street theatre with their al fresco demonstrations of athletic masochism.[43]

Different explanations have been offered as to why we can see the sole of one foot. Some, such as Rodney Hoare,[44] assume that the body was lying completely flat, and speculate that the cloth was folded up around the feet, which were pressed against the wall of the tomb. Or it may be that the body simply retained the position it held on the cross, with its knees raised slightly, allowing the feet to be placed flat on the ground when taken down.

The Hungarian-born American religious artist Isabel Piczek has made a special study of the shroud-man's anatomy, particularly with regard to the apparent foreshortening of the image. She concluded that the body shows the position of crucifixion, presumably retained by rigor mortis, with the arms being forced down across the body. The foreshortening is accurate to a degree which argues against it being the work of an artist of average skill.[45]

The VP-8 Image Analyzer work caused great excitement when John Jackson claimed that the 3-D images showed what appeared to be small coins over the eyes. Soon, an enthusiastic researcher, Francis Filas (a Jesuit theologian from Chicago) claimed to be able to read part of an inscription around the edge of a coin – just four letters, UCAI, which could be the middle of a Greek version of 'Tiberias Caesar' (*Tiberiou Caisaros*).[46] He was the emperor in Jesus' day, and this was an inscription known from leptons in use during Pilate's governorship. However, most other researchers ascribed this to Filas' imagination, and when STURP made a special search for the coins, they could not find them.[47]

So we are faced with an astonishing enigma. The carbon dating tells us that the Shroud is a fake, but if it has been pronounced dead then this is one relic that resolutely refuses to lie down. In fact, most of the above characteristics are as incompatible with a fourteenth-century origin as they are with a first-century date.

At first our task seemed daunting, to say the least. If it were not for the carbon dating, we might have been tempted to fall in with the believers, for the evidence – as listed above – appeared to be still on their side. And had it not been for the astonishing events of the last few years, we might still have been part of that uneasy coterie who the rest of the world too glibly describes as 'flat earthers'.

But first we had to look at the known history of the Shroud, to glean from an often biased and selective story where the most awesome relic in Christendom could possibly have begun its career. Had it actually originated in a cold tomb in first-century Palestine – or was it created much nearer to our time, and even nearer to us geographically?

Where did the Turin Shroud come from?

THE VERDICT OF HISTORY

'The case [against the Shroud's authenticity] is here so strong that . . .
the possibility of an error in the verdict of history must be accounted as
almost infinitesimal.'

Herbert Thurston, Society of Jesus 1903

THE BELIEVERS' biggest problem has always been that there is no historical
evidence that the Shroud is older than – at the very best reckoning – 650
years. It simply appears, unheralded and without the slightest explanation
of how it got there, in the middle of France some time in the second half
of the 14th century. Both the mystery of its previous whereabouts and the
very manner of its appearance tell against the Shroud's authenticity. If it
were genuine, where was it for the thirteen centuries after the crucifixion?
And how could the relic to end relics just drift casually into history? Surely
something so potent, with so much potential for seizing the hearts and
minds of the masses, would have been ushered in with fanfares, prayers
and feasting.

Those worried by this glaring gap have made several suggestions to
account for it, while others take the stance that the missing years can
just be ignored, since the scientific evidence alone (apart from the carbon
dating, of course) is, they claim, enough to guarantee the Shroud's
authenticity. Before the carbon dating, the believers could argue that
the weight of evidence was in favour of the Shroud being genuine, but
now the scales have tipped the other way, and the only way in which
the results can be undermined is by showing that the Shroud existed at
least before the earlier date-limit of 1260.

Another line of attack is to point to examples of the unreliability of carbon
dating, or to argue that the samples taken were contaminated in some way.[2]
But, while it is true that carbon dating has provided a good few howlers in its
time, and that the tests are so sensitive that contamination is a recognized
and constant problem (exposure to cigarette smoke, for example, renders
it useless), it is not an argument that is relevant to the Shroud.

First, the same dates were arrived at by three separate laboratories.

Secondly, where a date agrees with independent evidence of the object's age it must be accepted – and the Shroud's dates pinpoint exactly the time of its debut in history. This cannot be a coincidence. Nor can it be anything other than desperation that makes the same believers who argued most vociferously for the carbon dating to be done the very people who are now most active in criticizing the technique.

The pro-authenticity lobby, then, sees the Shroud's history in two parts: first the period of total mystery from the first century to its appearance in fourteenth-century France, followed by its accepted history from that time to the present day. But as our own researches progressed, we discovered that there were grounds for disputing even the second part. However, first we had to familiarize ourselves with the main events of the accepted history, especially those surrounding its sudden and dramatic appearance.[3]

Until 1983 today's Turin Shroud was the property of the House of Savoy, Italy's royal family. Their ownership can be traced back to the mid-fifteenth century, when they acquired it from the de Charnys, minor members of the French aristocracy, who owned it in the last part of the fourteenth century. The first documented reference to the de Charny Shroud dates from 1389. Before that there is total silence – nothing to show where and how the de Charnys had come by it.

Clearly that first document is critical to our understanding of the Shroud's origins. It was a letter from the Bishop of Troyes, Pierre D'Arcis, to Pope Clement VII – and it unequivocally denounces the Shroud as a fake, a cynical forgery created to defraud gullible pilgrims.[4]

The circumstances that compelled D'Arcis to pen his letter (which is generally known as the 'D'Arcis Memorandum' among Shroud researchers) were as follows: in his diocese was the insignificant village of Lirey, the family seat of the de Charny family and the site of a small collegiate church (one that houses an endowed chapter of canons). Those canons, with the approval of the head of the family, Geoffrey de Charny (known as Geoffrey II to avoid confusing him with his more illustrious father) had just begun to hold public expositions of a cloth that they claimed was the Shroud of Jesus, and upon which his image could be seen, miraculously imprinted. After investigating the matter, D'Arcis was convinced that it was a hoax and, incensed by such blatant exploitation, wrote to the Pope demanding that he ban the expositions.

They had certainly been theatrical; lit by torches, the Shroud was held up by priests on a specially erected platform, high above the heads of the huge throngs eager to see the wondrous image. Later, to demonstrate his support for the canons in their dispute with D'Arcis, Geoffrey II took to raising the cloth with his own hands. The bishop's description of the image is all too brief, '[it is] the two-fold image of one man, that is to say, the back and the front,' but it does sound like today's Turin Shroud.

D'Arcis denounced it in the most forthright terms, accusing the Dean of Lirey of deceit and of being 'consumed with the passion of avarice', even going so far as to accuse him of hiring 'pilgrims' to feign miracle cures when the cloth was raised aloft. He was also angered because in gaining Pope Clement's approval for the displays Geoffrey had gone over his head and made the request directly to the Papal Nuncio to France. When D'Arcis tried to intervene and threatened the Dean with excommunication, Geoffrey appealed to King Charles VI of France for a warrant to confirm his right to exhibit the Shroud – which he duly received.

But for later historians the most damning claim made by D'Arcis was that the image was painted. One of his predecessors, Henry of Poitiers, had carried out his own investigations and had, D'Arcis said 'discovered the fraud and how the cloth had been cunningly painted, the truth being attested to by the artist who had painted it, to wit, that it was a work of human skill and not miraculously wrought or bestowed'.

Unfortunately for D'Arcis, Pope Clement was related to the de Charny family – Geoffrey II's stepfather was his uncle – and instead of supporting his local representative he sided with the de Charnys, going to the remarkable length of commanding the bishop's 'perpetual silence' on pain of excommunication. He did, however, compromise to the extent that he decreed that the cloth could only be displayed as a 'likeness or representation' of Christ's Shroud.

The whole episode could be dismissed as a local dispute over just one of the many alleged holy relics that proliferated in Europe at the time – feathers from the wings of angels, countless splinters from the True Cross and a whole wardrobeful of the Virgin's chemises – were it not for the fact that seemingly the same relic would, 600 years later, perplex twentieth-century scientists.

Even at this stage there seems to have been something going on behind the scenes beyond a mere tussle over a lucrative relic, or a local power struggle between bishop and lord. Geoffrey II's direct approach to the Pope, even given their kinship, was unusual and suggests it was a tactical move on his part. And Clement's threat of excommunication has a distinctly malodorous air of downright blackmail. As Ian Wilson remarked in his first book, 'One cannot escape the feeling that there is something missing, something more to the affair than meets the eye.'5

For those opposed to the Shroud's authenticity, the 'D'Arcis Memorandum' is proof that the Shroud was, and is, a painted fake. Believers have countered that it is equally correct to interpret that most damning phrase of D'Arcis as meaning that Henry of Poitiers had found not *the* artist who had painted the image, but *an* artist who had made a copy of it.[6] It is, however, a specious argument; it is true that the original Latin does allow such an interpretation, but in the context the accepted version must be correct. What possible reason would the bishop have had for mentioning it otherwise? How would the man's confession not further Henry's case against the Shroud?

Nor was D'Arcis the only one to make the claim that the image was painted. At one stage in the dispute Charles VI sent the Bailiff of Troyes to confiscate the Shroud, pending a judgement. (The Dean refused to hand it over.) The Bailiff's report survives to this day – and it, too, states bluntly that the image was a painting.[7]

The memorandum also yields another clue. The bishop states that the exhibitions were a revival of earlier displays that were held 'thirty-four years or thereabouts' before – that is, around 1355. It was on that occasion, according to D'Arcis, that Henry of Poitiers found the guilty artist and stopped the expositions. If true, this would make the first known owner of the Shroud Geoffrey II's father, also Geoffrey, in his day a famous knight and war hero of France.

There is no direct corroboration of the existence of the Lirey Shroud in Geoffrey I's day, and there are several reasons to doubt that it was being displayed in 1355. It was that Geoffrey who founded the Lirey church, and the records of its original endowment in 1353 (which still exist)[8] make no mention of the Shroud among the relics he donated. The church was consecrated by Bishop Henry of Poitiers in 1356 (again with no mention of the Shroud in the records),[9] something that seems unlikely if Henry had only a year before disciplined the canons over such a serious offence. However, D'Arcis' 'thirty-four years or thereabouts' does allow some leeway. Geoffrey I was, in fact, killed in battle less than four months after the consecration ceremony, dying a hero's death at the battle of Poitiers while shielding his king, Jean II, from an English lance-thrust with his own body. He had no opportunity to present the church with the Shroud in the intervening months, and public pilgrimages could not have been organized in such a short space of time. Some have therefore speculated that it was actually his widow, Jeanne de Vergy, who, left in financial difficulties after her husband's death, first displayed the Shroud to swell her coffers – even though Geoffrey himself had sought to keep it secret. This would put the date of the first expositions at 1357 or 58.[10]

The only independent testimony that the Shroud was exhibited at Lirey during the time of Geoffrey I or Jeanne de Vergy is a solitary pilgrim's badge recovered from the bed of the Seine in 1855 and now in the Musée de Cluny, Paris, which shows a Shroud-like image (unfortunately too small for any of the details to be properly made out).[11] It has not been dated precisely, but because it includes the coats of arms of both the de Charny and de Vergy families – they were only united by the marriage of Geoffrey I and Jeanne – it has been suggested that the badge belonged to one of the first pilgrims who made the journey to Lirey to see the Shroud.

Throughout the historical dispute, however, neither the first nor the second Geoffrey de Charny ever described – at least in writing – how the Shroud came into his family's possession. How could the ultimate relic have virtually sidled into their hands? If it had been a trophy of war, they might be expected to have boasted of their bravery in capturing it. If they had bought it, or even won it in gaming, they might be expected to seek some congratulation, if only for their shrewdness. Even if the de Charny family made a fetish out of modesty – and there is no evidence that they did – surely they would have spoken out to clear their names when accused of maintaining a hoax by D'Arcis and Henry of Poitiers. But of the Shroud's provenance there is silence. It is almost as if they had found it lying in the attic – or as if they had conjured the image up through the skills of an unscrupulous artist the likes of whom have occurred not infrequently through the ages.

After the Pope silenced the bishop with his threat of excommunication, Geoffrey II continued to exhibit the Shroud at Lirey (although as 'a likeness or representation' only) until his death in 1398, when it was inherited by his daughter Margaret. She was married and widowed twice – her first husband falling at Agincourt, her second being the wealthy Humbert of Villersexel (whose other titles included Lord of St Hippolyte sur Doubs and Count de la Roche). She remained childless.

In 1418 Margaret and Humbert removed the Shroud from Lirey Church, ostensibly for safekeeping during the troubled times following the English victory at Agincourt – and were promptly sued by the canons for making off with what they regarded as their property. Until 1449 the relic was kept in a chapel on Humbert's land at St Hippolyte sur Doubs in the Franche-Comté region, where annual expositions were then held.

Humbert died in 1438; eleven years later Margaret took the Shroud to Belgium, where it was displayed at Liège. The local bishop appointed two professors to investigate the Shroud: they concluded it was a fake.[12] Three years later it was exhibited back in France, at Germolles. It is usually assumed that, despite being seventy and presumably frail, Margaret insisted on travelling because she was seeking a suitable guardian for her family's treasured possession. She was the last of her line, after all – but this is just speculation.

Finally, some time before 1464, she gave the Shroud to the wealthy dukedom of Savoy, then headed by Louis and his wife Anne de Lusignan, Queen of Jerusalem, in return for a castle and land. At least, it is presumed that they were exchanged for the Shroud; selling a holy relic would have been regarded as improper, so there is no proof of this supposed grand barter. (The land may have been a gift, however, for Margaret's second husband was known to have been closely associated with the Savoys.)

Was Margaret genuinely concerned that the greatest relic of all should find a good home? And if so, is that in itself evidence that she believed it to be authentic? Or was she merely lining her pockets as the chill of her declining years began to bite? We will never know, but each action of the historical guardians of the Shroud has been – and will continue to be – mulled over and interpreted in strikingly different ways depending upon the beliefs of the interpreter. There are many such examples of this selective reading of history.

For example, in the pro-authenticity literature, the Shroud's subsequent owners – Louis, Duke of Savoy and his wife Anne – are usually described as being extremely pious and noble; Anne especially being singled out for her spirituality. The reason given for this uncritical view is simply the fact that they surrounded themselves with monks and priests. Historians generally, however, are less kind – and less naive – seeing Louis as a weak man completely under the thumb of his dominant and ambitious wife. Indeed, one commentator goes so far as to call her 'the evil genius' of the Savoy family[13]. The *Encyclopaedia Brittanica* describes Louis as 'indolent, incapable and ruled by his wife',[14] while the Siennese poet and diplomat Aeneas Sylvius states that Anne was 'a wife incapable of obeying married to a man incapable of commanding'.[15]

The House of Savoy had grown steadily in wealth, influence and territory since the early eleventh century, until by Margaret de Charny's day they controlled large areas of the old kingdom of Burgundy, covering parts of modern France, Switzerland and Italy. Louis' father, Amadeus VIII – who died in 1449 – was the first to be granted the dukedom (until then the Savoys were mere counts), and was one of the most remarkable characters of the period. An archetypal early Renaissance prince, Amadeus was a patron of the arts who was equally respected as a soldier and peacemaker, and was renowned throughout Europe for his piety. In 1434 he renounced his title in favour of his son and went into retreat at the monastery of St Maurice at Capaille. But five years later he reluctantly came out of retirement when he was declared Pope Felix IV, despite the fact that he had never taken holy orders.

Louis clearly had a lot to live up to; no doubt he felt the strain of maintaining such notable piety. But for aspiring noble families of the Middle Ages the best status symbols were undoubtedly the rarest of holy relics; what could be better than the Holy Shroud itself?

Unfortunately, Anne's scheming, Louis' weakness and the continued war with France (or Italy – Savoy was trapped halfway between them) meant that the family suffered a decline. And so did the Shroud. Between the year they acquired it and its public exposition at Vercelli on Good Friday, 1494, it seems to have disappeared from public view, precisely at a time when its pulling power might have helped them financially.

Although it was known to have remained among the Savoys' possessions, it was remarkably quiescent during a full forty-year period. It is not even certain where it was kept, although it was certainly at the forefront of their minds – they enlarged their principal church at Chambéry specifically to house the Shroud between 1471 and 1502. Or perhaps it was to be the home of a new, and better, Shroud? Could it be that arrangements were underway throughout this 'silent' phase to provide the world with a more impressive holy relic?

Certainly, following its 'reappearance' in 1494 there was an enormous change in the way it was publically perceived. Until then the only official line was that it was merely a 'representation' of Jesus' Shroud. However, during the 1470s this view was challenged by Pope Sixtus IV (Francesco della Rovere), who championed it as the true Shroud in his book *On the Blood of Christ* (written in 1464, but not published until 1471, after he became Pope). On his election he accorded special honours and privileges to the Chambéry church, to him the last resting place of the cloth that had held Christ's body. It was especially important to him because he laid great emphasis on the redemptive power of Christ's actual blood – and did not the Shroud itself hold this power?

It is unlikely, however, that Sixtus ever saw the Shroud. Its real apotheosis came when his nephew, Julius II, granted the title 'Sainte Chapelle of the Holy Shroud' to the chapel at Chambéry and gave the cloth its own feast day, 4 May. Annual expositions followed, on a far grander scale than those at Lirey a century and a half earlier. All this, of course, proved extremely lucrative for the dukes of Savoy and the clergy of Chambéry; huge revenues from pilgrims and gifts from Europe's nobility poured in to swell their coffers. Fifty years on, Louis of Savoy's investment had finally begun to show a dividend. Not surprisingly, the Shroud became the family's most prized possession, almost taking on the role of a protective talisman.

But disaster – almost – struck. During the night of 3–4 December 1532, a great blaze swept through the Sainte Chapelle in Chambéry. The Shroud was kept in a locked silver casket (rather as it is today), which was itself locked behind a metal grille. Ironically, this elaborate security arrangement nearly brought about the relic's destruction – the fire spread too quickly for the terror-stricken nuns to fetch the key-holders. Luckily, the town blacksmith managed to reach the chapel in time and prised open the grille. The precious casket was carried to safety by one of the Duke's officials and two priests. The silver casket had, however, begun to melt in the intense heat, and a drop of molten silver had set the cloth alight. The flames were quickly doused, but the scars of the fire, and the tidemarks of the water, are still clearly visible.

The fire is important, not only because of the damage it caused to the cloth, but also because it is constantly cited as evidence for some theory or another about how the image was formed, and it is regularly quoted as a reason for the 'freak' carbon dating results. Some have speculated that before the fire the image had been painted, and that the image visible today was caused by a reaction in the pigment or some other effect due to the heat.[16] More recently there have been claims that the chemical changes in the linen interfered with the carbon dating results, making the cloth appear much younger than it was.[17] It has also been proposed that the original Lirey Shroud was destroyed in the fire, and that today's Turin Shroud was a Renaissance replacement. The idea is not new.

Rumours circulated within weeks of the fire that the Shroud had not survived, and they grew to such proportions that a papal commission was sent to investigate. It was almost a year and a half later that the Shroud, with patches over the burnt parts and a new holland cloth backing, was returned to the Sainte Chapelle. The Shroud had not been destroyed in the fire: the Lierre copy, made in 1516, shows the 'pokermarks', which must have been made before 1532, and other earlier evidence of damage.

In 1578 the Shroud was transferred to the Cathedral at Turin – which is dedicated to St John the Baptist – something that, in the light of our later discoveries, was to prove singularly significant. Turin was the new capital of the Savoy lands, and the Shroud was to remain there except for the years of World War II, 1939–46, when it was taken to the Abbey of Montevergine at Avellino in the south.

The Duchy of Savoy gradually shifted their affiliations, becoming steadily more pro-Italian, a process finally complete in the middle of the seventeenth century when Savoy became an independent Italian state. On the unification of Italy the House of Savoy was elected to be the new state's royal line. The Shroud remained their greatest treasure, even after the monarchy was abolished and the family exiled in 1946. Even when living in Portugal, the last king, Umberto II, continued to be consulted about its care and display, while the clergy of the cathedral acted as its custodians until Umberto's death in 1983, when he bequeathed it to the Vatican. (His widow, as we shall see, was considerably more sceptical about it, and had no hesitation in denouncing it as a fake.)

The Shroud was moved to a specially built chapel, designed by Guarino Guarini in 1694, where it still is. In its early Turin days it was displayed on its feast day – 4 May – but later it become the custom to do so only for special occasions, often with a gap of decades.

The Shroud's journey through history was not all smooth, and there were many sceptical voices raised at every opportunity. One of the most frequently voiced objections to its authenticity is the fact that a miraculously imprinted Shroud is not mentioned in the New Testament at all. It does not figure either in the story of the resurrection, which relies heavily on miracles, nor is it mentioned in the Acts of the Apostles or in the Epistles, where every possible evidence of Jesus' divinity is used to effect. Surely, say the sceptics, if such a thing had existed, it would have been one of the most heavily promoted aspects of the whole Christian story. Yet it is not there at all.

With distinctly Jesuitical logic, some have even managed to use this argument in support of the Shroud's authenticity. They argue that a medieval forger would not have faked a relic that was not mentioned in the gospels – although quite how this accords with the popularity of, say, Our Lady's chemises is not explained.[18]

As usual, interpretations of the original Greek gospels are combed for supporting material. The Synoptic Gospels – Matthew, Mark and Luke – describe Jesus being buried in a single piece of cloth. The Gospel of John – arguably the only eyewitness account of the burial[19] – has the body being wrapped in several 'linen bands' or othonia, and a soudarion (sweat cloth), that was separate from them. No one knows how big these bands were, or what their precise function was. It seems unlikely, however, that a strip of cloth would match the dimensions of today's Turin Shroud, which is a quite massive 4m 37cm long.

Some contend that the soudarion fits the bill, while others shrink it to no more than a sort of holy face-cloth. But the real point to the Gospel story is that they never describe the cloth as being bloodstained, nor do they mention a miracle Shroud at all. On these grounds alone are we justified in condemning the Shroud as a fake? Many think we are, but there are several other objections to be dealt with first.

Debate also rages about whether or not the image of the corpse conforms to, or contradicts, first-century Jewish burial practice. It is unlikely, however, that any conclusion will be reached, as our knowledge of this esoteric area is limited, and again, somewhat speculative.

Sceptics say that the disciples would have viewed Jesus' shroud with the abhorrence all Jews felt for objects contaminated by the grave. Believers counter this by citing the special nature of the dead man; the disciples might well have made an exception in his case. However, in general the Jews were anti-relic, and always have been. The only holy object mentioned in the entire Bible is the Ark of the Covenant, and there is every reason to believe that the Jews who surrounded Jesus never deviated from such traditional thinking. There were no relics bandied about in the earliest days of the Church – a fact that in itself immediately casts doubt on those that surfaced abruptly in the golden age of relics, some 1300 years later.

Then again, believers claim that the image – perhaps due to some anomalous chemical reaction between the body and the spice-impregnated cloth – could have 'developed' over time, and may not have been visible for months, even years, after Jesus' death. But in this case, why would the bereaved disciples have kept it in the first place, when there was nothing remarkable to see on it? The 'developing' process would hardly take over 100 years, roughly the time it took for the New Testament to have been written. Surely a miraculous image of Jesus would have deserved even the most last minute of 'stop presses'?

If a miraculously-imprinted Shroud had been somehow accidentally omitted from the New Testament, might a rumour of such a relic not have circulated among the wonder-hungry early Church? As far as we know, however, there was not so much as a whisper of such a holy artefact. The early Church was Shroudless.

Then again, did Jesus actually look like the man on the Shroud of Turin? There is no physical description of him in the New Testament, but the Biblical commentator Robert Eisler[20] has found evidence in the Apocryphal texts to show that Jesus was short, possibly even hunchbacked. This is not, of course, our idea of what Jesus looked like. Enter almost any Western church and you see a proliferation of statues, engravings, stained-glass windows and so on showing a tall, strapping man with a handsome, narrow face, forked beard and hair parted in the middle: an image that has entered the collective unconscious, but which almost certainly came at least in part from the Turin Shroud. The fact that it owes nothing to historical accuracy is almost neither here nor there. To most people, this is what Jesus looked like, and to challenge it, perhaps putting in its place a pitiful hunchback, is to chip away at the very foundation of the emotional hold of Christianity. Whoever faked the Turin Shroud created a template for our concept of Jesus, either deliberately or accidentally. Whoever faked the Turin Shroud used a model who was to become in time the Jesus of our very dreams.

The Shroud only surfaced in 1357. If it were genuine, where was it before that? If it had existed, it would have been the most prized and sacred relic in Christendom; how could it have remained anonymous and unmentioned for well over a thousand years?

However, between the sixth and thirteenth centuries there were references to supposed shrouds of Jesus. Relics of the Son of God himself were naturally the most sought after, but seeing as he was believed to have ascended bodily into heaven, believers had to make do with associated relics, such as bits of the True Cross or the Crown of

Thorns, and even parts of his body. Alleged milk teeth and his foreskin – actually seven foreskins – went the rounds.

Bits of shroud, or mummy-like wrappings, had been venerated since the fifth century, when one such relic had been brought to Constantinople, and another was seen by a Frankish bishop in Jerusalem in the mid-seventh century. Others were brought into Europe by returning Crusaders, such as the Shroud of Cadouin (which was shown recently to be an eleventh-century Muslim cloth). Another European contender was the Shroud of Compiègne in France, acquired by Charlemagne (742–814) at the end of the eighth century and preserved until its destruction during the French Revolution in 1789.

Naturally the two greatest collections of relics in Christendom would not have been considered complete without their own 'Shrouds'; that of the Byzantine Emperor in Constantinople boasted one from the late eleventh century, and the thirteenth-century collection of Saint Louis IX housed one in the Sainte Chapelle in Paris. Altogether there were more than forty rival claimants for the title of 'Holy Shroud' – and the claims of every one of them have been minutely examined by historians.[21] Yet in only one case – that of an isolated reference dating from 1203 – is there any possibility that it might have been the Lirey or Turin Shroud in an earlier guise. In all the other cases, the dimensions are completely different and, most signficantly of all, in no instance (except in that 1203 reference) is there any mention of a miraculous image. In other words, alleged shrouds of Jesus may have been relatively thick on the ground, but in almost all cases they were blank pieces of cloth. Clearly this was because the exhibitors did not know they were supposed to fake an *image*, and because the story was completely unknown.

Of course that single 1203 reference has excited interest in predictable circles as the only potential precursor of the Lirey Shroud. It is a significant factor in providing answers to questions about why the Shroud had managed to be completely unknown for so long.

In the Middle Ages, the single greatest collection of relics was kept not in Rome, but in the centre of the Eastern Orthodox Church – in the Pharos Chapel of the Byzantine Emperor, in the grounds of his imperial palace in Constantinople. In 1204 the city was looted by soldiers of the Fourth Crusade (fellow Christians), and soon afterwards Europe was flooded with stolen relics. Shortly before the ransacking of Constantinople, the French knight Robert de Clari recorded seeing in the church of St Mary of Blachernae: '. . . the *sydoine* in which our Lord had been wrapped, and which stood up straight every Friday so that the *figure* of our Lord could be plainly seen there'.[22]

He goes on to say that, after the city was sacked six months later, this *sydoine* disappeared. Was it destroyed in the fighting or was it absorbed into the booty of some European knight?

De Clari's memoir is beloved of Shroudies everywhere, for it is seen as proof that a shroud bearing an image existed well before the time of Geoffrey de Charny, and therefore before the period indicated by the carbon dating. But there are problems with it.

The chronicler is not regarded as being reliable; the preferred account of the Fourth Crusade is that of Geoffrey de Villehardouin. Not only was he a meticulous observer, but he was also a veteran diplomat who actually worked with the leaders of the Crusade. And he never mentions such a *sydoine*.

Although de Clari describes a shroud complete with image, he gives too few details for it to be compared at all objectively with today's Turin Shroud. There is even some dispute over whether the Old French *figure* refers to a full-length image or, as in modern French, it simply means a face. (The consensus is, however, in favour of the former.) It is not even certain that de Clari is claiming that he actually saw the *sydoine* with his own eyes, since he only describes visiting the church 'in which it was displayed' – he might simply have been told about it.

At the same time a plain – unimaged – Shroud was among the relics catalogued for the Pharos Chapel, and it had definitely been there since the 1090s. And just to confuse matters further, Geoffrey de Villehardouin[23] states that St Mary's Church escaped the looting of the city. So, tantalizing though de Clari's story may be, it is inadmissible evidence for the existence of the Shroud before the time of the Geoffreys of Charny.

Shroudies are not so easily put off; all attempts to reconstruct a pre-Lirey history for the Turin Shroud still include de Clari's note. But how did the Shroud find its way from first-century Palestine to the Constantinople of 1203, then on to Lirey in the 1350s – and all against a background of its official (that is, Biblical) non-existence? There is one idea that may just save the day for the Shroudies here: Ian Wilson's famous Mandylion theory, which was developed from the work of Father Maurus Green.

In his 1978 bestselling *The Turin Shroud*, Wilson claims the Shroud had indeed appeared throughout those early years, but under another name, that of the Holy Mandylion of Edessa.[24] (Henry Lincoln's film, *The Silent Witness*, based on an idea by Wilson, also makes this claim.)

The Mandylion was a cloth that bore a miraculous image of Jesus' face – an object referred to from its first appearance as *acheiropoietos*, Greek for 'not made by human hands'. Like the Turin Shroud, some of its history is documented fact, while some remains in the realm of legend. It emerged as the most sacred relic of the city of Edessa in what is now Turkey, in the second half of the sixth century, where it remained until 944. It was then forcibly removed – despite violent protests from the local faithful – to Constantinople to join the Emperor's huge collection of relics in the Pharos Chapel. There it stayed until the looting of 1204, when de Clari's *sydoine* also vanished. Superficially at least, it does seem as if the hypothesis that the Mandylion and the Turin Shroud were one and the same has something going for it. After all, neither were 'made by hands', and they had been missing for the same period of time. (Although even here the holes in this evidence are clear: the shared *acheiropoietos* label is a matter of faith, and trying to prove similarities between two things that were missing seems to be clutching at straws.)

The immediate objection is that the Mandylion bore the image of Jesus' face only – the word implies a small, handkerchief-sized cloth. It was supposed to be a towel imprinted during his lifetime, unlike the Shroud which was created after his death, and held the image of his whole body. Wilson has supplied counter-arguments; but first some background is needed.

During the life of the Mandylion, relics had a different function in the Middle East from that of their European counterparts. In Europe they were officially objects of devotion, while being enormously lucrative for the Church. In the Middle East they represented political status and power, and often had a talismanic potency, being seen as protectors of the city that owned them, warding off foreign invasions and natural disasters alike. Known as *palladia*, every city had such a holy prophylactic, and Edessa's was the Mandylion – a fitting honour for the first city to be evangelized in Byzantium.

The relic was first mentioned by the chronicler Evagrius in the 590s when he told how its miraculous powers repelled an attack by the Persian army fifty years previously.[25] Before that date, there were only legends that linked the cloth to a King Abgar V of Edessa – a contemporary of Jesus.

According to the legends, Abgar wrote to Jesus asking him to come to Edessa to cure him of a terrible illness. Jesus' letter in reply was in itself deemed Edessa's most holy relic – until the Mandylion appeared. Shortly after the Crucifixion the Apostle Thaddeus travelled to Edessa and cured the king, converting him to Christianity.

In fact, once the cloth was established as the primary relic towards the end of the sixth century, the legends were adapted to link it with King Abgar. There are two versions: in one Jesus had caused an image of his face to appear on a towel with which he wiped his face, and which he then sent along with his letter to King Abgar. The second is that the image was created during the Agony in Gethsemane, and it was taken by Thaddeus to Edessa. Either way, it was a miraculous cloth that healed

Abgar and brought about his conversion. Abgar's successors, however, reverted to paganism, so the Mandylion was hidden – bricked up in a niche above one of the city's gateways. Here it remained for 500 years until it was rediscovered and came to the aid of the city.

The story can be dismissed as a fable that had been concocted after the discovery of the cloth to give it a suitably holy and miraculous pedigree. If it does have similarities to the Turin Shroud, it may be argued – as Wilson has done – that the legends preserve a memory of genuine events involving an imaged cloth taken to Edessa shortly after Jesus' death.

Although this relic shows only a face and not a whole body image, Wilson argues that before it was hidden, the cloth had been folded so that only the face showed. It is a fact that if the Turin Shroud were folded in half four times, the face would fit exactly into the uppermost section, showing nothing of the body. If the Shroud were then fixed to a board and covered with some kind of ornamental metalwork – and there is some evidence that the Mandylion was – the cloth could easily have gone through history without its owners knowing that it was a full-length shroud.

Support for this theory comes from one of the earliest texts to describe the Mandylion, the late-sixth-century Acts of Thaddeus.[26] Telling how Jesus dried his face on a towel, the cloth is described as *tetradiplon*. This is a totally unknown and untraceable word – indeed, this is its only known use – and because of the context it is usually translated as 'towel'. But its literal meaning is 'doubled in four' . . . could Wilson have been right?

He says that the later Abgar legends are based on the true event of the Shroud arriving in Edessa soon after the crucifixion, and that it really was preserved bricked up in a city gateway for 500 years. He believes it was discovered thanks to rebuilding work needed after the great flood of 525, and that the city fathers kept its discovery a secret until the Persian attack nineteen years later.

During its time in Edessa, the Mandylion was not known to be merely part of a larger image, but some time after its arrival in Constantinople – says Wilson – its true nature was rediscovered, although not made public. It then became the *sydoine* seen by Robert de Clari in 1203. Looted by Crusaders in the next year and brought to Europe, it eventually made its way into the hands of Geoffrey de Charny in the 1350s.

While it was in Edessa it was deemed too holy to be copied, and was never displayed publicly, so there are no eyewitness accounts of it. Even in Constantinople it was kept strictly for the Emperor and his honoured guests. There are no known firsthand copies, so it is impossible to reconstruct its true appearance.

The plausibility of this theory hangs on the veracity of Evagrius' story, and Professor Averil Cameron of King's College Ancient History

Department in London has pointed out that there is every reason to treat his account with caution.[27] Evagrius said that the Mandylion was used to repel the Persians in 544, but he was writing fifty years after the event. And another chronicler, Procopius, writing just five or six years after the event, makes no mention of it at all. Even more significant is the fact that Evagrius based his account on that of Procopius. Presumably Evagrius invented the story to give Edessa's holy relic more eminence than those of rival cities, and therefore there is no proof that the Mandylion existed in 544.

Other cities used their *acheiropoietos* images in the years between the accounts of Procopius and Evagrius: for example, one at Memphis in Egypt in the 570s and another at Camuliana, Cappodocia in the 560s. If the Mandylion had been discovered in 544 it may well have been the original that inspired them, but the 590 date makes it just another in a long line of similar relics. And if the story was an invention, then there was no link between Abgar and Jesus.

The term *acheiropoietos*, however, does appear to indicate that the image was mysterious, until one realizes that even quite blatantly manufactured images were also said to be 'not made by hands'. It was one of the quainter traditions of the medieval Church. In the Lateran Palace in Rome, for example, a painting of Jesus is known as 'The Acheropita' (the Latin equivalent). Even a mosaic was given this title. Obviously it came to refer to a specific genre of religious art; it cannot be used to uphold the authenticity of the Mandylion or of anything else.

There is also a serious contradiction in Wilson's argument about the meaning of the word *tetradiplon* in the Acts of Thaddeus. If, when this was written in the 6th century, no one knew that the Mandylion was actually the folded Shroud, then the word cannot mean 'folded in four'. Or, if the writer knew it was a much larger cloth, why was he alone in this knowledge? And why does he use the word in a story about a face-towel? The Turin Shroud is 13 sq m – surely it would have been somewhat bulky for a facecloth? Even the most dimwitted removal man would have wondered at its sheer weight.

There are other problems with Wilson's hypothesis. He says that at some stage the Mandylion was discovered to be the full-sized cloth bearing the image, and it then became the *sydoine* seen by Robert de Clari in the St Mary of Blachernae Church. But the inventory of relics for Constantinople's Pharos Chapel listed the Mandylion *and* an unimaged shroud – so the *sydoine* could not have been the Mandylion.[28] In fact, de Clari actually mentions the Mandylion in an earlier passage about the Pharos Chapel.[29] Wilson counters that after the discovery of the full image the Mandylion became the *sydoine* and a fake Mandylion was put in its place, although there seems to be no earthly reason for this elaborate subterfuge. If you have the real thing, why try to make it something else (or vice versa)?

In fact Wilson himself relies on the Shroud having been worshipped as just a head in his reconstruction of what happened to it between 1204 and its appearance at Lirey 150 years later. He says it became the infamous idol head worshipped by the Knights Templar (a religious order founded in about 1118 and suppressed in 1312) – although Jesus' shroud image would, so our researches indicate, be the very last thing the Templars would want to worship.

Another episode in the Mandylion's career indicates that it was a simple painted image. It was pawned in the eighth century by the Edessan rulers to pay taxes to one Athanasius, a member of a rival Christian sect, the Monophysites. But when it was redeemed he gave them a copy he had had painted and gave the original to his Monophysite baptistry.[30] The Edessans were completely fooled by his trick: so was the original just such a painting? Significantly, the best modern artists have failed to reproduce a convincing Shroud image, and a painted copy would be very obvious immediately.

Philip McNair, a professor of Italian with an interest in the Shroud, has objected to the Mandylion theory. He suggests that if it had been the Shroud with just the head section on display, then the cloth would have yellowed and the image on it faded, and the difference would be noticeable today.[31] In fact, although the background of the cloth is evenly coloured, the head image itself is actually darker than the rest.

Is there any way of proving the Shroud's history? A great many people who we have talked to during the course of our research have cited the work (published in 1976) of Dr Max Frei, the forensic scientist, as ultimate proof of the authenticity of the cloth. (In fact, at one point the phrase 'but what about the pollen?' was, not entirely seriously, considered as a title for this book.) Frei's work was, however, as we hope to show, very flawed from a scientific point of view.

Frei identified pollen trapped in the fibres of the Shroud as belonging to species of plants found only in Palestine, the Anatolian steppes surrounding Edessa (modern Urfa) and around Constantinople (Istanbul). From this it was reasonable to conclude that the cloth had, at some time in its chequered career, been in each of those three places – exactly, in fact, the places proposed by Wilson. This was not a coincidence.

Accounts of Frei's work give the impression that he took his samples from the Shroud and identified the plants from which they came by comparing them to catalogued pollen from around the world. Then, it is believed, he compared the identified samples to their known geographical distribution, and independently arrived at the same conclusion as Wilson. Not so.

Before Frei's work there had been virtually no systematic collection and classification of pollen, so he himself had to build up the database with which to compare his own samples. One of the most important criterion of scientific investigation is that results should be verifiable by others; in this case it was impossible to do so.

There were also no controls to which his results might be compared. Frei's work was based on the premise that pollen grain husks are virtually indestructible, and this also implies that they could be carried great distances over a period of milennia. Any ancient piece of cloth would be bound to pick up stray pollen husks from a great many places. This factor would have had to be allowed for: finding grains from say, Urfa, is not significant unless they exist in such a proliferation on the cloth that they are definitely above the level that might find its way there by accident over the years.

No one knows where the cloth was woven, although it is likely it came from the Middle East. Neither is it known where and when it was kept before being imprinted with the image. It could have been kept directly in the path of a wind blowing straight in from Urfa almost constantly, for all we know.

There are also some clues as to how Frei's work seems only too neatly to reinforce Wilson's reconstructed history of the Shroud in the background to his research. After taking the samples in 1973, it seems Frei's work ground to a halt for lack of funds. Then in 1976, producer David Rolfe began to work on the film The Silent Witness, which was based on a script by Ian Wilson, and had the Mandylion theory at its centre. Rolfe and Wilson roughed it in various inhospitable parts of the Middle East (heroically coping with the puzzling but complete lack of sanitation at Urfa), looking for locations for the film: Rolfe paid for Frei to go with them. It was from samples collected on this trip that he completed his work and presented his conclusions.[32]

True, Frei did match pollen found on the Shroud to plants unique to the three locations suggested by Ian Wilson, but then he only looked in those three places. The Mandylion theory demands that the Shroud had been in those three places – and those three only. If, for example, there was evidence that it had been in Toledo, the entire theory would be invalidated. Yet for all we know there is Australian pollen on the Shroud: Frei did not look for it. Both Wilson and Rolfe, however, must have been pleased with his work, which justified the gamble of Rolfe's funding of Frei's trip, and one could easily conclude that the latter may have regarded it as a loan repaid. Perhaps his sponsors would not have been so keen to enlist his help if they had known that he was, in the years to come, to authenticate the 'Hitler diaries'.

Frei's work has been criticized by other experts as being too selective.[33] And it received scant support from STURP – they found 'little pollen' on the samples that they took.[34]

The Shroud is not, then, another incarnation of the Mandylion. But where was it from 1204 to its sudden appearance in Lirey in the late 1350s? Again, Wilson endeavoured to provide the answers. He believed that the Shroud was taken to France by Crusaders who sacked Constantinople. To explain the bewildering silence on the subject that followed, he invokes that most enigmatic military order, the Knights Templar.

Historians complain that this organization is brought in to fill any gap in history; and it is true that they are ideally suited for the purpose, for very little is known about them – academically, at least.

The Templars were, ostensibly, an order of soldier-monks founded to safeguard the passage of pilgrims to the Holy Land in the early twelfth century. Soon they became influential and wealthy, with branches in most European countries, but as their power increased, so did the machinations of their enemies.[35]

They have, with varying degrees of plausibility and lunacy, been put forward as custodians of the Holy Grail, the progenitors of Freemasonry, protectors of the bloodline of Jesus – and, most recently, they have been persuasively implicated in the search for the lost Ark of the Covenant. To a certain extent, the historians' complaint is valid, but the Templars' background is so murky, and the rumours surrounding them are so extraordinary, that it is no wonder that they are invoked by anyone keen on the shadowlands of history.

The Order of the Temple of Solomon – to give the Templars their proper title – was founded in Jerusalem in 1118, shortly after the First Crusade, by just nine knights. They soon grew to immense wealth and political power, acting virtually as a separate European state during the twelfth and thirteenth centuries. They were a mixture of military/chivalric and monastic orders, each of them being bound by strict oaths of loyalty, personal poverty and celibacy, while also being the most highly trained and feared fighting force of their day.

Proud and aloof, acknowledging only the Pope as superior, the order owned lands and fortresses across Europe, and operated the first international banking system. But on Friday 13 October 1307, every single Knight Templar in France was arrested and imprisoned on the orders of Philip IV, on – even for that day – quite sensational charges of heresy and diabolical practices. They were tortured, and confessions that supported the charges were wrung out of them.

Over the following months, under the orders of Pope Clement V, much the same happened in other European countries, and the order was dissolved by 1312 – as far as most historians are concerned, that was certainly the end of that. However, the authorities in countries outside France tended towards greater leniency; the detained knights were released – as long as they rejected the order and repented of their 'crimes'. But those who insisted on their innocence were burnt to death. This included the Grand Master of the order himself, Jacques de Molay.

History has it that Philip simply wanted their money, but were the charges against them trumped up completely? It is suspicious that so many knights, even given the horrific circumstances of their confession, told tales that tallied in detail. The most serious accusations levelled at them were that they denied Jesus as Christ, spat at and trampled the Cross, indulged in ritual homosexual practices, and that they worshipped a mysterious idol known as 'Baphomet', whose exact form differs depending on the confession, but which is generally taken to be a demonic head.[36]

Ian Wilson's theory[37] is based on the fact that one of the highest ranking Templars – their Norman Preceptor, who was executed with Jacques de Molay – was called Geoffrey de Charnay. This is, of course, the same as that of the first recorded owner of the Lirey Shroud forty years later (the variation in spelling is not significant). Wilson's original speculation about a possible family connection between the two Geoffreys rested on just the similar name – there was no genealogical evidence one way or the other. But in 1987, genealogist and BSTS member Noel Currer-Briggs[38] established that there was a relationship between the two historical figures; Templar Geoffrey de Charnay was the uncle of the Geoffrey of Lirey fame. On this, Wilson was proved right.

For him, this relationship helps to explain where the Shroud/ Mandylion was between 1204 and the 1350s. If the cloth were in the possession of the Templars then no wonder its whereabouts were unknown – the order was obsessed with secrecy. And after the fall of the order, it passed into the possession of the de Charny family, whose failure to explain its provenance may well have been a natural reluctance to have it linked with the disgraced Templars.

There is, of course, one immediate objection to Wilson's theory here. In his eagerness to find the Shroud a pre-1350 location, he seems to have unavoidably linked it with Baphomet, the demonic idol head of the Templars. We shall come to our own understanding of that order and their beliefs later, but for Wilson, with his own well-publicized Roman Catholic views, this is an astonishing connection.

Suspending disbelief for a moment, how did the Shroud get to France after the sacking of Constantinople in 1204? The Templars were not involved in any action there during the Fourth Crusade. Building on Wilson's ideas, Currer-Briggs suggested that it could have found its way into Europe through the good offices of the former Empress of Constantinople, Mary-Margaret of Hungary.[39]

She was of a Frankish noble family who were related to some of the Crusade's leaders, and was the widow of the deposed Byzantine Emperor Isaac II. It was his overthrow (for reasons that are not relevant here) that led directly to the sacking of Constantinople. Within a month of the fall of the city, Mary-Margaret married one of the Crusade leaders, Boniface de Montferrat – with whom she went to Greece – and after his death, with yet another husband, to Hungary. Currer-Briggs believes that it was this Elizabeth Taylor of the Byzantine world who took the Shroud/Mandylion out of the sacked city, possibly giving it to the Templars as security for a loan.

An ingenious retrospective – but it is a theory about an article that may well not have even existed, or which was being deliberately kept secret, so it must remain speculation. And, throughout the unwinding of these elaborate historical theories, one must always bear in mind that the Mandylion could not have been the Shroud – and that the carbon dating proves it. (In fact, Currer-Briggs himself has difficulties with Wilson's Mandylion theory, yet is unable to suggest how the Shroud came to pop up so abruptly in Constantinople without any mention at all of it in the previous twelve centuries.)

In the absence of any hard-and-fast evidence for the existence of the Shroud before the Lirey displays, several researchers turned instead to indirect clues.

For example, many believers say that because the man on the Shroud fits the image of Jesus in pre-fourteenth-century Christian art, it must prove the cloth's authenticity. True, before the sixth century there were many variations in the depiction of Jesus – he was sometimes shown beardless, for example – but the sudden consensus image does not itself prove that the Shroud had come to light and inspired all art thereafter. Of course if the Shroud is a forgery it could well have followed established artistic traditions, especially if the forger had a keen eye for detail and was a meticulous master hoaxer.

Some researchers, however, have claimed to locate specific characteristics on the Shroud itself that establishes that it influenced artists before Lirey. Frenchman Paul Vignon, one of the most celebrated sindonologists, claimed that some characteristics of the face of the man on the Shroud match depictions of Jesus dating back to Byzantine times, which have now become known as 'Vignon marks'.[40] The most famous

of these is the downward pointing 'V' shape between the brows, which
Vignon believed matched exactly the tradition in early iconography of
showing Jesus with what looks like a distinct frown-mark. Vignon claimed
to have isolated twenty similar marks which he matched with those on
early Christian paintings. No icon had them all – a twelfth-century
Sicilian painting had the most at fourteen – but it was enough to
convince Vignon that the Turin Shroud had been around since at least
the eighth century.

There is, however, still a major chicken-and-egg problem here. Surely
there is no reason why our putative master forger could not have used
his power of observation – just as Paul Vignon did – to create a fake
Shroud complete with downward pointing 'V' shape between the eyes?
The answer to that is that he could not, however, unless he had a camera
handy. Until 1898 pilgrims could see very little detail on the Shroud, and
certainly no 'V' shape. It is only in photographic negative that this detail
can be seen at all clearly, so how could sixth-century icon artists possibly
have copied it?[41]

The minute inspection of the cloth went on: after Vignon came Alan
Whanger, Professor of Psychiatry at Duke University, North Carolina.
Using a device for superimposing one picture on another that he had
developed specially for the purpose, he compared the face of the
Shroudman to various pre-thirteenth century paintings of Jesus. He
concluded that they fit with such precision that the pictures must have
been copied faithfully from the Shroud.[42]

Whanger's criteria were the 'points of congruity', such as those used
by US police forces to judge whether or not two pictures are of the
same person. He claimed that some of his examples actually showed
more points of congruity than are required by the police and the FBI
to establish identity. The trouble with this kind of work – as we were to
find out for ourselves – is that it is very subjective, and rapidly becomes
a kind of Rorschach inkblot test. The other problem is that such fine
detail tends to blend in with the weave of the cloth (again, we speak
from experience). And, of course, in order for any of these comments
to be valid, they have to be applicable to the image as seen by the naked
eye, and not using the negative.

There are other difficulties here: as we were to find out to our cost,
there are indeed none so blind as those who won't see, and nowhere
is this adage more relevant than when applied to Shroudies. They have
seized on Vignon's work with great excitement, taking it as yet more
evidence for the Shroud's authenticity. But an objective appraisal of it
is nowhere near as conclusive. They point, for example, to similarities of
one raised eyebrow – and of course the 'V' shape – between the Shroud
image and earlier icons. But where the more obvious detail is concerned,

earlier icons show a marked difference from the Shroud. For example, they show the shape of Jesus' face as being anything from long and narrow (as on the Shroud) to full and round.

Again, subjectivity ran riot in Whanger's work. One of his most congruous 'fits' (match for the Shroud image) is that of Christ on a Byzantine coin from the reign of Emperor Justinian. He has found no fewer than 145 points of congruity here – surely a superhuman feat, for the image on the coin is only 9mm high (smaller than the Queen's head on a 5p piece). But if Whanger showed virtually paranormal powers of observation, then what about those of the putative Byzantine copier, who slaved away without benefit of computer microscope and super-strength contact lenses? And even if this unknown genius of a draughtsman had the technical prowess to do such a thing, why would he have needed to, when a much vaguer copy would have done just as well?

Perhaps not surprisingly, Whanger's claims have been met with some scepticism from the more objective of Shroud scholars, as 'Ian Wilson joked in a lecture to the BSTS in April 1991, 'all this [Whanger's claims] from a psychiatrist . . .!'

Yet other researchers argue completely the reverse. They look for characteristics that are *different* from artistic convention, believing that these would show that the Shroud image was taken from a real image. One such is the nakedness of the man on the Shroud, and the unusual and unnatural way his hands are crossed. Wilson cites examples to underline this, such as an illustration in a late twelfth-century manuscript in Budapest and a tapestry sent to Pope Celestin II at about the same time: both show Jesus's hands crossed as on the Shroud, and the former also shows him completely naked.[43]

The trouble with this argument is that there are also paintings showing people other than Jesus with these characteristics. In a church at Berze-la-Ville in south-east France, for example, a wall painting dating from 1110 shows St Vincent naked and in a pose exactly like that on the Shroud.[44] Using Shroudies' logic, this proves that the man on the Shroud is in fact St Vincent.

Recently an ingenious attempt has been made by Ian Dickinson, one of the more active – and reasonable – members of the BSTS, to show that the Shroud existed at least before the earlier limit indicated by the carbon dating. He has tried to find the missing parts of the cloth's side strip. This 8cm wide section, of separate origin from the Shroud proper, is 5cm or so too short at either end. Most Shroudies have just shrugged: maybe it was always too short, who cares? But Dickinson believes that the missing bits were deliberately cut off – perhaps as a gift to some honoured person – and reasoned that, if they could be traced and proved to have existed before 1260, the carbon dating would be cast into doubt.[45]

He thinks he has found one of them in the cathedral in Pamplona, Spain. Unfortunately it is kept inside a sealed reliquary: attempts are being made to persuade its guardians to open up in the spirit of scientific enquiry. However, it is known that the reliquary and the cloth inside it were there before 1260. But even if the cloth did match the missing parts of the Shroud's side strip, what would it prove? Just that the strip existed before the earlier limit of the carbon dating – so what, if it came from another piece of cloth anyway? It could have been any age and from anywhere, and proves nothing.

All this evidence, especially when set against the carbon dating, is simply speculation – in some cases fuelled by the near desperation of the believer to prove the cloth authentic. None of it shows that the cloth we call the Turin Shroud existed before the later limit of the carbon dating – indeed, before the 1350s.

Perhaps there was a series of 'holy Shrouds'; today's Turin Shroud being just one of a line of them . . . but whatever the background of the fake's emergence (and we will be coming to that shortly), there was no doubt that the time was absolutely ripe for producing such a thing.

Although there was no early report of an imaged shroud ever being exhibited to pilgrims, there had long been traditions of cloths imprinted with Jesus' face. Apart from the Mandylion, there was also the Veronica.

Again, although significantly omitted from the New Testament itself, the story of its creation figured largely in early Christian tradition, and is part of the Catholic Stations of the Cross. It was said that, as Jesus staggered up Calvary under the weight of the cross, a sympathetic woman rushed out of the crowd and wiped away the sweat from his face with her handkerchief. It was then seen to bear the imprint of his image. The woman's name was Veronica.

A cloth said to be the same one, and which is called the Veronica – had been kept in Rome since at least the twelfth century. It was seen publicly very rarely, but one of those rare occasions was just a few years before the first appearance of the Lirey Shroud – in the Holy Year 1350 – when it was displayed to a rapturous audience of pilgrims. It was the talk of Europe.[46]

But it was only Jesus' face. Imagine how gullible Christendom would react to a cloth bearing the image of his entire body; one that showed him crucified, about to come into his godhood through the final glory of the Resurrection. How could the unscrupulous and avaricious resist such a temptation? And we believe that all the evidence points to such a fraud – or a series of frauds – being perpetrated.

There remains, however, the Shroud's essential paradox. On the historical evidence alone no one should have the slightest hesitation about dismissing it as a fourteenth-century fake. But on the scientific evidence – at least on its superficial appearance – alone, we have to admit that there is something truly strange and inexplicable about the image. What arguments about how the image was formed do the authenticists put forward to underpin their beliefs? And if the Shroud is not the winding sheet of Jesus, how else could the image have been created?

— 3 —

THEORIES

'The dilemma is not one of choosing from a variety of transfer mechanisms but rather that no technologically-credible process has been postulated that satisfies all the characteristics of the existing image'
Lawrence Schwalbe and Ray Rogers, STURP scientists, 1982[1]

IF THE Shroud of Turin is authentic, how could the image have been formed? And, by the reverse of the same token, if it is a fake, by what process could it possibly have come into being? These are questions that have vexed thousands of thinking people since the true extent of its detail became known in 1898.

Surprisingly, however, few Shroudies regard the image as literally a miracle. Of course, if it were, all the effort put into the scientific studies would be pointless, since, by definition, miracles are outside the scope of science. If God can accomplish anything simply through an act of divine will, he could easily have caused an image of the crucified Jesus to appear spontaneously on a piece of medieval French linen, or hurled the genuine burial cloth through a time-warp from first-century Jerusalem to fourteenth-century Lirey, thus bypassing 1300 years and skewing the carbon dating.

There have been similar images reported by the faithful over the years. The most holy relic of Mexican Catholicism is the image of Our Lady of Guadalupe. It is a cloth bearing the image of the Virgin Mary, which was said to have appeared on the cloak of an Indian who had an encounter with the Virgin in 1531 (conveniently for the Church: she appeared complete with Indian features and dress and urged the natives to convert to the religion of their new overlords). Although the image is known to have been overpainted, there is still some mystery about the underlying image (there is, in the USA, an Image of Guadalupe Research Project). Although the arguments are outside the scope of this book, many do point to this image as a clear example of miraculous imprinting. And if it could happen in the case of this cloth, why not in the case of the Turin Shroud? Yet nobody has felt the need to trace this particular icon back to the earthly life of the Virgin Mary.

Part of the Shroud's appeal to the believers is that it is, apparently, something between a miraculous and a mundane object, a souvenir left by Jesus that is now open to the scrutiny of twentieth-century science. More than one writer has suggested that this is deliberate; a conundrum set by God to bring the atheistic age of science back to the right path. Why, they ask, would the Shroud display characteristics that could only be appreciated in our technological age, when photography and computer-aided image analysis are available? One leading researcher, while advocating a strictly scientific approach to the enigma, has even stated that the Shroud has been divinely protected throughout its long life for just such a purpose.[2]

Labelling the Shroud 'a miracle' is perhaps a fail-safe – or just an excuse – for those who wish to ignore the carbon dating, but those who have devoted themselves to its investigation and uphold the laws of science, will have no truck with the easy way out.

Some see the origin of the image on the Shroud as paranormal, rather than miraculous. They suggest that supernatural, rather than Divine, forces may be at work. Mexican parapsychologist César Tort has raised the possibility that the image is a 'thoughtograph'. There is evidence – controversial, but not easily dismissed – that some psychics can create recognizable images on film by the power of thought alone. The most famous case is that of Ted Serios, an alcoholic Chicago bellhop, whose abilities were studied intensively in the mid-1960s by the eminent researcher Jule Eisenbud. If it exists, the ability of the mind to affect the highly sensitive chemicals of photographic film would seem to be a natural variant of psychokinesis (PK) – the alteration of the state of a physical object by mental influence alone – as exhibited most famously by Uri Geller.[3]

Tort[4] points to a similar phenomenon, that of images appearing spontaneously on the walls and floors of buildings. He cites a well-documented case from the 1920s, when the image of the late Dean John Liddell appeared on a wall of Oxford Cathedral. Such pictures are usually of people of special sanctity, but not always. In one case in Bélmez de la Moraleda in Spain, which was investigated by the veteran parapsychologist Professor Hans Bender one-time mentor of Elmar Gruber, co-author of The Jesus Conspiracy, leering, demonic faces have appeared regularly on the walls and floors of a house for more than twenty years.

César Tort's starting point was the paradox between the historical and scientific evidence that we had already noted: the image on the Shroud is more consistent with actual crucifixion (and so, to most people, with the first century), than with a medieval artistic forgery, but the carbon dating and the documented history show it to be medieval. How, asked Tort, could a fourteenth-century cloth show a first-century image? So he speculated that it was a thoughtograph, projected onto the cloth by the collective minds of the pilgrims who came to meditate on a (then plain) cloth that they believed had wrapped their risen Lord.

Tort admitted the main objection to this scenario: even suspending disbelief about the reality of thoughtography, we would expect the image to conform to the beliefs and expectations of those who unconsciously created it. To a medieval mind, there should be nails in the palms (not the wrists), Jesus should look younger, and he would certainly not be naked as here. To explain this, Tort has to invoke another paranormal phenomenon – retrocognition – where the past can be psychically perceived.

The pros and cons of these phenomena are outside the scope of this book, but in the case of Tort's hypothesis it is enough to say that neither effect has ever been reported as working on the scale needed to make the Shroud image, and that the use of two such unknowns – thoughtography and retrocognition – is simply stretching credulity far too far. Neither does it explain why a negative image was projected, or why the bloodstains should be so different from the rest of the image. It is a bold and open-minded attempt to reconcile the contradictory elements of the Shroud, but in the end it creates more questions than answers.

One of the favourite theories of scientific Shroudies is that the image is not in itself a miracle, but that it was the by-product of one – the Resurrection. This is the 'nuclear flash' theory, promoted by STURP co-founder John Jackson (a physicist with the USAF) and taken up enthusiastically by many others[5]. They suggest that, as the image resembles a scorch-mark, it was caused by a split-second burst of high-energy radiation emanating from Jesus' body as it regenerated. Since the carbon dating, believers have hastily capitalized on this theory: they claim that if the Shroud had been subjected to a blast of radiation, the amount of radioactive carbon-14 would have increased and the Shroud would appear to be much younger than it really is.

We have heard variations of that theory from virtually every Shroudie we have talked to – and it seems crazy. We think it is astonishing that such a theory could have been seriously advanced by a trained physicist, and supported by other scientists, since it should be obvious to anyone with even the most elementary understanding of the nature of radiation that this hypothesis violates the very laws of physics that it invokes[6].

For the 'nuclear flash' theory to be valid, the energy released would have been so great it would have destroyed not only the cloth itself, but also a large part of Jerusalem. But even if we accept, for the sake of argument, that the phenomenon was somehow controlled by Divine will, there are still fundamental objections to be considered.

Such a process could never have imprinted the kind of image we see on the Turin Shroud. All radiation – nuclear, thermal or electromagnetic (which includes light) – spreads out from its source in all directions, and therefore would have scorched all parts of the cloth equally. Even if the linen were in close contact with the body, the best that could be expected is a scorched silhouette of a human form, featureless and of equal intensity – certainly not the detailed and recognizable Shroud image. If the cloth were draped over a body, we should be able to see the sides and the top of the head. As it is, they are not there.

It is like holding a sheet of photographic film a few inches away from a light bulb and expecting to see a picture of the bulb itself when the film is developed: all that would be seen is a fog where the light had uniformly hit the film. Light shining from any source is known as incoherent, with the rays spreading out equally from the point of origin. Without some mechanism for turning it into coherent light – where the rays are made to travel in the same direction, towards a specific point – no image can be captured. We can see the light bulb because the eye has such a mechanism: the pupil. A camera has its lens. These laws hold good for any kind of radiation.

To produce the Shroud image, the radiation would have had to travel directly up, perpendicular with the body, and also directly down to produce the back image, and in no other direction. This breaks the laws of physics. Even if the radiation behaved in this way, it could never have reproduced such fine detail of the man on the Shroud. Radiation can only make a picture by being blocked by something, thus creating a shadow. Different kinds of radiation are blocked by different materials; visible light will not pass through a human body, whereas x-rays will pass through the skin and internal organs but not through bone. If the 'nuclear flash' theory were correct, we ought to see the same effect as an x-ray – a skeleton – not the detailed outer body. Proponents of this view have pointed out that the fingers do appear to be skeletal, but in that case why is the rest of the body natural in appearance? It can be argued that the hands have that look due to 'degloving' – the draining of the blood from the hands during the process of crucifixion.

Some books on the Shroud reproduce pictures of images produced by the aftermath of the atom bomb at Hiroshima – for example, the 'shadow' of the wheel of a hand valve etched onto the wall of a nearby gas tank – and they attempt to draw a parallel with the Shroud image.[7] In fact, there is no such thing. These images are literally shadows – the wheel was between the source of radiation and the wall, blocking or altering its passage. In the case of the Shroud the theory is that the source of radiation was within the body. We are seriously asked to believe that it was blocked only by the skin and hair, which it then faithfully reproduced.

The only way in which a recognizable image can result from a three-dimensional body, using any form of radiation, is if the radiation is reflected from its surface, not shining through it. The source would have to be outside the body. Take this example: imagine making a glass model of a human head with a bright light bulb in its centre. Turn the light on and what do you see? Only the shining shape of the head: the features would not be distinguishable. Now imagine a solid bust lit from an external source, reflecting the light. Everything about it would be clearly visible. Even so, we can only make it out because our eyes focus the rays of light; a cloth coated in light-sensitive chemicals and suspended in front of the bust would never capture the image.

Finally – as pointed out by BSTS member Peter Freeland – the process would have burned away, or at least caramelized, any blood on the cloth.

So, the much-quoted 'nuclear flash' theory is the least tenable of all, and would deserve less attention even than the thoughtograph hypothesis of César Tort, were it not for the fact that it continues to be taken seriously in Shroud circles: in fact, a paper was given on the subject at the 1993 Rome Symposium. Many unscientific Shroudies accept it as the most likely explanation, or at least as a serious contender. But the scientific Shroudies also tend to cling to this theory, which surely says more about their desperation to believe than their faith in the laws of science. The theory is as full of holes as the Shroud would have been, had it been exposed to such a process.

There is a second category of theories to account for the formation of the image: rare natural processes, chemical reactions between the body of Jesus and the cloth of the Shroud.

The first such idea was Paul Vignon's 'vapourographic' theory, put forward in the early years of this century.[8] He speculated that the cloth was impregnated with aromatic oils that contained myrrh and aloes which reacted with ammonia gas given off by the body. (The corpses of people who die after prolonged torture are covered with sweat with an unusually high urea content, in which ammonia is abundant.) Vignon carried out some experiments with these substances and, after much trial and error, he was able to produce vaguely Shroud-like stains, but with nothing like the detail of the real image.

Recently Elmar Gruber and Holger Kersten returned to this hypothesis, and in their experiments, which are described in their book *The Jesus Conspiracy*, they applied concentrated heat to Kersten's body, which had been soaked in a mixture of aloes and myrrh. This was to test their idea that Jesus was still alive while in the Shroud. They managed to obtain images, but had to admit, because of the resulting distortion, that 'the original could not have been formed in this way.' Despite this failure, they still believe that some similar process must have been responsible for the formation of the image on the Turin Shroud.

Since Vignon's experiments, many other reacting agents have been suggested, which include: an extract from the soapwort plant used to clean fabrics in Roman times, a turpentine-like extract from the terebinth tree, and even common salt. Fortunately it is not necessary to discuss them all as they all share a basic flaw.

Any chemical reaction would have continued through the cloth as the rising vapour seeped through, whereas the Shroud image is only on one side of the cloth. (This was not known in Vignon's day.) And to produce the perfectly-graded image, the gas would have had to travel in parallel lines and lessen in density the further it moved from the body. Gas does not however behave like that: it diffuses in all direction. The best that we would see is a uniformly-coloured, man-shaped silhouette.

To deal with some of these problems, BSTS Chairman Rodney Hoare introduced what he called the 'thermographic correction'.[9] As we have seen, this also formed the basis of Gruber and Kersten's hypothesis. Noting that all chemical reactions need some degree of heat, he argued that perhaps Jesus was actually alive in the tomb and warmer than his surroundings: from this he developed the idea that the Resurrection was, in fact, simply a recovery from coma, which led him to make some extraordinary claims for the 'message' of the Shroud.[10]

Hoare argues that, if the body were warm, the underside of the cloth would have been warmer than the outside, which would explain why only one side is darkened. The fabric closest to the skin would have been warmer than that slightly further away, hence the grading of the image. Both arguments, however, fail to convince: the fall off in temperature would, once again – by some uncanny coincidence – have to have been exactly right to produce the recognizable human form. The fact of the back image also presents a problem. If the man's back were pressing down on the cloth it should have trapped the warmth, or at least pushed the cloth nearer the body, making the image visibly darker than the front. Yet both back and front images are of equal density. Critics have also pointed out that, had the man been alive, the cloth around the nose and mouth would have been distorted – and therefore so would the image – where it had been sucked in as he breathed.

A serious objection, which applies to all the chemical theories, was raised by STURP. If the image is composed of chemical by-products from the original reaction, it should (as with pigment), have changed colour near the areas that were burned in the fire of 1532. (STURP also made a specific search for the chemical by-products predicted by Vignon's theory, and failed to find them.)

Any process involving vapour rising from the body would depend on factors such as the texture of the body in any given spot. For example, for Vignon's theory, the entire body must have been uniformly drenched in urea-laden sweat, otherwise the intensity of the image would vary. Conceivably, the skin was, but the hairs of the beard and the head do not perspire – and even if they were soaked in sweat they would still have got in the way. The vapour would also rise at a different rate from the hair than the skin, so the image of the face and the beard should be very different. They are not.[11]

The chemical vapour theories also fail to explain the lack of distortion of the image. We saw earlier that attempts to reproduce the image by putting a cloth over a model covered with paint ended up with a distorted, unlife-like image when the cloth was flattened out. The same would apply to an image created by any chemical reaction.

None of these theories accounts for the presence of the blood. If it is real blood, it must have transferred to the cloth through contact with it, yet we know that the body image was, at least in part, the result of action at a distance. (We will discuss this highly significant point in greater detail below.) So a second, equally rare process would have to be invoked, and the odds against two such phenomena coming together are astronomical. Significantly, the believers frequently say at this point, 'But it is Jesus we are talking about – anything could have happened.' Perhaps this is true, but then they have no right to cite known scientific laws as any of their evidence. They cannot have it both ways.

A case cited as support for the 'natural process' hypothesis emerged in 1986, from a hospice in Thornton, Lancashire. Five years before, a patient, identified only as 'Les', died there of cancer of the pancreas. On stripping his bed, the nurses found a stain on the mattress, forming the clear outline of the back of the unfortunate man's body: shoulders, back, buttocks and upper legs, and, most strikingly, the left arm and hand on which he had been lying. A faint, distorted image of part of his face could also be seen. Remarkably, the image had formed on the mattress through the man's pyjamas and the bedsheet (both of which were routinely burned before the image was discovered, although the imaged mattress cover was kept). Although it was five years before the case was brought to the attention of medical and forensic experts, Professor James Cameron of the London Hospital, who had studied the medical details of the Shroud image, was able to show that the image was due to the action of enzymes present in alkaline fluids. Because of the condition of the patient's pancreas, they were released in his urine and, due to his incontinence, collected in the hollows created by his body.[12]

The case caused a stir in the Shroud world, but in fact the parallels between this case and that of the relic are merely superficial. Les' image was clearly made through contact, and was distorted by the weight of his body pressing against the mattress. The difference between the two images is, on the one hand, if you looked through a window from a few feet away, and on the other, if you pressed your face up against the glass.

If the two cases were truly the same phenomenon, the back of the Shroud image ought at least to show similar evidence of contact. It does not. The Thornton image is that of the outline and hollows of the body only, where the liquid collected, whereas the Shroud shows all areas of the body equally. If the image on the Shroud were caused by similar enzyme action, the fluid would have had to jump across the gap between body and cloth where the cloth was not actually in contact with the man's flesh.

The two images do not even look alike, and the enzyme theory cannot be applied to the Shroud. The case does, of course, demonstrate that human bodily fluids can create images that do not wash off – in the Thornton case even bleach failed to budge it.

Another intriguing parallel, this time from the plant world, is that of the 'Volckringer patterns'. These were described in 1942 by Jean Volckringer, a chemist colleague of Pierre Barbet at the Saint-Joseph Hospital in Paris.[13] He discovered that when plant specimens are kept pressed between sheets of paper in botanical collections, negative images sometimes appear on the paper – even, on occasion, upon a second undersheet. Like the Shroud image they are negative and sepia in tone, and show parts of the plant not in direct contact with the paper. They can take years – sometimes decades – to appear, yet the image must have been 'caught' early on, since they show the sample as it was when first pressed, even when it later shrivelled up. The patterns also appear without exposure to light.

The cause of the Volckringer patterns remains unknown, as indeed does their relationship to the Shroud image. Certainly they represent the only parallel found in nature, yet on a much smaller scale and involving vegetable, not human, tissue. The 'action at a distance' exhibited here also involves far smaller distances, and pressed plant samples are of course much flatter than a human body, so helping to create an undistorted image. It is hard to see how the Shroud image could be created by the same process. And although the time it takes the Volckringer images to appear might explain why no image was described as being on the empty burial linen in the Gospel stories, it also provides no reason for the cloth to have been kept and treasured in the first place – especially by Jews, for whom burial linen was deemed so unclean as to be untouchable.

This phenomenon did inspire some original work by BSTS member

Dr Allan Mills, a lecturer in planetary science at Leicester University. He suggested that the Volckringer patterns were due to the effect of free radicals, unstable atoms that are given off by some substances and which, after running loose for a brief life, bind together with other molecules, causing a reaction. He thinks that free radicals are given off by plants and react with lignin, a polymer present in plant and vegetable products such as paper. His experiments showed that lignin was particularly sensitive to the effects of free radicals. And as it is also present in linen, he proposed that the Shroud image was caused by what he terms Free Radical Catalyzed Polymerization – stable currents of warm air rising from the body that carry with them free radicals, which then permeate the cloth. (He disagrees with Hoare about warmth necessarily implying life; he suggests that the warmth of a living body would produce currents that are too turbulent to create a sharp image.)[14]

When Mills gave a talk on this effect to the BSTS in October 1991, however, he did admit that his theory could not explain the back image. And discussing some other aspect of his research he also said, 'I stopped the experiment when I realized it wouldn't work in a tomb . . .' An increasing number of people point to a studio of one sort or another as the original location of the Turin Shroud, and for Mills' work to be at all valid, he should at least have considered this possibility.

All the problems discussed above go to prove that no single known chemical process could create the Shroud image, at least not without requiring highly controlled and/or coincidental conditions. So we are left with only one possible category of explanation: forgery. But even this is almost equally problematic. Even setting aside the stylistic arguments discussed in Chapter 1 – the un-medieval realism, the anatomical excellence, the negative effect and so on – there are still enormous difficulties.

Most of the experiments conducted by the STURP team were designed to detect artificial pigments – inks or dyes – on the image. The results were negative, except in the view of one member of the team, Dr Walter McCrone. He received a good deal of publicity in the months after the testing by claiming that he had not only found and identified paint that made up the image, but also that he had worked out the actual method used by the forger. (The qualification 'that made up the image' is important: there is no dispute that there are microscopic traces of pigment on the Shroud. It is known to have been in contact with painted copies, which were often held against it to 'sanctify' them.)

Walter McCrone is a microanalyst with his own research company, Walter C. McCrone Associates Inc, based in Chicago. His method of identifying substances is to study them under high magnification, and sometimes to supplement that with chemical tests. He has been involved in the forensic work of many criminal cases and is often consulted by art dealers about the authenticity of their *objets*. Allegedly an independent, even abrasive character, McCrone seems to love controversy and publicity.

The case that established his international reputation and brought him to the attention of the Shroud world was his unmasking of the 'Vinland Map' forgery. In Barcelona in 1957 an American antiquarian book dealer found a map, apparently dating from the fifteenth century and copied from an earlier Viking one, which showed parts of north America. For years there had been speculation that two tenth-century Norse sagas telling of the discovery and colonization of an unknown land to the west were in fact describing America. This would mean that the Vikings had beaten Columbus to it by over 500 years – and the Barcelona discovery seemed to be proof of this at last. At first sight it appeared to be genuine: wormholes in it matched those in two books of known fifteenth-century provenance, indicating that the map had once been kept between them (a common practice of the time).

Yale University bought the map in 1965, but after some historians had expressed doubts about its authenticity, they decided to bring in Walter McCrone. He removed particles of the ink and examined them under an electron microscope. His conclusion, announced in 1974, was that the ink contained a substance – anatase (titanium dioxide) – that had only been invented in the 1920s. The map was therefore a forgery.[15] The case brought McCrone international publicity, and it was this that led Ian Wilson to approach him on the possibility of applying his techniques to the Shroud.

Ironically, serious doubts have recently been raised about McCrone's debunking of the Vinland Map.[16] In 1987 physicists at the University of California examined the map using a well-tried technique for analyzing chemicals, particle induced x-ray emission, and found that the ink contained only minute amounts of titanium – more than 1000 times less than that claimed by McCrone – which one would expect to find in medieval ink. It appears that the Vinland Map is genuine after all, but (perhaps predictably) the finding has been almost completely ignored by the archaeological world, even though, before McCrone's announcement, archaeological discoveries in Newfoundland had proved that the Vikings had indeed discovered the New World.

This case is interesting because of the insight it offers into McCrone's character. He dismissed the University of California's results as being mistaken. Contrary to the detachment supposedly exhibited by scientists, he appeared to take their findings as a personal attack, writing to the

Californian team that their work was 'the first shot in a declaration of war'.[17]

Despite his field of expertise, McCrone's interest in the Shroud initially centred on the possibility of carbon dating it, and it was to this end that he first began to work with STURP. However, in 1977 he made an independent approach to King Umberto II to try to get permission for the tests, which effectively antagonized both the custodians in Turin Cathedral and STURP itself – and as a result, he was banned from the tests when they did take place.[18]

After the 1978 STURP tests he was given access to the samples of threads that were taken back to the USA, examining them first under a conventional microscope before turning to the more powerful electron microscope. His conclusions were extremely provocative and profoundly distasteful to the believers: he claimed he had found artificial pigment – paint – on the threads taken from the Shroud. And predictably, although challenged by all the STURP team and the Italian scientists present at the tests, McCrone received more publicity than all of them put together.[19]

His final conclusion was that the samples contained a pigment known as Venetian red, which was made by grinding iron oxide into a powder. He claimed that this alone was responsible for the Shroud image. The ground pigment would have been mixed with a liquid medium for application; his chemical tests revealed the presence of a protein, collagen, that he interpreted as being just that medium. To reinforce these observations, he got an artist, Walter Sanford, to reproduce the Shroud face using the same materials, with tolerably good results, although nowhere near the quality of the original. But McCrone's findings were good enough to convince David Sox, then General Secretary of the BSTS (and up to that time a supporter of the Shroud's authenticity), that the image was painted. As a result of his sudden conversion to the anti-authenticity camp, Sox left the BSTS in the words of Ian Wilson 'amid a brouhaha of publicity' – being, as we were to discover to our cost, neither the first nor the last to fall foul of that supposedly neutral organization.[20]

The dispute between McCrone and the rest of STURP turns on two questions: the origin of the particles of iron oxide on the threads, and whether or not they were responsible for the creation of the image.[21]

Iron oxide – ordinary rust – is one of the most common substances on earth. It is present in dust, and so it is hardly surprising that it was found on the Shroud. But from ancient times it has been ground down by artists as pigment; McCrone's opinion was that the particles were of a shape and size that indicated they had been ground, and that they were present in too great a concentration to be due to accidental contamination.

It was not the presence of iron oxide that was disputed by the STURP scientists (chiefly biophysicist John Heller and chemist Alan Adler), but rather McCrone's belief that it actually created the image that led to their disagreement. So they tested it without resort to microscopy to see if it was present in sufficient quantities to account for the image. X-ray fluorescence scans during the 1978 tests had revealed traces of iron, but there was no detectable difference in its density between the image and the non-image areas – although there was more in the bloodstains.[22]

Several suggestions were made to account for the iron oxide; it could have come from the blood, spreading across the cloth due to years of folding and rolling. On the other hand it could be a by-product of the manufacture of the linen itself (probably the most plausible explanation[23]), or it could have been due to atmospheric contamination. In view of these objections, STURP declined to include McCrone's two papers in their final report. Their selectivity raises some interesting questions about their own position.

The tests that McCrone had used to detect the protein medium were criticized on the grounds that they produce false positive results when used on cellulose, a component of linen. Alternative tests were tried by Adler. They failed to find protein in the area of the body image; although, again, they did in the blood areas.[24]

Many harsh criticisms have been levelled at McCrone's method and conclusions. Most cynically, some have pointed out that, of all the STURP team, he was the only one to have benefited financially from the tests – due to the publicity for his research company. Others have noted that his papers were published only in his own journal, *The Microscope*, whereas other members of STURP chose to publish theirs in independent journals, thus fulfilling a major criterion of scientific respectability. All papers have to be examined and the results confirmed by a panel of experts before being accepted for publication. McCrone said that he published in his own journal only because it could guarantee the necessary high quality colour reproduction of his photomicrographs.

Of all people, we admit to some fellow feeling for McCrone. Even before his findings were complete he had to endure a barrage of criticism from the Italian scientists that verged on pure abuse.[25] But it has to be admitted that his work is open to serious question. To start with, McCrone had produced figures showing the number of particles of iron oxide present in the image areas compared to those in the non-image areas. They appeared to indicate that there was much more iron oxide in the image than elsewhere on the cloth, supporting the idea that it was the result of faking the image.[26]

However, he made no distinction between those particles from the body image and those from the blood, having concluded that the difference was simply due to the amount of pigment applied. However, this is an over-simplification: the blood has many other different characteristics, most of which cannot be explained in this way.

When John Heller pointed out that the number of iron oxide particles quoted by McCrone, even on the image area, was so low that an image made by them would be too faint to be seen, McCrone's response was that, in that case, 'there must be more'.[27] Ian Wilson also challenged McCrone's published data, pointing out that it appeared to contradict the scientist's own conclusions by saying that there was less iron oxide on the blood image threads than on those of the body image. McCrone admitted that the apparently precise number of particles he had given previously, were in fact estimates.[28]

The most reasonable conclusion is that McCrone was wrong. In any case, there are good logical reasons against the Shroud being a painting. For example, the 1532 fire would have made the paint crack and the subsequent dousing it received would have caused water damage that could be compared to that of other paintings. History has shown that the image, unlike any known painting, is not changed by either fire or water.

After McCrone, the leading pro-painting voice is that of American Joe Nickell. He is a private investigator, and a member of the Committee for the Scientific Investigation of Claims of the Paranormal (CSICOP), a scientific pressure group that campaigns against belief in any form of paranormal phenomena. In 1983 he published *Inquest on the Shroud of Turin* (revised in 1987), in which he proposed his own method for reproducing the Shroud image.[29]

Nickell soaked a cloth in hot water and then pressed it over a bas-relief statue. When dry, the cloth was fitted closely over the statue's contours. He then rubbed the cloth with powdered pigment of the type suggested by McCrone (although before he read McCrone's hypothesis he had tried powdered myrrh and aloes). He claimed that the result is an image that looks very like that of the Shroudman. It has a similar negative effect, but no three-dimensional quality.

It must be said that Nickell's results, like those produced by Walter Sanford under McCrone's direction – although more recognizable in negative – are nowhere near as impressive as the Shroud, even though both attempts were produced by modern artists deliberately trying to create a negative image. Although they were much more familiar with negatives than any medieval artist would have been, the hypothetical early hoaxer managed to outdo them.

Nickell's suggestion has been criticized for being too convoluted for any putative medieval artist and as having no parallel in art of that period.[30] César Tort also points out that Nickell cites McCrone's work in support of his own.[31] In fact, apart from the link with iron oxide pigment, McCrone's method is totally incompatible with Nickell's – McCrone believed he had found evidence that the pigment had been applied as *liquid* paint.

Although they do reproduce some of the characteristics of the Shroud image, neither McCrone's nor Nickell's methods – or that of any other technique yet suggested – are satisfactory, and both researchers are forced to deny or belittle the significance of some of the Shroud's features, such as the negative effect.

Techniques other than painting have been proposed. One idea is that the scorch-like effect was created by heating a life-sized metal statue and wrapping the cloth round it. But the end result, once again, is a distorted and bloated image. Others have suggested that the image was the result of block printing using clay, and yellow ochre, or that it was drawn in red chalk. None of these work – although the last two ideas invoke Renaissance, not medieval, techniques.

To be fair, we found that the believers (who have the lion's share of Shroudie literature on their side) were often too quick to dismiss such ideas. For example, at one time a suggestion was made that the scorch effect could be due to something like 'invisible ink' – lemon juice or something similar – which looks clear when applied, but darkens when heated. This was dismissed, not illogically, on the grounds that it would be impossible to paint such a huge and detailed picture in invisible ink. The suggestion that some of the characteristics could be explained by some form of block printing was turned down because STURP had looked specifically for inks, and had found none.

However, nobody (to our knowledge) has ever put the two ideas together and realized that you can print with invisible ink. Not that we think this was the method used – even though, as we shall see, the invisible ink idea does have some bearing – but it just shows how wary one should be about accepting the believers' arguments unquestioningly.

We had looked into all the theories, both for and against – including some too bizarre to be mentioned – and in our view none provided a watertight case. We had noticed, however, that the same problems came up time and time again, whether you were looking at the pro or the anti material.

The most significant problem was the lack of distortion of the image. No attempt to explain the image – be it contact with the body, heating a metal statue or even the nuclear flash theory – would provide a totally undistorted image. And why do we see only the front and back of the body, not the top of the head or the sides?

The inescapable conclusion is that the Shroud had never been draped around a body, living or dead. However the image may have been formed, the cloth had to have been perfectly flat at the time. This has long been recognized by the believers, but has been rather cannily played down by them. To explain it they have argued that the Shroud must have been supported by something on either side of the body. The most popular idea is that the corpse was surrounded by blocks of spices, intended for use later when proper burial rites could be carried out after the Sabbath – and so the Shroud was stretched across the top of the blocks and kept flat.[32] But this can only work if the body was laid on one half of the cloth, the blocks placed round it, and then the top half pulled over the front. Even given the haste that the Gospels tell us surrounded Jesus' burial (because of the imminent approach of the Sabbath), why choose such a complicated arrangement?

Another version, proposed by Rodney Hoare,[33] that the body was in a lidless stone sarcophagus and the cloth stretched over the top, is even more absurd. Presumably it would still also be under the body – in direct contact with it – yet there is no difference in quality, colour, intensity or 'focus' between the back and front images.

The absurdity of these suggestions just goes to show to us that faith often moves even the mountain of common sense with seamless ease. If the cloth had been supported over the body, there are immense problems with the bloodstains. Unlike the body image, they are caused by some substance – real or fake blood – being added, so they could not have somehow been transferred across the gap from body to stretched, flat cloth. Yet the bloodstains are arguably the most perfect of all the anatomical details. They could only have been put on the cloth by direct contact.

Time and time again in our reading of the previous research, we kept coming back to the difference between the body and the blood images. The nuclear flash theory, for example, might explain the scorch-like nature of the body image, but the temperatures needed would probably have destroyed all blood (and flesh) within miles, let alone that on the cloth. And none of the chemical reaction theories explains how the blood got there.

Some theorists, as we have seen, try to invoke two unique processes working at the same time, rather like Tort's double paranormal phenomena. But not only are the processes different, as cited by their apologists, they are mutually exclusive. Any process that could explain the formation of the body image would actually prevent the blood image from forming, and vice versa. These anomalies could only be reconciled if someone deliberately put them together in faking the Shroud.

Other oddities about the bloodstains reinforce the idea of a fake, many of which were suggested in the late 1970s by BSTS member Peter Freeland – but which have been studiously ignored by the believers.[34] The bloodstains are just too perfect. Yes, they behave exactly as one would expect, given the nature of the wounds, but what state would the blood have been in when the image was formed? If the blood had congealed, then it could hardly have been somehow transferred to the cloth. On the other hand, if it was liquid, it would have soaked into the cloth and run along the fibres. And it certainly would not be so sharply defined in the way that has impressed – and puzzled – the forensic scientists.

As might be expected, the believers have a ready answer. They suggest that the body was wrapped in the Shroud at the very moment that the blood was the right consistency; not too congealed to stick to the cloth, not so wet as to lose its definition. But we know that the blood soaked through the cloth, so it must have been fairly fluid. And their argument assumes that all the blood, from all the wounds, had reached exactly the same consistency at the same time. But even if the body had been wrapped in the Shroud immediately after being taken down from the cross, some of the blood would be fully congealed, some semi-congealed and some still fairly liquid. After all, according to the Gospel accounts, the various wounds were made at different times of the day.

The Crown of Thorns wounds were made in the morning, as were the marks of flagellation (which show traces of blood).[35] The nail wounds, obviously made when Jesus was first put on the cross, would have continued to bleed throughout the day, and the angle of the blood flows confirms this. The last wound was the largest, caused by the centurion's spearthrust to the ribs; the blood flow there was so liquid that it ran across the back, apparently as the body was laid on the Shroud.

Yet all these bloodstains, regardless of their condition, look exactly the same on the Shroud. And the case against their authenticity is underlined by a closer look at the scalp wounds, as suggested by Peter Freeland: yes they are particularly impressive at first sight, hardly the rough-and-ready daubs one might expect from an artist. They well up from pin-sized wounds, filling out into large drops. And the largest forehead wound has even stained the creases of the brow over which it trickled. Doctors have confirmed that real blood behaves just like this when running from real wounds of that size, on that part of the body.

Yet, as every reader of crime fiction knows, blood does not run from the wounds of a dead man. Here, however, it appears that fresh blood is welling up almost as the observer looks on. This feature, so often conveniently ignored, is central to the story. Even so, there is something terribly wrong with the blood on the scalp. Those 'perfect' blood flows, particularly on the back of the head, are visible through the hair. This is, of course, impossible. Blood running from pricks in the scalp would mat the hair and the wounds would lose their definition; all we should be able to see would be a bloody smudge. Instead, on the Shroud, we can actually see the tiny head wounds individually. Equally puzzling is the fact that some of the blood flows appear to extend well beyond the face.

Whoever did this was no journeyman artist. Whoever did this, however, was – where the blood flows are concerned at least – just too much of a perfectionist. For once with this amazing image, aesthetic considerations overrode strict accuracy.

Then there is the back image. It has the same intensity as the front. If it was authentic, it must have been in direct contact with the cloth and should show some distortion, as in the Lancashire hospice case. It does not. And if it were due to some kind of chemical reaction, it should be darker than the front, since it would have pressed harder on the cloth and would have trapped whatever vapours were responsible for the image. But it is exactly the same shade as the front. And some theories – such as that of Allan Mills – allow for no back image at all.

As we came to look at the evidence of the Shroud as it stood in 1988, its mystery seemed more perplexing than ever. Everything points to it being a fake – the carbon dating, the historical evidence, the tell-tale anomalies in the lie of the cloth and the bloodstains. Yet it is not a painting. We could not ignore the sterling work of STURP and other scientists. And while most other Shroudies are influenced by their own religious bias, it was not the case with us. Neither are we known as sceptics in matters paranormal (which includes so-called 'miracles'); put simply, we had no axe to grind one way or the other.

We kept coming back to the data. The sheer realism of the image and its anatomical excellence is totally at odds with what might be expected from a medieval forger. It was the 'nuclear flash' theory that helped to steer us towards a certain path by making us realize two major factors. The first was that, if the image really was created from a human body, whatever energy was used – nuclear radiation, rays or just ordinary light – had to be reflected from the body, not emitted from within it. The second was that the energy must have been directed or focused in some way, otherwise there would be no recognizable image.

In summing up the results of the 1978 tests, STURP scientist Lawrence Schwalbe wrote: '. . . elimination of all known methods does not prove that a clever artist or hoaxer did not think of a method unknown to us.'[36] Those words were to prove prophetic where our work was concerned, although the description of the hypothetical forger as 'clever' was, we discovered, definitely something of an understatement! Even at that early stage, we realized that even if the Shroud was the work of an artist, it was still far from being the simple fake that was dismissed so brusquely by detractors such as Teddy Hall. Whoever created it possessed knowledge far, far ahead of his time, and had used a method so effective that it continues to confound even the cream of the twentieth-century scientific community. Clearly this was no ordinary artist, no ordinary person.

In the months that followed the announcement of the carbon dating results, we were to discover that the creator of the Turin Shroud was much more than even a brilliant artist. He possessed, in ways hitherto unguessed at, one of the most extraordinary minds the world has ever known.

— 4 —

CORRESPONDENTS

'The shroud is still an object worthy of contemplation and the identity of the unknown, brilliant author is the greatest remaining mystery.'

Professor Paul Damon of the Arizona radio-carbon laboratory[1]

SO FAR we have dealt with the historical and scientific background of the Shroud, and with all the theories put forward to account for the image as objectively as we can. But this story is inevitably also our own story, and this is where it really begins.

The carbon dating results were announced on 13 October 1988, Templar Day. And within two months, I (Lynn) was to begin a two-year on and off relationship with Ian Wilson. During this time I was asked to be consultant for an exhibition of images from the world of the paranormal at the Royal Photographic Society in Bath, which was entitled 'The Unexplained'. The Society's Administrator, Amanda Nevill, and I spent many hours discussing the content of the exhibition, and our conversations often spilled over into other topics. We both agreed that the carbon dating made the Shroud more, rather than less, fascinating, but I was unprepared for her sudden instinct that the Shroud image should be included in 'my' exhibition. By this time I felt as if I were somehow being invaded by the thing – with Ian's presence in my life and thoughts it seemed that everywhere I turned there the Shroud was. At first, I was adamant that the Turin Shroud should not be part of the exhibition.

However, very soon I – still somewhat grudgingly – agreed not only to its inclusion, but to its being the focal point of the entire room. Of course the cloth itself remained firmly in its holy casket in Turin, but Ian arranged for us to borrow a full-sized transparency. Amanda had a lightbox specially constructed on which to exhibit it: as the image is over 4 m long, it cost approximately £900 to build (and was later bought by the British Museum, where the transparency was shown in their exhibition 'Fake: the Art of Deception', some months afterwards).

We also fixed a life-sized photographic negative of the image on an adjacent wall, so visitors could check the detail after seeing the 'real' thing on the lightbox. It was an enormous success. In the first few days of the exhibition I often fluttered nervously around like a mother hen, and many visitors came up to me and chatted about the exhibits. The Shroud, in its place of honour, was the first thing you saw on entering the exhibition, and, so soon after the 'disgrace' of the carbon dating, was a favourite topic.

A few visitors expressed their doubts about the carbon dating, saying that the image was obviously miraculous and that scientists could be wrong. I could only nod in part agreement, having some strong views on the arrogance of scientists myself. But several visitors I talked to told me, rather vaguely, that they had 'heard somewhere', or 'read somewhere' that the Shroud had been faked by Leonardo da Vinci, or by 'his studio team'. It is an odd phenomenon; many people seem to know that Leonardo was connected with the Shroud but could not remember where the information came from. One person who did, however, was my neighbour Helen Moss who said she clearly remembered being *taught* that the Maestro had faked the Shroud by her teachers at her Jewish School in Leeds.

I had known Clive for some time – we had been members of the same research groups – and he came to the opening of the exhibition and to other activities connected with it. For him as for me, the groundswell of the various visitors' opinions about Leonardo and the Shroud meant very little in those early days. We both reflected, however, that it did make sense that the only known man clever enough to have perpetrated this astonishing fraud may actually have done it.

The exhibition had caused a minor flurry of publicity, and I found myself on radio and television doing a whistle-stop tour of the exhibits. Having appeared many times on the Clive Bull and Michael van Straten shows on London's LBC Radio I felt at home with a microphone. John Sugar from the BBC World Service was one of the interviewers who came up to Bath, and after we had breezed through the exhibition on tape, we had a long discussion about the Shroud. As a result of my growing enthusiasm about it, he invited me to appear on a magazine programme specifically to discuss the post-carbon dating Shroud. Little did we realize just what fate had in store, thanks perhaps to that broadcast. I say 'perhaps' as at the same time I had also expressed much the same views on LBC, and subsequent investigation has failed to isolate which one of those broadcasts initiated the coming events.

Over the years, like anyone who has appeared a few times on radio and television – and especially someone who deals in the paranormal – I have had more than my fair share of crank letters. Some of them are obvious: written in three different coloured inks, for example, and on neatly cut-out, minute squares of paper, while others appear to be perfectly sane until the punchline. Suspicion of an alien intelligence that lurks in their television set is usually something of a giveaway, I find.

Shortly after doing both these broadcasts, I received a letter from a complete stranger. I was more alarmed, to begin with, by the fact that this mail was addressed to my home, than with its contents. I was furious: heads would roll at LBC or at Bush House! But both sets of staff emphatically denied giving out my personal details to one of their listeners.

The letter was intriguing. Signed simply 'Giovanni' it dealt with Leonardo and the Shroud, but took the story much further into the realms of what appeared to be fantasy. On the radio I had simply said that the Maestro may have been implicated in the fake, but this man claimed to have inside knowledge that Leonardo had been responsible. Giovanni said that I should read *The Holy Blood and the Holy Grail* (1982) by Michael Baigent, Richard Leigh and Henry Lincoln, as background to the story of Leonardo and the Shroud, and that he would be in touch again.

I have to admit that, even though I had been fascinated by the book in question since reading it only six months beforehand, I was no wiser about Leonardo and the Shroud, although he does figure in the story as Grand Master of a secret society. The only reference by those authors to the Turin Shroud is found in their second book, *The Messianic Legacy* (1986), when they muse on a strange phenomenon among their readers:

'There were . . . numerous people who, quite inexplicably, persisted in confronting us with the Shroud of Turin. 'What about the Shroud of Turin?' we were asked repeatedly. (What indeed?) Or, 'how does the Shroud of Turin affect your thesis?' It was extraordinary how frequently this non sequitur occurred.'[2]

Clearly there was a feeling that the events and theories outlined in *The Holy Blood and the Holy Grail* had some connection with the Shroud, although quite what they were eluded everyone. In due course, however, it became clear that we would make that connection.

Our mystery man, 'Giovanni', had made some astonishing claims about Leonardo and the Shroud. When we first read his letter there was, of course, a lot of nervous laughter. However, there was also a distinct feeling under it all that what was being said would really start the ball rolling. As we have seen from the views of visitors to the exhibition, Giovanni's claim that Leonardo had faked the Shroud was hardly news. There appeared to be a rumour in the collective unconscious to that effect. But Giovanni had much more dramatic details to flesh out this story. He offered extraordinary pieces of information that, although seemingly outrageous, gave us real food for thought.

He said that Leonardo had put the image of his own face on the Shroud.

That serene, gaunt, bearded face so widely believed to be that of Jesus himself was in fact Leonardo da Vinci, perpetrating a sacrilegeous joke on posterity. If this were not enough in itself, he went further, much further. He claimed that the body on the Shroud from the neck down at the front and all of the back image was that of a genuinely crucified man, a fifteenth-century victim of the first-century legacy of man's inhumanity to man (or to God, depending upon your views of the nature of Jesus). Giovanni had no information on the central question: had Leonardo actually tortured someone to death in this horrific manner for the sake of historical accuracy, or had he used an already-dead body?

Still more was to come. Our informant also told us that Leonardo had not created the Shroud image by painting it or using any other known technique such as brass rubbing. He said that it represented the Maestro's greatest and most daring innovation, as the image had been created using 'chemicals and light, a sort of alchemical imprinting'. He was saying that the Shroud image is actually a composite photograph of Leonardo da Vinci together with some hapless crucifixion victim whose every contusion had been recorded for posterity by a 15th-century camera.

At least he had not claimed that the Shroudman was an alien from Betelgeuse, but we felt that what he had claimed was so outrageous as to be in that category. Besides, why the semi-anonymity of signing himself just 'Giovanni'? At this stage we kept his letter in a file marked 'Loonies and Cranks', where we felt it deserved to be.

However, his words niggled away at us. The idea of the Shroud image being some kind of a photograph did make sense as the most inexplicable feature of the Shroud is that it behaves like a photograph.

Whoever Giovanni was it soon became evident to us that he had made comments worth paying attention to. As we have seen, several visitors to the exhibition had expressed the idea that Leonardo had been involved in faking the Shroud, and Giovanni just took the idea further. Although we were never to make up our minds about him or his true motives, and to this day we are healthily sceptical about everything connected with him, we are grateful for his tip-offs, which provided us with valuable short-cuts to the research that culiminated in this book.

There was another special moment, another sort of tip off, and one that I look back on with a certain wonder and a great deal of affection. Walking round the exhibition in a daze some days after having received my first Giovanni letter, I invited Amanda Nevill's then seven-year-old daughter Abigail to join me. An intelligent and lively child, she was delightful company and made considerably more pertinent comments about the exhibits than most of the adult visitors rolled into one. We rounded a corner and found ourselves staring straight at the life-sized negative of the man on the Shroud on the opposite wall. I thought perhaps the image of such great physical torture was not appropriate for a child (having Cathar-like views on images of martyrdom), and tried to steer her away from it. But Abigail cocked her head to one side and stared at it solemnly.

'Why is his head too small – and why is it on wrong?' she asked immediately. I looked at the image and felt distinctly faint. Suddenly this was like the critical moment in the story of the Emperor's New Clothes. 'It doesn't *fit*,' she announced emphatically, with a certain disgust at the bad handiwork that was presumably involved. Then she lost interest. I did not. Somehow I managed to turn the conversation and keep her remarks to myself for a short while. But inside I was exulting at what was clearly a highly significant insight – a real breakthrough. If you want the truth, ask a child.

This insight appeared to reinforce Giovanni's comments about the Shroud image being a composite. If Leonardo had superimposed his own face over someone else's body, it may not, of course have made a perfect match. (At this stage we had no idea just how difficult his technique was: later, when we tried to replicate it, we got a taste of his problems.)

Clive was also stunned by Abigail's comments and at the speed that so many things were falling into place. Yet if we were ever going to present anything like a coherent case for this radical viewpoint, we had a very long way to go.

We got on with our lives, although I admit to sneaking into a library and looking Leonardo up. I really wanted to know what he looked like: I was ashamed to admit it, but my long years of education had not provided me with even a vague mental picture of the Florentinian Maestro. I had to check; after all, if he was fat and bald he would be an unlikely candidate for the thin-faced bearded Shroud man. I remember clearly having to take a deep breath as I opened a standard art history book and flicked the pages. But there he was: thin-faced, bearded.

Some weeks after this, I went into a shop to buy a birthday card and was puzzled to see a vivid image of Leonardo on a stack of cards out of the corner of my eye. Intrigued as to why anyone would want them – perhaps there was a sudden craze for the Old Masters I knew nothing about – I investigated. In fact, what I was looking at was a reproduction of the 1935 portrait of the man on the Shroud by Ariel Aggemian. On the back of the postcard it read confidently 'You are holding a picture with . . . the Holy Face of Jesus . . . taken from the Holy Shroud of Turin.' I certainly could not fault the last statement, but as for the first, my initial reaction was, even at this early stage, a vehement: 'Oh no I'm *not*.'

Clive and I hurriedly arranged a lunch, and I showed him a Leonardo reference book and the postcard. I had no need to point out the purpose behind this impromptu show of visual aids – he could see for himself.

A pattern was clearly emerging, but even so we had to go very carefully indeed. We needed some corroboration by someone who was totally unconnected and unconcerned with the Shroudie world. At the time I was a freelance feature writer on a women's magazine, and that afternoon they were organizing a mammoth photo shoot for their fashion pages. I took the portrait of Leonardo and the postcard into the models' dressing room, knowing that anyone connected with women's magazines is used to being asked odd questions, whether it be about their most intimate personal habits or their views on the latest mascara. So I just showed them the two pictures and said, 'What do you think?'

The response was instant, and extremely gratifying. Out of fifteen who came and went during the afternoon (I did manage to do some work from time to time!), eleven of them said straight away: 'It's the same man.' Two said words to the effect of, 'I don't know what you want me to say . . . apart from the fact that it's the same man.' One said she didn't know what I was after and was busy, and the last one said she recognized the man on the Shroud because she was a Catholic and she hoped I wasn't going to say anything upsetting about it. If she is reading this, which I doubt, I apologize.

This unofficial vox pop was hardly evidence, although it is true that the human eye is a better judge than almost any other monitoring, imaging or matching equipment, from the camera to the computer. I had been careful not to give the models any clues as to what reaction I was looking for. We regret not having taken their details for future reference, but even so that episode certainly added to the growing enthusiasm we felt for further investigation into Leonardo and the Shroud. And it certainly made us smile when, months afterwards, Rodney Hoare and Michael Clift of the BSTS said, respectively, 'I can't see the similarity myself,' and 'The man on the Shroud looks nothing like Leonardo.'

Over the months we received a total of thirteen letters from Giovanni, which gave us a great deal of information about Leonardo and the

Shroud, most of which we have shown to be the case through independent research and our own experiments. To sum up, these are his main points.

Leonardo faked the Shroud in 1492. It was a composite creation: he put the image of his own face on it together with the body of a genuinely crucified man. It was not a painting: it was a projected image 'fixed' on the cloth using chemicals and light: in other words it was a photographic technique.

The Maestro faked it for two main reasons. First, because he had been commissioned to do it, by the Pope, Innocent VIII, as a cynical publicity exercise. But the reason he invested it with such concentration, daring and genius was that it represented for him the supreme opportunity to attack the basis of Christianity from within the Church itself (and perhaps he rather liked the idea of generations of pilgrims praying over his own image). He imbued it with subtle clues that, if understood, would be profoundly challenging to the Establishment. However, Giovanni said, Leonardo was never paid for his work on the Turin Shroud because, to the naked eye, it was very disappointing! Perhaps Leonardo can now be said finally to have collected his reward. All this information had been given to us as a statement of fact. Was there any evidence to back this up?

We have seen that Giovanni's first letter urged me to read *The Holy Blood and the Holy Grail* by Michael Baigent, Richard Leigh and Henry Lincoln.[3] In fact I needed no urging, having finally got round to reading it shortly beforehand: years previously, when I was Deputy Editor of the weekly publication *The Unexplained*, we had carried a short series about the book, but I have to confess that at the time it held no interest for me and, as I did not actually edit the series myself, I didn't read it.

Fate can be very quirky: the story of that book was to parallel ours to some extent, and was to be the background for much of our research, though it was three years before I was to make contact with one of the authors, Henry Lincoln, with whom I had a brief telephone conversation.

The Holy Blood and the Holy Grail began with the mystery of Rennes-le-Château, a remote village in Languedoc in southern France, close to the Spanish border. In the last years of the nineteenth century its priest, François Berenger Saunière, began excavating the church and found some documents in a pillar, and, so it was said, two skulls, under the altar. The scrolls were in code, and seemed to point to the involvement of local aristocracy in some kind of plot. Whatever else Saunière found, it seemed to be extremely valuable, for quite abruptly he became immensely wealthy, attracting the cream of Parisian high society to his parish – although, again, we can only guess what the attraction was. Saunière rebuilt the church to house many extremely bizarre decorations, including a plaster demon guarding the entrance, over which there is a sign that reads: 'This is a terrible place'.

The priest, although apparently totally healthy, ordered a coffin to be delivered ten days afterwards, and indeed that was the day on which he died: 17 January 1917. His corpse was set in a sitting position, and many mourners, including some from as far away as Paris, who also seemed to have prior knowledge of this death-day, filed past, each plucking a red pom-pom off his robe. The priest who had been called in to hear Saunière's last confession had, it was rumoured, fled in horror, and Rennes' priest went to his grave unshriven.

In the 1970s Henry Lincoln had researched this story for three BBC television programmes,[4] and had uncovered possible connections with other murky groups in history, including the Knights Templar. Some years later he and his colleagues Baigent and Leigh collaborated on a book project that set out to research this bizarre story yet further. It was to be something of a Pandora's box, eventually leading them through a maze of secret societies and controversy, and which culminated in *The Holy Blood and the Holy Grail*, an international bestseller.

They had discovered that behind the Saunière story was a shadowy organization called the Priory of Sion, who allegedly had existed since the eleventh century. Members of the Priory, including the then Grand Master, Pierre Plantard de St Clair, had made themselves known to the three authors and had helped them in their research, which rapidly widened in scope until the original mystery was almost forgotten. The avowed aim of the Priory was, it seemed, to uphold the bloodline of Jesus and Mary Magdalene, who they believed had been married. They claimed that Jesus had not died on the cross, but had perhaps lived for many years afterwards, and that the Magdalene had taken their children to the south west of France, where she lived out her long life. Their descendants became the Merovingian dynasty of French kings. It is a strange, compelling – but of course 'heretical'– story and has received considerable criticism and downright abuse. (Ian Wilson always provides the prefixes 'notorious' or 'infamous' when forced to discuss *The Holy Blood and the Holy Grail*.)

The idea that Jesus was married made perfect sense to us; as the authors pointed out, it would have been so unusual for an adult Jew of that time to be a bachelor that it would have excited comment, but no special reference would have been thought necessary if he had been married. The prejudice against marriage came much later in the Church's history, together with an implicit condemnation of women in general. And, as

we were to discover, early Christian writers referred to the Magdalene as
'the bride of Christ', which may have been symbolic in the way that the
phrase is used of nuns today, but as it was not applied to any of his other
female disciples, it may have been the literal truth. We think it was.

That Jesus and Mary had children is also completely understandable,
although perhaps it is strange that they were not mentioned in the Bible,
a work that is so replete with often arguably gratuitous genealogies. Then
there is the matter of the 'bloodline', which the Priory of Sion are alleged
to protect. Surely there can be no such thing, certainly not by the time
of the twentieth century, 2000 years after Jesus and Mary would have
had their children? There must be thousands, if not millions, of their
descendants by now, and not all of them can be aware of their lofty
pedigree.

There is a good deal of evidence outside the Bible to reinforce the idea
their Jesus and Mary were at least lovers, if not officially married.[5] The
Gnostic Gospels – early Christian writings that were not included in the
New Testament – offer some clues. The Gnostic Gospel of Philip, for
example, depicts the disciples expressing jealousy at how Jesus preferred
her to them, and was always kissing her on the lips.[6] Simon Peter was
especially angered by her, and may have become her implacable enemy.
The very fact that such Gospels dwelt on tales about the Magdalene's
lofty position among the disciples may well give an indication as to why
they did not form part of the established Christian canon.

The more one applied logic to the situation the more obvious it became
that Jesus' wife is not mentioned in the New Testament not because the
Gospel writers had the profound antipathy to marriage that the Church
later possessed, but because they actively disliked the person who was his
wife. It was not the fact of his marriage that they hated, but the identity
of the woman he had married that they deemed so unacceptable that they
simply avoided mentioning her wherever possible.

Over the centuries the Magdalene has been portrayed as a whore, if
a repentant one. There is very little internal evidence in the Gospels
for this assumption; it is merely an enduring tradition. Yet we were to
discover another, hitherto underground, tradition that not only upheld
Mary as a very special teacher in her own right, but which explained the
idea of her former prostitution.

Baigent, Leigh and Lincoln allege that over the centuries, the Priory
of Sion had boasted many great names as Grand Master.[7] In fact, a
few of them had been women, for the Priory had always been an
equal-opportunities secret society. Among the male Grand Masters
listed in the organization's documents, known as the *Dossiers Secrets*[8]
were Sir Isaac Newton, Victor Hugo and Leonardo da Vinci. Da Vinci,
it seemed, took over the leadership in 1510 until his death in 1519

when he was a guest of Francis I at his château at Amboise in the Loire valley.

Like many other readers of *The Holy Blood and the Holy Grail* we felt twinges of scepticism about some of its claims, although we thought that the logical structure of the book was convincing enough. On the surface it did seem too good to be true that the Priory had as its Grand Masters some of the most famous names in history; others included Claude Debussy and Jean Cocteau, for example. However, in recent years less than famous people have taken over that lofty role, including Pierre Plantard de St Clair and its present incumbent, a lawyer from Barcelona.

Giovanni also claimed to have been high in the ranks of a schismatic faction of the Priory of Sion. There are indications that the organization has undergone internal upheavals in the last decade: the Grand Master at the time of the publication of *The Holy Blood and the Holy Grail*, Pierre Plantard de St Clair, is reported to have resigned – the first ever to do so. According to one source the official headquarters of the Priory is now in Spain. Giovanni claimed that his faction were purists who believe that the modern organization had moved too far from its original aims and beliefs.

Many critics of *The Holy Blood and The Holy Grail* have underlined its reliance upon often mysterious – and therefore uncheckable – sources. Although we had been tempted to take the critics' side at first, very soon our own situation began to parallel that of those three authors to some extent, and we were rapidly humbled by it. As we found out the hard way, a mysterious source does not necessarily mean a fictitious one, although there is never any lack of critics to hint otherwise.

What evidence is there for the existence of The Priory of Sion? Opinions vary between two extremes. The first is that the claims made by the organization – namely, that they have existed since the eleventh century and that they are the custodians of secrets from long before that – are literally true. The other extreme is that it is all an invention of Baigent, Leigh and Lincoln. The latter can be shown to be false, as the Priory had achieved some notoriety in France during the 1970s and its existence is a matter of public record from the 1950s onwards. This does not, of course, prove its claimed pedigree.

A middle view is that the Priory are a modern group who are trying to claim a lengthy history for motives best known to themselves. Some writers on esoteric subjects have expressed scepticism that the Priory could have remained unknown for so long – the existence of even the most secret political, religious and occult societies eventually becomes known. The American writer and expert on secret societies, Robert Anton Wilson,[9] has concluded that the Priory are of twentieth, or perhaps late-nineteenth century origin, and were created as a form of elaborate practical joke. A similar view seems to prevail within today's esoteric circles. We heard from a modern Templar contact that the Priory was invented by Pierre Plantard in occupied France during World War II (as 'a cover for atrocities committed by the Allies and the French Resistance', whatever that might mean).

There is a major problem here: proving the existence of a secret society is similar to trying to prove a negative. Logically, the most successful secret society is the one that nobody knows about, and it seems that when we are dealing with the Priory, we are at least up against past masters in manufacturing misinformation, cover stories and mischief. Yet in their case, there is evidence – albeit indirect – that backs up the Priory's claims as reported by Baigent, Leigh and Lincoln. Their research has found clues that suggest that the Priory has existed under a number of other names, including 'front' organizations that are known to history – such as the defunct Compagnie de Saint-Sacrament which had been headquarted in the seminary of St Sulpice in Paris – and that the aims of these groups are consistent with those of today's Priory.10

As our own research progressed, we realized that there was a thread, an historic continuity that seemed to point to the existence of a highly organized conspiracy dating from roughly the same time as the Priory is supposed to have been formed. This discovery on our part was initially perplexing, for by the time we came to make it, we had become rather sceptical about that organization. With hindsight we realize, however, that the one thing one can say definitely about the Priory of Sion is that they are extremely clever and infinitely inscrutable. (See Chapter Six.)

However, one can find evidence of a less tangible, but equally compelling nature that shows a continuity of esoteric symbolism if nothing else. Themes such as Arcadia, the number 58, Black Madonnas and Mary Magdalene are found in noticeable profusion where the Priory is supposed to have had influence, and in the works of artists, writers and poets who are said to be connected with that organization. These recurring themes would seem to indicate an 'underground stream' of esoteric belief.

If Leonardo was once Grand Master of the Priory of Sion, then he must have been a very different character from the rational, scientific genius of popular imagination, for one characteristic of the Priory is their passion. Their devotion to the Magdalene and to their cause is remarkable both in its intensity and its durability. In fact, little has been known of the real Leonardo – perhaps a state of affairs that was deliberately fostered by persons unknown – over the centuries.

In all of my thirteen letters from Giovanni, one phrase cropped up more than any other, and that is 'For Those Who Have Eyes To See, Let Them See'. We discovered that this was not only a version of the well-known Biblical quotation 'If any man have ears to hear, let him hear,' Math 8:

16, but also an alchemical adage. We were being told to look beyond the surface, to accept no standard texts, no glib answers. We soon came to realize that where the work of the Priory is concerned we were dealing with people who had – and still have – the finest of minds, and with an organization that is as intelligent as it is 'heretical'.

On one level, these bits of information from an anonymous source were not any more significant than say, receiving the answers to crossword clues (without always knowing the clues themselves) through the post. There was something rather disturbing, however, about being picked out by a stranger who had decided to unburden himself of some rather murky historical and religious secrets. For some time I was in danger of becoming paranoid; unexpectedly hearing a male Italian voice behind me would make me jump – I jumped a lot during the tourist season in London – and I was not over keen on hearing my letterbox snap open and shut. I was not exactly scared by Giovanni's letters – indeed they often enthralled me – but I wondered what it was all leading up to.

Then in March 1991, we met Giovanni. Somehow he had discovered my home telephone number, although it is ex-directory, and to my utter amazement got in touch. Clive and I met him in the bar of the Cumberland Hotel off Marble Arch in central London for three hours of rambling conversation over drinks.

Giovanni was not a disappointment, although he could be said to be too good to be true. Looking like a rumpled Tom Conti, with a creased designer suit and a shock of greying black hair plus beard, he was an Italian of middle age and middle height. Talking to Giovanni was like talking to the Queen: there was no small talk. After providing us with a bottle of very good Muscadet, he launched immediately, if idiosyncratically, into what our friend Craig Oakley was later to describe as 'heavy stuff'.

If we thought that we were being flattered by this attention, then we were rapidly disabused of this illusion. Giovanni seemed not to be interested in us personally, as his repeated questions about Ian Wilson revealed. Strangely, while he did know that I was no longer in touch with Ian, he also seemed to think that this was merely a temporary state of affairs. Whenever he brought up the subject of Ian he scrutinized my face and mannerisms very carefully, being particularly satisfied – or so it seemed – when I once found myself blushing. It began to dawn on us that Giovanni's prime interest was not in us, but in Ian, and that the reason he had been feeding us all the information about Leonardo and the Shroud was in the hope that it would get back to him.

After some long silences and exchange of glances between us, Clive asked Giovanni whether or not this was the case. With a private chuckle, our Italian contact admitted this was so. We asked why he had not approached Ian directly.

To our amazement, he said straightaway that 'we' had tried it once before, but had not succeeded and Ian was now suspicious of any such approaches. When we asked why Ian was so important, Giovanni sniffed that he was the foremost Shroud scholar (laughingly adding 'so far') in the UK, if not in the West, and that he is considerably less pro-authenticity than his public stance would have people believe. We were frankly sceptical.

He went on to say that, as he had clearly failed to get to Ian Wilson either directly (whatever that might mean) or through me, he had decided to choose us to promote what he called 'the truth' about the Shroud. Put like that, it was hardly complimentary and the whole scenario was, we were beginning to feel, distinctly unsavoury. Rather sharply we told him that if we were to take his Leonardo story further, we would do so with open minds and we would not agree at any stage to act simply as a mouthpiece for him and whoever he might represent.

At this first sign of real anger, the whole tone of the conversation changed. Giovanni visibly relaxed, and began to ask us what we thought about The Holy Blood and the Holy Grail in terms that suggested he knew something that the authors of that book did not. He asked us what we thought of the evidence for the existence of the Priory of Sion, and when we said rather politely that it seemed intriguing but hardly conclusive, he laughed.

The conversation then moved to secret societies in general and Clive and I expressed our views that conspiracy theories might be fun, but that way madness lies. Giovanni shrugged and murmured that such opinions were odd coming from us, considering just how many members of such organizations we actually knew. As we sat stunned, he listed several of our acquaintances by name, giving their rank in groups such as alchemical movements, the Templars, the Freemasons and the Priory itself. It was particularly chilling to hear him list a publishing consultant with whom I had worked many years before as a fellow member, and a former creative director who had been my boss on a long-running partwork (and with whom I had had several dramatic rows) as a master alchemist. Although by this time we were in a state of shocked denial, what was truly chilling about these apparently wild statements was the ease with which we later discovered at least some of them to be true. For example, it transpired that the creative director not only writes on the subject of alchemy, under the name Neil Powell, but he also has a home at Rennes-le-Château – and shortly after this I found myself working with him again.

Giovanni said that he had arranged to meet us because as far as he was personally concerned, 'things were hotting up' and he deemed it prudent to go back to Italy. Although he refused to elaborate, he seemed to be implying his contact with us had made his departure rather urgent.

Almost as an aside, he asked us to destroy his letters, in case they could be traced back to him. An expressive silence followed this statement. We agreed, but to our shame did not actually get rid of the Giovanni file until certain circumstances hinted heavily that such a course of action might be wise (see below).

As he gathered up his crumpled raincoat, he said over-casually, 'This is not a game, you know, for children. You will find yourself the subject of unwelcome attention and not just from those who worship Leonardo's face without knowing it.'

He turned to go, and with perfect dramatic timing, he said, 'Why are our Grand Masters always known as John? Leonardo was, of course, a Giovanni. This is no small point, but it is the key. Just think about it.'

When we had sat there in silence for a few more minutes and discovered that we had not turned back into pumpkins, we finally began to unwind. We simply did not know what to make of Giovanni or his obsession with secret societies.

In the following weeks and months we had just begun to come around to the idea that Giovanni was a sad case, even though our independent research had already confirmed many of his apparently wilder statements. Then events, some of them already disturbing, began to form a pattern.

There had already been one worrying incident which may have had some connection with something that was a sign of 'unwelcome attention', although we had tried to push it, and its implications, to the back of our minds. In June 1990, Ian and I were still seeing each other, until there was a sudden – and final – silence. A friend telephoned him to ask why he was no longer in touch with me. He replied that he had 'come into some information'. Of course this may have been some gossip about me that had no bearing on anything other than my character, but in the light of what was to come – the attempts to discredit our work – it was certainly provocative. We later gathered that this was an anonymous letter which seemed, as far as we could tell, to link me with some satanic subculture. Such was the impact of this missive that Ian later wrote to Clive warning him in the strongest terms that 'if you have any personal regard for Christian values you are doing yourself no favours by following the path on which Lynn is leading you . . . playing around with the "Leonardo" theory is a mere minor gambit of hers in a game that is much more sinister.' Despite our repeated insistence that he tell us what I was accused of, he steadfastly refused to say 'for legal reasons'.[11] I have been told that he then telephoned at least one leading British Shroudie to hint that I was involved in occult practices.[12]

Shortly after our meeting with Giovanni, in March 1991, by which time our research was already quite advanced, I was walking around

Hampstead Village in north London with my friend Peter. We were looking in art galleries and window-shopping, and therefore wandering all over the place quite randomly. At first we thought we were imagining it, but there did appear to be a man following us. Whenever we turned round there he was, abruptly looking in shop windows; when we crossed the road, so did he. Whenever we stayed for any length of time inside a shop or gallery he kept looking in at us, presumably checking to see if we were still there, or whether we might have left by another door. The peculiar thing was that he was bad at it, so obvious. In the end we turned round to face him and stared: he disappeared into a pizza restaurant rapidly. But when we walked past and looked in, he was sitting by the window peering over his newspaper: seeing us stare, he looked away. To this day I can describe him perfectly.

Clive and I had a similar experience in a wine bar off Great Portland Street in central London, where we used to meet regularly for lunch, to discuss our research. A different man sat in the shadows behind us and was quite clearly listening to what we were saying to such an extent that we made pointed references to it and very obviously changed the subject. It was all so blatant, but being typically British we found it impossible to challenge this man. When we left he followed us, and when we parted he followed me, even to the extent of trailing me round every department of Marks and Spencers in Oxford Street, where I went quite deliberately. I only lost him when I was the last one to be allowed on a full bus, leaving him standing in the queue. I watched to see if he jumped in a taxi to 'follow that bus', but he shrugged and disappeared into the crowd. Whoever was on our trail, they wanted us to know that they were.

There have been many occasions when we felt as if we were being followed, but they were less clear-cut than the episodes we have just described. Shortly after that I had telephone calls from several people I had dealings with, checking to see if I had suddenly moved house. Apparently their letters to me had been returned, with 'not known at this address' scribbled on them. Checking with the local sorting office I discovered that they had received two letters which had been addressed to me with 'gone away' written on them, had concluded that I had moved, and had returned all my mail subsequently. I never got to the bottom of this, but it was a somewhat chilling experience.

There were several similar incidents, none of them adding up to anything very much in themselves. But then, one Saturday in July 1992, came the most dramatic of them all. Because of the nature of a writer's lifestyle, I am almost always at home. However, on this particular day, Clive and I were visiting the church of Notre Dame de France off Leicester Square with our friends Craig Oakley and Tony Pritchett. While I was out, there was an attempted break-in at my flat, the only one in my nine years' residence. Curiously, the would-be burglar made his attempt in full view of a busy road in bright sunlight on a Saturday afternoon, perhaps simply because this was the only time he found that I was out. The next door gardener had chased him away, and the police were called who promptly became suspicious about the apparent bizarreness of this very public crime. They asked if I had any enemies because there are many more secluded premises in my road which are easier to break into. To smash your way into my flat you have to cross a garden that can be clearly seen from the main road and there is only one entrance with no means of a quick gataway. It seemed as if I had been singled out personally.

It was after this that I destroyed the Giovanni letters, with more than a little sense of relief.

Perhaps the most worrying of these incidents took place at the Rome Symposium of the international Shroud community in June 1993. Although – for obvious reasons – we were not there ourselves, a few days after it finished Clive received a letter from the wife of one of the BSTS members, crowing that 'all your tricks have backfired', and accusing him of mounting some kind of campaign against Ian Wilson. We had learned to take this particular correspondent less than seriously, but after making some enquiries among others who had attended we were able to confirm that, shortly before the symposium, letters had been sent to various leading lights in the international Shroud community making allegations about Ian Wilson – and apparently signed by Clive. Despite our efforts, we were unable to obtain copies of the letters, and never discovered the exact nature of the allegations.

Clive had sent no such letters, and we had not the slightest knowledge of them before the symposium. However, the intention of the forger was obvious – and successful. The Shroudies closed ranks around Ian Wilson and we became effectively *personae non grata*. Several previously cordial correspondences stopped abruptly. The serious side of this was the effect it had on our research, as access to a lot of the more obscure literature was made more difficult. This, presumably, was the intention of the forger, as well as discrediting us in the eyes of the Shroudies.

Taken individually, none of these incidents is particularly significant. After all, strange things do happen in big cities these days, and we were well aware that we could have been accused of being paranoid. However, taken together, these events seemed to point to some kind of concerted effort to harrass and intimidate us, and also to discredit us and our work in Shroudie circles.

It might be thought that these were the actions of some of the more fanatical Shroudies, but this sort of energetic campaign is hardly their style (waspish exchanges of letters being as far as they generally go), and several of the earlier incidents took place before we were known to them.

Interestingly, we were not the only sindonologists to experience odd, if not sinister, goings on. Holger Kersten in *The Jesus Conspiracy* reveals that the BSTS are quite used to such attentions.[13] He describes how on a visit to London in January 1989, when he was trying to find evidence against the carbon dating, he was warned by the then Secretary to be careful in his investigations as he might find himself hanging under Westminster (it was actually Blackfriars) Bridge, like 'God's banker' Roberto Calvi. She stressed that the BSTS had had a disturbing experience when overtures were made by a Templar organization in 1979. Ian Wilson had tried to investigate them, and managed to gain an informant, only to back off when this woman completely and mysteriously disappeared.

We became aware ourselves of that organization's interest when we were approached by one of the BSTS' founder members, who not only claimed one of the grander Hapsburg titles, but also announced to us that he was an active Templar. After showing a marked interest in us and our work (which was not very advanced at that stage) he abruptly dropped us and has not been seen at any BSTS meeting since.

The Templars were not the only candidates for this strange little campaign against us. If Giovanni were really part of a schismatic group of the Priory of Sion, and if he had passed on to us some of their secrets, then we might well have found ourselves under such scrutiny. As we were to discover (see Chapter Six) the Turin Shroud has always been an object of great fascination to the Priory, and perhaps the closer you get to the reason why, the less they like it.

It may be that it is not the Priory that we need to be wary of. There are, after all, other vested interests in maintaining the mystery of the Shroud. However, we have come to realise that, once the true message of that image is understood, there will be considerably more at stake than a few academic reputations. Even discovering the identity and purpose of the Shroud's creator is, we have discovered, tantamount to opening Pandora's box, because within the mystery of that cloth lies another, infinitely greater secret.

— 5 —

'FAUST'S ITALIAN BROTHER'

'Leonardo formed . . . a doctrine so heretical that he depended no more
on . . . any religion . . .'

Lives of the Artists, by Giorgio Vasari, 1550
(this sentence was removed from subsequent editions)

CONSPIRACIES, REAL or imagined, may seem beguiling, even a little
romantic, but we soon realized that they really served as nothing more
than a distraction. Here we were, a commonsensical systems analyst and
a hard-headed journalist who were concerned with investigating the
Shroud, and our research into it soon became the focus of our lives.

We could hardly overlook the apparent lead given to us not only by
Giovanni but also by young Abigail and several visitors to the exhibition
at Bath: namely that the Shroud had been created by Leonardo da Vinci
and that he used himself, at least in part, as the model. Since those early
days there have been many dismissive comments about our mysterious
source of information. Shroudies have called all our work 'worthless' just
because we have admitted we acted on a tip-off. Yet no one ever berates
the police, for example, for doing the same if they solve a case as a result.
The effect of their information is to make them search for admissible
evidence. We think this analogy is particularly apposite here.

Unlike many other Shroudies, we were not sceptical about the carbon
dating (while admitting that it can sometimes be inaccurate) and believed
it to be just as valid as any other scientific research into the Shroud,
including STURP's work in the 1970s. The carbon dating results told
us the period of history we should be concentrating on, and immediately
we realised that not only did this timespan include the heyday of faked
relics, but it also included the lifespan of Leonardo da Vinci.

The Leonardo scenario certainly made a lot of sense to us, although
there did appear to be one problem with chronology. As we have seen,
most of the historical literature traces the Shroud back to the 1350s, and
Leonardo was not born until 1452. However, the history of the Shroud's
early days before it achieved renown as a relic is remarkably hazy and

theories that the Lirey Shroud was replaced by a new and better model are not unknown. We were to find that there is persuasive evidence such a substitution did indeed take place (see Chapter Six).

It would have been obtuse and ungrateful of us to disregard all the helpful comments that had come our way about Leonardo's part in faking the Shroud, and so it was natural for us to begin by researching this extraordinary and enigmatic individual.

Leonardo is the perfect, perhaps the only, candidate for creator of the Shroud. Pierre Barbet attempted to demonstrate the improbability of the image being the work of man by summing up the attributes which would be required of the perpetrator in these words: 'If this be the work of a forger, he must have been a super-genius as an anatomist, a physiologist and an artist, a genius of such unexcelled quality that he must have been made to order.'[1]

Citing Leonardo as author of the Shroud has long proved irresistible to the more open-minded sindonologists as it is obvious that if it is a forgery, someone of genius must have been behind it. The forger had to have been someone with spectacular gifts, and whose method in this case was unique and so advanced that it still refuses to yield its secrets to art experts and scientists. It had to be an innovator, someone who thought beyond all obvious and conventional methodology, and also it had to be a real researcher, someone who had actually tested the method of crucifixion, for example. For the same reason, this faker had to have a working knowledge of anatomy. Leonardo, as Peter Brent and David Rolfe put it in their film The Silent Witness, was 'the only man with the blend of artistic ability, technical ingenuity and psychological insight who might plausibly have forged so powerful an icon'.[2]

Of course to most believers the idea that the Shroud was created by human hands is nonsense. Yet Leonardo's name does come up time after time in the literature. Ian Wilson has mused that the creator of the Shroud must have been 'an obscure Leonardo of his time'.[3] Noel Currer-Briggs has declared that the putative artist's 'knowledge of human anatomy rivals that of Leonardo da Vinci . . . yet he must have lived and worked in total obscurity in fourteenth-century Burgundy'.[4] The big question here is: is it possible that someone of such genius could have remained unknown to history?

Sometimes Leonardo's name is invoked by the pro-authenticity lobby but only to damn him with faint praise. Recently, German researcher Holger Kersten wrote: 'Even a genius commanding skills and talents greater than those of a Leonardo da Vinci would clearly have been incapable of such a masterly feat.'[5]

The regularity with which Leonardo's name is mentioned in this context is a sure indicator that these writers realize that not only is he the best candidate for the forgery – he is the *only* candidate. In fact, once one realizes that there are good reasons for believing that the Lirey Shroud is not the same as today's Turin Shroud, the identity of the latter's creator becomes almost self-evident. Add to that the remarkable similarity between Leonardo's own face and that of the man on the Shroud and coincidence begins to stretch too far.

Leonardo has been proposed by others as the genius behind the Shroud. The earliest was Noemi Gabrielli,[6] a member of the Archbishop of Turin's secret commission of 1969–73 (see Chapter 1), and formerly director of Piedmont's art galleries. To be strictly accurate, she thought that an artist of Leonardo's school was responsible, as she detected a similarity in the shading of the face of the man on the Shroud to a technique invented by Leonardo and used by his pupils, and even went so far as to draw a parallel with the face of the Redeemer in Leonardo's 'The Last Supper'. As to method, she suggested that, rather than being painted or drawn directly on to the Shroud, the figure was the result of a block print, first painted in clay and yellow ochre on a separate piece of cloth which was then pressed against the Shroud with a padded block, a technique used in the early days of printing. Her ideas were given short shrift by the believers, who brushed them aside without bothering to try to analyse their merit, often with extremely patronizing comments and thinly-veiled slights on her competence and even her mental health. However, although we are broadly sympathetic for the abusive treatment she received at the hands of the believers, her suggestion could not account for the characteristics of the image as later isolated by STURP.

Gabrielli, like others before her, had failed to notice the resemblance between the Maestro and the man on the Shroud. To our knowledge, the first to do so was Anthony Harris in his 1988 book, *The Sacred Virgin and the Holy Whore*.[7] The theory that it was an ingenious self-portrait is just a small part of this book, which is an investigation into the underground church of Mary Magdalene that flourished in France. The fact that he made the connection that had been literally staring researchers in the face is to his credit, but unfortunately he fails to explain just how Leonardo committed this dangerous and blasphemous act. He believes that the image was created using red chalk – a technique of which Leonardo was master – or possibly powdered pigment à la Walter McCrone, neither of which work. And, unconvincingly, he argues that Leonardo drew himself while looking in a mirror, balancing on tiptoes to create the effect of a stretched-out body.

Finally, we learned that, by a remarkable coincidence, an Italian research group, Project Luce, had arrived at a very similar conclusion to ours at the very time that we were researching the subject. In March 1993, *Oggi* magazine carried an interview with the founder and president of the group, Maria Consolata Corti, under the headline 'Clamoroso: L'Uomo della Sacra Sindone è Leonardo!' Corti and her co-researchers had noted the uncanny similarity between Leonardo and Shroudman, and their work had convinced them that the image was indeed a self-portrait. They believe that he had been commissioned for the work by the Turkish Sultan of Constantinople, Bajezid, although they offer very little evidence to support this idea. Neither have they any answers about just how he might have done it. They speculate that the image was created using blood, sweat and other bodily fluids, but are unable to say exactly how they were applied. Corti also notes that Leonardo experimented with the camera obscura and muses that the image may have been 'the first experiment in photographic negative', in the sense that he attempted to create such an effect by painting.

This is an odd example of the well-known phenomenon wherein a similar idea surfaces in two completely unconnected places at once. The *Oggi* article appeared just three days before a similar piece on our work appeared in the *London Evening Standard*. The timing – and the fact that both pieces carried photographs of, respectively, Maria Corti and Lynn Picknett, holding enlargements of the face of Shroudman/Leonardo – raised the paranoia level among Shroudies, particularly the French CIELT, who took it as evidence of some form of conspiracy, apparently on the grounds that both of these exponents were women!

In searching for the identity of the forger we were looking for someone capable of devising a technique so advanced and unparalleled that twentieth-century science has yet to unravel it. This unknown genius must have had a great knowledge of anatomy, and an obsession with perfection that went beyond the mere need to satisfy the uncritical public of his day.

Leonardo's advanced ideas and inventions – flying machines, armoured cars, diving suits and contact lenses to name but a few – are too well known to need us to elaborate further. Curiously, however, Leonardo's bicycle, one of his most far-sighted inventions, is relatively little known.[8]

Fifty years after the Maestro's death, the sculptor Pompeo Leoni, horrified by the way Leonardo's manuscripts and papers had been allowed to be scattered, bought all that was left and did what he could to recover the rest, ordering and cataloguing what he collected. Loose sheets were glued into an album, which is now known as the *Codex Atlanticus*. The reverse sides of these sheets were therefore hidden for almost 400 years. In the 1960s the sheets were carefully unglued to see what was on the back. One of them revealed crude (in both senses of the word) drawings by one of Leonardo's young pupils, including some obscene sketches aimed at his young servant Salai (and presumably Leonardo himself), an unflattering sketch of the boy – and, in one corner, by the same hand, a bicycle. Clearly this was drawn from life.

Some scholars were so flabbergasted by the overtly modern design of the instrument that they refused to accept it, declaring it a modern addition put in as a joke (despite the known history of the *Codex*), until some historical detective work showed that it really did date from Leonardo's day. The proof is that the chain mechanism appears in one of his notebooks (the *Codex Madrid*), dating from the same period, around 1493. The pupil must have copied one of Leonardo's inventions. The design is almost identical to that of modern bicycles, with two equal-sized wheels and pedals linked to a chain to drive the rear wheel. The most astonishing thing of all is the way it anticipates all in one go the major steps in the evolution of the bicycle.

The first modern bike was invented in 1817 and was propelled by the feet of the rider, something like a scooter. It developed over time: pedals were added, although they were used to turn the wheel directly: one turn of the pedals made one revolution of the wheel, hence the enormous front wheels of the penny farthing. They were slow, and riding one was very hard work. Eventually, shortly before 1900, the chain and gear mechanism was added, enabling the wheel to be turned several times for one turn of the pedals, as on today's bicycles. This slow evolution, involving many factories, entrepreneurs and inventors, took no less than eighty years, yet Leonardo got there in one leap, 400 years before. Arguably, the concept of travelling by bicycle was more original than that of flight.

Leonardo was also a pioneering anatomist, being one of the first to dissect corpses in an attempt to discover how the human body worked. His perfectionism is summed up by one writer: 'Leonardo would spend hours, days or even weeks studying the muscle of an animal appearing in the background of a painting so that it could be drawn perfectly.'[9]

Had Leonardo been commissioned to paint a crucifixion there is no doubt that he would have researched the anatomy of the physical position and the dire physiological changes that result from this particular mode of execution. He would have discovered, among other things, the proper position for the nails to be hammered in at the wrists and ankles. However, he never painted a crucifixion – yet there are indications in his notebooks that he had actually studied its anatomical requirements. A note that has long puzzled the biographers, dating from 1489 or 1490, refers to a specimen that Leonardo had borrowed: '. . . the bone that Gian Giacomo de Bellinzona pierced and from which he easily extracted the nail . . .'[10]

It seemed quite clear to us that it was in some way a self-portrait: not only had Giovanni said as much, but the recent computer work on the Mona Lisa had shown that he was not averse to using his own image in works that were allegedly depictions of quite other people. Besides, despite the curious notions of BSTS officers, it obviously looked like him, as our vox pop had shown. It had been hinted that he also had used some kind of basic photographic technique to create this dark masterpiece for posterity. Plus, we had been told that he had been motivated by a profound distaste for the Church, arising partly from his own secret magical and alchemical activities, and partly from his own anti-Christian nature. Somehow we had to provide persuasive evidence for all that. We had to show, as in classic crime detection, that Leonardo had the 'means, motive and opportunity' to create the ultimate fake relic.

For a start, there was no accepted evidence that Leonardo was involved with magic, alchemy or any underground organisation. He did not appear, on the surface, to be enthusiastic about such matters as divination, which are normally (although often erroneously) linked with the whole subject of magic. Yet his name was included in the *Dossiers Secrets* of the Priory of Sion as one of their Grand Masters, and although evidence for the authenticity of those documents themselves is by no means concrete, it did at least hint that Leonardo was known in 'heretical' circles to be one of their number. We also came across a nineteenth-century Rosicrucian poster depicting Leonardo as 'the Keeper of the Grail', Joseph of Arimathea (see illustration). Again, this was proof of nothing except perhaps a familiarity with his reputation as an occultist in esoteric circles. It has also been reported[11] that occult historian, the late Dame Frances Yates (1899–1981), described Leonardo as being of a 'Rosicrucian frame of mind.'

The Rosicrucian movement, which was closely associated with alchemy and the development of Freemasonry, as such did not begin until 1614, when documents began to circulate from Germany that told of a secret brotherhood of Magi.[12] It was claimed that the order had descended from one Christian Rosenkreutz who had lived until the age of 106 and been buried in an extraordinary tomb in 1484. Rosicrucians, it was said, were alchemists and magicians, Cabalists and Hermeticists. Modern commentators claim that there never was a Christian Rosenkreutz and that the whole early pedigree was an invention, perhaps a metaphor. The Rosicrucians are generally thought to be the immediate precursors of modern Freemasons.[13]

'Rosenkreutz' means 'Rosy cross', a powerful alchemical symbol that owes little to Christianity,[14] and one that is not unknown in the symbology of the Priory of Sion.[15] And with its roots in alchemy, there is no reason why it should not have been known in Leonardo's day. Presumably the Rosicrucians themselves had a precursor – which may or may not have been the Priory – and this other order or organization must have been known to hermeticists and esotericists when Leonardo was alive.

Yet perhaps this is not quite what Frances Yates meant. To have had a 'Rosicrucian frame of mind' obviously hints at 'heresy', to a wide range of esoteric knowledge and a questioning, daring, intellect. This then, was Leonardo in a nutshell.

Significantly, the works of the Rosicrucians reveal that they attached some importance to the Shroud image. In a book of theirs dating from 1593 there is a diagram labelled 'Ark of Noah'[16] (see illustration), which shows a naked, bearded figure superimposed on a plan of the Ark, which is divided into compartments with astrological associations. The figure is very similar to the Shroud image.

Less immediately obvious is the figure that recurs in the complex diagrams of the great English Rosicrucian (and Grand Master of the Priory, if we are to believe the *Dossiers Secrets*), Robert Fludd (1574–1640). Taken to represent Adam, the primal man, the figure lies on his back, with his knees raised and hands crossed over the loins. This position is exactly the same as that reconstructed by artist Isabel Piczek (see Chapter 7). What all this means is by no means certain to those outside of that organization, but it does show that there was a Rosicrucian thread running through Leonardo's life, one that can be detected in those very Rosicrucian depictions of the Shroud itself.

Frances Yates was also to muse in her *Giordano Bruno and the Hermetic Tradition*: 'Might it not have been within the outlook of a Magus that a personality like Leonardo was able to co-ordinate his mathematical and mechanical studies with his work as an artist?'[17] Obviously either the whole business was a complete fabrication, or it was going to open the ultimate can of worms.

Given Leonardo's cast of mind and his place and time in history, it would have been very odd if he were not interested in esoteric and alchemical experiments. As we shall see, to the informed and questing thinker of his time and place there was no problem with being both scientist and magical adept, with on the one hand denying Jesus as God and on the other invoking archangels and ancient archetypes. There was no discrepancy to them in being cynical about established religion and also throwing themselves, heart, mind and soul into ceremonies that were designed to bring them into profound and challenging contact with the terrifying world of the 'Abyss' – what may be seen now as the innermost and uncharted reaches of the unconscious mind.

One problem that many people today have in linking Leonardo with magic is the notion that the Renaissance was essentially a 'scientific' revolution, where hocus-pocus and ritual had no place. In fact, this is completely wrong.

The early Italian Renaissance was an explosion of art, science and culture that effectively obliterated the intellectual darkness and crippling timidity of the Middle Ages. New techiques were developed in art and architecture, new discoveries made, new ideas sought and eagerly discussed.

A great many would-be free thinkers had been frozen in their tracks by the implacable and forbidding power of the Church, like rabbits caught in the headlamps of onrushing vehicles, only to collude in their own death through the terror of moving on. In Leonardo's time it was not unusual for anyone who dared to study beyond the confines of the Church's corpus of knowledge to find themselves guests of the Inquisition.

What lay behind this explosion of thought and enquiry was nothing less than a sudden and dramatic change in man's concept of himself and his place in the world and the causes of this abrupt shift have not been satisfactorily explained by standard authorities. The invention of the printing press was an important factor in the dissemination of new ideas: it was not, however, in itself a cause. Traditionally, the origins of the Renaissance have been traced back to the collapse of the Byzantine Empire – thanks to the military might of the Turks in 1453 – which resulted in an influx of classical works into Europe: however, this is a simplistic view.

Dame Frances Yates has shown in her books that the major influence in the intellectual flowering of the Renaissance was an upsurge of interest in ideas that are now termed 'occult'.[18]

To us, the very idea seems incongruous, at least at first glance. We tend to think of the Renaissance as the start of the age of science – Leonardo himself is spoken of as 'the first scientist', which is, to the modern mind, the very antithesis of magic and the occult. But to a very large extent this is the result of the way our culture has developed. To understand the Renaissance we must first abandon our tendency to comparmentalize knowledge, and to sneer at those compartments that lie outside our own understanding.

The very essence of the typical Renaissance mind was that nothing was compartmentalized: everything was part of one great store of knowledge. Today we regard science and the arts as two separate, irreconcilable activities, and our educational system is shaped by that idea, but in Leonardo's time that was far from true. Artists were philosophers, poets, engineers, musicians, scientists – and occultists. In fact, mechanics was then regarded as a branch of magic:[19] both pursuits were concerned with understanding and harnessing the laws of nature.

It was only later, in the second half of the sixteenth century, that there came a schism among the various branches of knowledge, one that has become an unbridgeable gulf. The new freedom of thought had led to the questioning of previously unchallenged dogmas of the Church, which culminated in the Reformation (many of the important figures in Renaissance occultism, such as Henry Cornelius Agrippa (1486–1535) were closely allied to the early Reform movement).[20] The Catholic Church fought back with the Counter Reformation, enlisting the aid of the Inquisition and loyal Catholic monarchs, such as those in Spain, and Europe was engulfed in a whirlwind of war and violence that drove the occultists underground. To survive, men of learning had to disown their occult roots. Even so, the distinction remained one of appearance only for many years afterwards. Isaac Newton (1642–172) devoted more of his life to alchemical pursuits than to the study of optics and gravity or the invention of the infinitesimal calculus. Gottfried Wilhelm Liebniz (1646–1716), the German mathematician and philosopher was a Rosicrucian who saw this mathematical wonder as only the first step in a system that would eventually be applied to spiritual, as well as mundane, affairs. Even the arch-rationalist René Descartes (1596–1650) flirted with Rosicrucianism.[21]

Yates argues persuasively that the debt owed by modern scientific thought to the occult has been undervalued. Just one of her examples[22] shows that one of the great triumphs of science over superstition, we are often told, was the discovery that the Earth is not the centre of the solar system, but that it orbits the Sun. However, when Nicolaus Copernicus (1473–1543) advanced his heliocentric theory, it first gained ground among the Hermetic philosophers, since it agreed with one of their fundamental principles, which stated that the Sun holds the ultimate magical power. Copernicus himself quotes the major Hermetic work, the *Asclepius*, in the introduction to his thesis, and he found his staunchest defender in Giordano Bruno, the greatest of the sixteenth-century Hermeticists. Yates questions whether or not the heliocentric theory would have received the same acceptance without its enthusiastic endorsement by the occultists.

She sees the elusive 'secret' of the origins of the Renaissance in an awakening of interest in occult ideas and what they taught about man's nature. Rather than ascribing it to the death throes of the Byzantine Empire, she sees the impetus as stemming from nearer home – in the increasing persecution of the Spanish Jews.[23] They had long been the guardians of various mystical and magical systems, the most important of which was the Cabala, an immensely complex esoteric tradition that claimed to represent the secret laws of the Universe.[24] Under intense pressure they began to migrate, taking their ideas with them. Matters came to a head in the fateful year of 1492 when all Jews were forcibly expelled from Spain, which had the immediate effect of making the Cabala, at least, known to a new, Christian audience. In fact, it was a Christianized version of the Cabala that became the cornerstone of the new and dynamic occultism.[25]

Two other major factors came into play at this point: Neoplatonism and Hermeticism, both of which were undergoing a period of renewal. Neoplatonism was a development of the classical philosophy of Plato (?429–347 BC), which most historians see as an essentially rationalist, proto-scientific philosophy. It was not so: it taught that man is a partly divine being trapped in an imperfect world, who can, theoretically, potentiate his godhood through the mastery of occult laws.[26]

Hermeticism is the philosophy based on two works said to have been penned by the great Egyptian magus, Hermes Trismegistus, the *Asclepius* and the *Corpus Hermetica*. The former had been known in Europe during the Middle Ages, but the latter only became known when rediscovered and translated into Latin by a Florentine, Marsilio Ficino, in the middle of the fifteenth century. Then, in 1486, another Italian, Pico della Mirandola (1463–1494) published a treatise on the Cabala. He had been taught by Spanish Jews, including a mysterious figure called Flavius Mithradates, who is now known to have altered Cabalist texts to make them more acceptable to Christians. Put together, the three systems – Neoplatonism, Hermeticism and the Cabala – were to transform the spirit of the age.

Throughout the Middle Ages, the Church, sole dispenser of truth, had taught that man is a weak, miserable creature, born in original sin and dependent solely upon God's mercy to keep him alive and – if he is lucky – save him from the fires of Hell. The medieval heaven was defined, not by the presence of pleasure, but by the absence of pain. Against such a background, there was nothing to inspire anyone to broaden their outlook, no point in developing a healthy, enquiring mind. But the Hermetic philosophy elevated the soul of man, teaching that each individual is a potential god. They said that everyone could actuate this personal divinity if only they could recover the secret knowledge that had been handed down throughout history, from adept to adept.

Suddenly anything seemed possible: the shackles fell off. The world became a fascinating place to be investigated fearlessly and, within the limits of the laws of nature, mastered. The glories of the Renaissance were nothing less than a surge of collective self-confidence due to the occult idea of man as divine being, coming into the world – as the poet William Wordsworth (1770–1850) was later to write – 'trailing clouds of glory'.

Occult ideas had been known of course before this time: alchemists in particular had a well-developed underground network. But suddenly these ideas were seized upon by enthusiastic young students who saw in them the end to the intellectual sterility of the ages, and the beginnings of a return to the exciting freedom of the classical world.

It was in Italy that the new Hermetic philosophy took shape, and it was also here that the Renaissance began. This was because, ironically, the Pope's authority was weaker here than anywhere else. The Italian states saw him as a political rival, and made sure they kept the Church's power to a minimum for that reason. From Italy the new age spread throughout Europe until the Church realized it had been too lax, and tried to bludgeon the world back into the Middle Ages. But wherever the new spirit went it flowered in paintings, architecture and literature, although its roots were firmly in the new occult philosophy, to use Frances Yates' term. She has traced a direct line of transmission and development from mid-fifteenth-century Italy, through the works of the German magician Agrippa, the great Hermetic prophet Giordano Bruno and the Elizabethan magus Dr John Dee at the end of the sixteenth century, to the origins of the Rosicrucian movement in the early seventeeth century, and beyond.[27]

The occult philosophy underscores all the manifestations of the Renaissance and should never be divorced from them, for it is in occult thinking that their often obscure symbolism lies. One of the key tools of Hermetic magic is the talisman – Ficino was obsessed by it. Although taken to be synonymous with an amulet or charm, a talisman is in fact much more. It was supposed to attract certain kinds of magical power to it, which it then channelled. Many Renaissance paintings and sculptures can be seen as talismans – 'Primavera' by Botticelli (1444–1510) for instance, is a talisman for Venus.[28] A century later, in Amsterdam, Rembrandt (1606–1669) was incorporating Cabalist elements into his paintings.[29]

Significantly, in the light of our research, it was in Florence that the three strands of Neoplatonism, Hermeticism and Cabalism came together most forcibly and most creatively. And the catalyst for this explosive intellectual transmutation was none other than Lorenzo de Medici (1450–1492), ruler of Florence and foremost patron of Andrea del Verrocchio (1436–1488) – who, as we shall see, was a prime mover in Leonardo's formative years.[30]

So eager was this court to establish Florence as a centre of culture and scholarship, that Lorenzo's father, Cosimo, had sent agents throughout the Mediterranean seeking lost manuscripts. The greatest prize they brought back was the Corpus Hermetica, which Cosimo rushed to translate. So great was the honour accorded this work that Marsilio Ficino was told to drop his translation of the complete works of Plato and get on with translating this instead.

Ficino also wrote or translated many of the classic works of Renaissance occultism, such as the *Orphica*, a collection of hymns to pagan gods, and *De Triplica Vita*, his treatise on astral magic and talismans, and was Lorenzo's tutor and mentor, later becoming the tutor of Lorenzo's children. Pico della Mirandola, champion of the Christian Cabala, wrote his famous treatise in Florence after Lorenzo offered him protection from the Inquisition. And, astonishing for his day, Lorenzo's Florence tolerated Jews: indeed, he often interceded personally to stop their persecution in other Italian states, making it an ideal haven for those threatened with the attentions of the Spanish Inquisitor General Torquemada in Spain.

We should not be surprised to discover that Lorenzo was also actively interested in the occult. According to historian Dr Judith Hook: 'His writings show a considerable familiarity with the Latin poets . . . a mastery of Hermetic literature, contemporary medical and architectural theory, and an interest in magic and astrology . . .'[31]

Florence was obsessed with groups and societies – guilds, committees, councils, religious cliques and so on. There was a network of secret religious organizations (although no one knows now what their views were), called the Companies of Night. A society especially associated with the Medicis was the Confraternity of the Magi, which was the nucleus of the Neoplatonic philosophers. Lorenzo, like his father and grandfather, was its president. Ostensibly orthodox, it nevertheless became more like a modern Masonic Lodge under Lorenzo, and those aspiring to influence were eager to be admitted to the 'rank of the Magi'.[32]

This, then, was the Florence to which Leonardo would become passionately attached, a centre of fervent occult discussion. It is inconceivable that Leonardo, who was interested in everything, would have passed these new and exciting possibilities over.

It was a world, however, that should not have been immediately welcoming to one such as Leonardo. By rights, he should have been subjected to the thumbscrews, the rack and the flaming pyre dozens of times over for his 'heresies'. Yet even apart from his radical beliefs we must also look at other habits of his that should easily have qualified him for the loving attentions of the Inquisition.[33]

Leonardo was left-handed; he was a strict vegetarian; he dissected dead bodies; he sought the company of alchemists and necromancers; he worked on a Sunday and only attended Mass when at court. The last two can be deemed obvious sins at a time when outward piety was all, but what of the others?

At that time, being left-handed was deemed to be evil, yet Leonardo, although technically ambidextrous, flaunted his left-handness.[34] He even wrote in 'mirror writing' in far from secret documents – devilish writing from the hand of the Devil.

He was also vegetarian.[35] To modern Westerners the idea that one's diet could be deemed heretical may seem surprising. Yet in many religions, such as Orthodox Judaism, Islam and Mormon Christianity, obedience to rigid dietary regimes is still mandatory, and any lapses are punishable.

The Church lays great emphasis on man's dominion over the animal kingdom, as given him by God in the book of Genesis. However, it goes further: if God gave us the beasts as ours, to do what we like with, then to eschew them in any way must be blasphemy. In Leonardo's day vegetarianism was referred to as 'the Devil's banquet', and to avoid eating meat (except on Fridays of course) was a sure way to be convicted of heresy.[36] But the question remains. How did he get away with it?

For most of his professional life, Leonardo had a special dispensation to dissect cadavers for purposes of anatomical research, something which normally carried the death penalty. Yet not only did he work long hours among stinking corpses, his hands wrist-deep in intestines (although he had invented a way of keeping his fingernails clean[37]), but he also frequently boasted – even, astonishingly, while in conversation with priests[38] – about how many men, women and children he had cut up. It was only towards the end of his life, c. 1513, when Pope Leo X took an active dislike to his anatomical researches, that he ceased practising them. Leonardo's charmed life was threatened, and it was around that time that he left for France, where he would eventually die.

While it is not generally known or accepted among standard authorities that Leonardo himself was an alchemist or a necromancer, there are several references to his frequent association with those who were known to be dabblers in these so-called 'black arts'.[39] For example, the only surviving sculpture in which he had had a hand was mainly the work of Giovan Francesco Rustici, who Serge Bramly, in his book *Leonardo: the Artist and the Man*, somewhat airily dismisses as 'an amateur alchemist and occasional necromancer'.[40] The work, depicting John the Baptist (who is raising one forefinger skywards), still stands in the Baptistry in Florence, the patron saint of which was also John the Baptist. Giorgio Vasari, the sixteenth-century art historian, says in his *Lives of the Artists*, that while Leonardo and Rustici worked on this figure no one was allowed anywhere near them. There could have been many possible explanations for this desire for solitude. Whatever they were up to, Leonardo and his friend Rustici did not want to be disturbed.

Necromancy was a very black art that required the use of corpses for divinatory purposes. Roughly a generation after Leonardo, Queen Elizabeth I's astrologer, the polymath Dr John Dee, was known to practise it with terrifying results.[41] It was a widespread practice among knowledge-hungry Renaissance men: certainly if Leonardo himself did not belong to that bizarre and unsavoury fraternity then he had absolutely no qualms about mixing with those who did. And he would, of course, have been an excellent source of raw material for them, having had such regular and unchallenged access to corpses for his anatomical researches.

While never for one moment considering Leonardo to have been either a necromancer or an alchemist, the cautious Serge Bramly writes: 'Leonardo no longer dared even to indicate clearly the ingredients of the alloys he had developed: he used code, or else borrowed the vocabulary of the alchemist, referring to Jupiter, Venus or Mercury, describing a metal as having "to be returned to its mother's breast" when he meant it had to be returned to the fire . . . But worse was to come: in order to discredit Leonardo at the Vatican, Giovanni accused him of practising necromancy: from then on Leonardo was forbidden to carry out the anatomical work he had been doing at the San Spirito hospital.'[42]

It seems strange that someone who did not 'dare' to commit details of his work to paper still 'dared' to use blatantly alchemical imagery: surely such language was considerably more dangerous than letting lesser brains puzzle over his work? And then there is the point that, when the Pope was faced with an accusation against Leonardo of heresy in the form of necromancy all he did was ban further anatomical research. Rumours have always abounded about Leonardo's secret work: he has been called 'Faust's Italian brother',[43] and Serge Bramly remarks 'there was the whiff of sulphur about Leonardo.'[44]

It was a cynical age and a power-hungry place. Perhaps it would not have mattered to his patrons – even to the Vatican – if he stank to high heaven of sulphur, as long as he he had something – some knowledge or some technique – that others did not, something that was uniquely useful in his time and place. In one of his notebooks he wrote: 'To dare to be the first, to make the dream a reality . . .': one can almost hear the tone of longing, of the passionate desire to be the ultimate innovator. But what made him the extraordinary man that he was? What drove him, what induced the restless energy, the power to create?

Leonardo was born at 10.30pm on Saturday, 15 April 1452 in Anciano, a village near the small town of Vinci in Tuscany. His grandfather, Antonio, eagerly noted down the exact time of the boy's birth: he may have wanted it for a horoscope to be drawn up.

His father was a notary, Ser Piero da Vinci, who had an important business in Florence. His mother was the mysterious Caterina (sometimes Chateria), a local woman who never married his father. Very little is known about her: local tradition has it that she brought the little boy up for the first five years of his life, then she married Attabriga di Piero del Vacca (possibly a soldier) and moved to Campo Zeppi, two kilometres from Vinci. They were to have three daughters and a son. She may have been the Caterina who was eventually to be the adult Leonardo's housekeeper, ending her days with him, but even this is debatable. This is all that scholars acknowledge about the shadowy woman who brought the tormented genius, Leonardo da Vinci, into the world.

However, there are traditions that do not belong to the historical mainstream. Giovanni laid great store by Caterina, who he sometimes referred to as 'the Cathar woman'[45] (Leonardo's vegetarianism may have been inspired by the Cathar tradition) and at other times hinted that she was herself no small fry in the underground movement of heretical belief and magic. Perhaps she was a 'witch' – a local wise woman with healing powers – or perhaps her abilities were more marked, more disturbing, more likely to influence the mind of a tiny boy with a magical world of enormous potential already burgeoning inside his head.

For just a few months Leonardo was the sole apple of his father's eye, then Ser Piero married Albiera, the first of his four wives. She was to die childless (in 1464), as was his second wife – but his last two wives between them were to present him with no fewer than twelve legitimate sons and daughters. Although it is likely that Piero's lusty nature resulted in several illigitimate offspring, Leonardo was the only one of them to be officially acknowledged by him; his illegitimacy was a state of affairs that was to cause the adult Leonardo enormous grief and rage, and perhaps was the single most important factor in what may be termed his inner torment in years to come.

Also living in the house near Vinci were Antonio, Leonardo's paternal grandfather, and his uncle, the amiable wastrel Francesco, sixteen years older than the boy. After Caterina's departure, the only women in the household were stepmothers, mothers of his father's legitimate children.

So the young Leonardo sought out the world of his mind, a world where anything is possible. There is evidence that young Uncle Francesco spent time with him, perhaps being almost the only playmate who could quite stomach the endless questions, the ceaseless mental activity, the frenetic energy. Perhaps, like most other geniuses, Leonardo was essentially lonely, isolated from other children by the inner powers that drove him, intimidating to those not so well equipped as he was to explore his inner space.[46]

His bastardy prevented him from entering the law, the family's profession, so the thirteen-year-old Leonardo was apprenticed to Andrea del Verrocchio, an artist in nearby Florence. At that time, artists were regarded as little more than craftsmen, and their studios were seen as rough-and-ready workshops. Apprentices – *bottegi* – were expected to master many artistic and mechanical techniques, often making their own materials. They lived 'over the shop' and rarely had time to venture into the outside world.

Verrocchio was fascinated by mathematics, music – and, more controversially – by magic and alchemy.[47] Leonardo was a quiet and studious worker, whose talents were evident from the first day. By the time a gilded copper ball, worked on partly by Leonardo and weighing over two tons, was placed atop the spire of Florence cathedral in 1471, the boy had become Verrochio's second in command.

At this time Leonardo met the geographer Paolo Toscanelli ('Maestro Pagolo'), who later charted Columbus' great voyage, and from whom he learnt much about machinery.[48] Another major influence from this time was Leon Battista Alberti (1404–1472), a polymath who experimented with the camera obscura. Like Leonardo, Alberti had almost superhuman physical strength; perhaps it was he who taught the apprentice the secrets of mind-over-matter, of martial-art-like control that appeared to lay behind the feats of both of them.[49] The adult Leonardo, for example, frequently straightened horseshoes as a party trick, and once casually lifted a heavy locked door off its hinges[50] – with, we are told, virtually no discernible exertion.

Another early contact was the artist Botticelli (Sandro Filipepi), who was seven years older than Leonardo and, if we are to believe the Priory's Dossiers Secrets, eventually became Grand Master of that organization (and whose esoteric interests are said to have found expression in his designing a Tarot pack).[51] It was upon Botticelli's death in 1510 that Leonardo took over at the helm of the Priory.

Florence at that time was a wealthy city state controlled by businessmen and ruled by the banking family of Medici. Verrocchio's workshop was kept busy making statues, decorations and portraits to add to their status. Leonardo was to write many years later 'The Medici made me and the Medici destroyed me',[52] although exactly what he was referring to in the latter part of that sentence is not known. Certainly contact with the Medicis was something of a mixed blessing in 1476, when the twenty-four-year-old artist was arrested on an anonymous accusation and charged with 'heresy', together with a group of other young men. This is generally taken to mean that the charge was sodomy; they were all released very rapidly, almost certainly owing to the fact that one of the accused was related to the Medicis. This may have got Leonardo off, but had this bad company got him arrested in the first place? And if the charge had not been sodomy, then just what was the heresy of which they stood charged? The punishment for both sodomy and heresy was the same in the law at that time anyway: death by burning.

Rumours of Leonardo's homosexuality were to follow him throughout his long life, and beyond. Apart from that brief and uncertain court case, and the fact he never married, there is little direct evidence for Leonardo being gay. His notebooks occasionally recorded his contempt for the sex act and it may be that his emotional life, so carefully subliminated in his work, never took on a physical expression. Or, as some commentators have suggested, his brush with the law over a sodomy charge effectively terrified him so much that he was never even tempted again.

However, salacious rumours continued to dog his name, even post-humously, and the recent discovery[53] of some pornographic doodles by his apprentices certainly reinforce the idea that he and homosexuality were not unacquainted. It is also true that his relationships with women were superficial and distant, and his comments on heterosexual relations frequently sneering and dismissive. Serge Bramly[54] points to the Maestro's strange drawing in section of a couple engaged in sex; while the man – with a curiously abundant mane of hair – is drawn in great detail, the woman is a mere sketch. Bramly also points out, however, that the man's penis, entering into her vagina, seems to have met another penis.

Over the years many commentators have cited the Mona Lisa as an example of Leonardo's tormented sexuality; there have always been rumours that it was, in fact, an ingenious self-portrait. Then in recent years two researchers – Lillian Schwartz of Bell Laboratories in the USA[55] and Dr Digby Quested of London's Maudsley Hospital[56] – have both demonstrated that this is indeed the case. Unlikely as this may seem, both these investigators have managed to show, using sophisticated computer 'morphing' techniques, that the female face is the mirror image of the Maestro himself, certainly when matched to his self-portrait as an old man which is now in Turin. All the major lines of the face – lips, tip of nose, eyebrows, eyes – match perfectly in both pictures.

Many people have seized on the 'Mona Lisa' as an expression of Leonardo's female side, his tortured anima that was so assiduously kept locked away from public view. But it certainly shows his propensity for subtly building his own image into the greatest of his works. Also, much has been made of Leonardo's pornography: sketches showing 'hermaphrodites in a state of sexual excitement', which have recently been returned to the Queen's Collection at Windsor after many years. (They were stolen during Queen Victoria's reign: it is said she was glad they had gone.) It is only too easy to ascribe Leonardo's apparent obsession with hermaphrodites to a perverse, perhaps even perverted, sexual craving, and to his fascination for dual gender, as expressed in his most famous self portrait, the 'Mona Lisa'.

There was another reason for a Florentinian of that era to be obsessed with sexual ambiguity, with the idea of intertwining one gender with the other. The hermaphrodite is a pure alchemical symbol, representing the perfect balance achieved in the Great Work, and the perfect being, in which the alchemist himself is transformed and transmuted spiritually – and, as many believe, physically as well. It was a 'consummation devoutly to be wished' and had little, if anything, to do with sexuality as we understand it today. The Great Work was an explosion of the potential into the actual, where the mystical quest takes on concrete form. As the alchemists said, 'as above, so below' – this process was believed to make spirit into matter and transmute one sort of matter into another. It made a man into a god.[57]

In the scientific and technological twentieth century an alchemist is viewed as a poor deluded fool, and all his practices, aspirations and beliefs were just so much mumbo jumbo that we can eshew with arrogance and confidence. And, to a large extent, when we first came to research it, that was also our stance. But we soon realized that alchemy may be apparently bizarre and laughable – the most serious alchemists deliberately fostered that image[58] to keep unwanted investigations at bay – but it is also extraordinarily powerful. It exerts a potent appeal to a person who wants to fulfil their physical, intellectual and spiritual potential and rise way above their fellows in understanding of the universe and their part in it. Alchemy is an often apparently bizarre fusion of philosophy, cosmology, astrology, physics, chemistry and even a form of genetic engineering. As Neil Powell, a modern authority on alchemy, says:

> The greatest alchemists were skilled in many fields. The scope of knowledge in those days was small enough that a person might hope to master all there was to know about subjects as diverse as medicine and religion, philosophy and alchemy, logic and magic. The seeker of knowledge would see nothing incompatible in the different fields of study. Magic would not conflict with medicine, or philosophy with religion. Knowledge was thought of as a unity, and all the different branches were different aspects of this unity. They all led to a greater understanding of the Universe.[59]

We came across the following story, which is a rich storehouse of meaning to 'those with eyes to see', and which helps to underscore the appeal of alchemy to a seeker such as Leonardo.

In the early years of the twentieth century the occult underground of Paris was agog when one 'Fulcanelli' published his book *The Mystery of the Cathedrals*,[60] a work purporting to show that the great Gothic cathedrals of Europe, in particular that of Chartres, were codes in stone that contained ancient alchemical and magical knowledge. The real identity of this writer was unknown, but soon stories began to circulate about his physical immortality, a by-product of the Great Work, as described above, the ultimate process of physical and spiritual transformation. In one such rumour, Fulcanelli was supposed to have changed sex. Preposterous as this may seem, this is part of the key principles of alchemy; male and female must be seen – perhaps merely metaphorically – in the same body at the end of the Great Work to represent the true balance, the ultimate physical perfection that is possible in this world. And Fulcanelli was not the only alchemist to be rumoured to have achieved physical immortality: an earlier adept, Nicholas Flamel of Paris, was believed to have lived to at least the age of 400, together with his beloved wife Perenelle. Flamel wrote that he had achieved the Great Work on 17 January 1392; some believe that he and Fulcanelli are one and the same. One may be sceptical of these stories, but there is more to them than meets the eye. As we have seen, the mysterious Fulcanelli/Flamel considered cathedrals such as those at Chartres and Nantes to be at the centre of alchemical symbolism: they do seem to contain such imagery in plenty. For example, one alchemical symbol that is widely acknowledged by modern scholars is that of an old bearded man, the back of whose head shows a young woman looking into a mirror.[61] A statue with this image graces the exterior of Nantes cathedral, as does a bearded king with the body of a woman, in the porch at Chartres that depicts the Queen of Sheba.[62]

One day in early 1993, I (Lynn) was sorting out my slides for a talk on Leonardo and the Shroud (since 1990 I have given many such talks) and found myself staring at one slide in particular, one with which I had thought myself very familiar. However, we had both failed to make a major connection.

The slide was of a sketch by Leonardo entitled 'Witch with Magic Mirror' (see illustration). I had regularly used it to illustrate Leonardo's secret fascination with magic, mirrors and dual gender, but I had completely missed the point. We had realized long ago that although it apparently showed a young woman looking into a mirror, if you look carefully you will see that the back of her head is actually an old man's face – Leonardo's own. It is nothing less than the same symbol as that of the alchemical statues at Nantes. I must have drawn hundreds of people's attention to points of interest in that sketch over the last few years, but I never realized that all that time I had been using what amounted to clear evidence for Leonardo's involvement with alchemy.

We also discovered, as mentioned above, that he used alchemical symbols in his notebooks, a dangerous practice indeed. This almost seems like an aberration, for they appear only briefly among the dozens of extant notes.

Leonardo would be unlikely to write at length anything that praised alchemy for obvious reasons of discretion. It is not enough to say that his notebooks were not intended for public consumption: he was famous in his lifetime and knew the value of all his scribbles. Besides, his young servant Salai was a notorious thief – who knew where his Maestro's valuable notebooks might end up? They could easily have fallen into the wrong hands during his lifetime.

The second important factor when considering Leonardo's writings on alchemy is to note their precise tone and content. As we have already seen, serious alchemists were primarily concerned with spiritual transformation, not with turning base metal into gold as is commonly believed. According to the occult scholar Grillot de Givry it is important to distinguish the true alchemist from 'the scrambling throng of the uninitiate, who have utterly failed to penetrate the secret of the true doctrine and continue working on anomalous materials which will never bring them to the desired result. These are the false alchemists, who are called Puffers.'[63]

It is clear that Leonardo's writings are directed at the Puffers. For example he asks them 'why do you not go to the mines where Nature produces such gold, and there become her disciple? She will in faith cure you of your folly, showing you that nothing which you use in your furnace will be among any of the things which she uses in order to produce this gold.' However, his attitude is not entirely hostile, for he also says that the alchemists 'deserve unmeasured praise for the usefulness of the things invented for the use of men.'[64]

Serious alchemists would agree with him. The contempt they felt – and still feel – for Puffers is on a par with many scientists' feelings towards those who still believe that the Shroud is really that of Jesus.

On the whole it is true that modern alchemists – there are alchemical institutes in both France and the USA – are just as keen on anonymity as their historical counterparts. This may seem odd, for surely the time is long gone when they would face the flaming pyre for their beliefs and practices. Some think that anonymity has simply become so ingrained in the psyche of alchemists that it is by now a tradition, but there is more to it than that. Put simply, alchemy is for initiates only, just as is any occult knowledge. Secrets must remain secrets. Or, as Neil Powell writes: 'Alchemists delighted in shrouding their writings with mystery and obscurity because they were always afraid the information would fall into the hands of the wrong people. Perhaps they enjoyed the secrecy for its own sake.'[65]

Alchemy still has elaborate and often impenetrable codes, employing fantastic imagery, but essentially it is a tough-minded system aimed at totally transforming not only the substances with which the alchemist works, but also the alchemist himself. Alchemists have a saying: 'There is no God but God in Man', not only a deeply dangerous axiom to bandy about in the days of the Inquisition, but also the perfect sentiment for one such as Leonardo.

We have come to believe that one of the most profound *raisons d'êtres* of the Priory of Sion is alchemy (at its lowest level perhaps a very apt discipline for those who are said to be among the world's top bankers). Nicholas Flamel is listed as one of their earliest Grand Masters, and January 17 – given by him as the date on which he achieved the Great Work in 1392[66] – is a day held sacred by them, a day specially set apart to honour alchemical perfection. Also on the list are Sir Isaac Newton, Robert Boyle (1627–1691) and Robert Fludd, all known to have been passionate alchemists. (Interestingly, Newton, like Leonardo, is now known as an arch-rationalist, but in his day there was nothing illogical about being an alchemist: all knowledge was valid.)

Alchemy is not a hobby like stamp collecting or growing orchids; it is a complete system for understanding both Man and the world which he inhabits. Leonardo's 'Witch with Magic Mirror' shows that he was familiar with alchemical imagery.

In our quest to provide Leonardo with the means, motive and opportunity to create the Turin Shroud, we were to prove that alchemy provided him with the means. Perhaps, however, his means and motive were inseparably linked. Alchemy may not only have provided the technical know-how for a bold and ingenious fake – one that, after all, could not be detected as a hoax in his lifetime – but it would also have put him in touch with a massive underground network of like-minded heretics. Including, of course, the Priory of Sion, of whom he was, allegedly, Grand Master (see Chapter 4).

Early in our research we kept coming up against the lack of logic implicit in the Priory's own avowed aims, and what they were currently making known of their background through a variety of sources, including the British Saunière Society. *The Holy Blood and the Holy Grail* maintains that the Priory exists to protect the bloodline of Jesus and Mary Magdalene, but speakers from the Saunière Society, of which Henry Lincoln is President, have repeatedly emphasized that Jesus was not remotely anything approaching a god. In fact, they tend to pour scorn on him, dredging the Dead Sea Scrolls and other sources to find comments critical of him. So why are they, as is widely believed, so keen on upholding his hypothetical bloodline? And why would such an independent and cynical thinker, and such a hater of cant as Leonardo, actually preside over their shenanigins?

For the authors of *The Holy Blood and the Holy Grail* their story had begun with the mystery of how Saunière, the priest of Rennes-le-Château, who had become massively rich virtually overnight. Hints about sex magic (in which occult power is supposed to be heightened if performed at the point of orgasm) and dark secrets proliferated; whatever went on in that remote Languedoc village must have been impelling, for even today it is a difficult and tedious journey from Paris (we speak from experience). Yet over eighty years ago the cream of Parisian society, including the beautiful and famous opera singer, Emma Calvé (who died in 1942), made that journey to see Saunière. Hapsburg princes were also among others who visited the tiny hamlet. We do not know why.

What motives would impel such persons to travel that distance: could it be to seek fame, fortune or secret knowledge? It could not have been fame that they sought, for many of them already had that. Could it have been the lure of immortality, the Elixir of Youth or any of the other chemical by-products claimed for the Great Work? Whatever Saunière had, real or imagined, was obviously deemed worth having. Let us not forget that Sir Isaac Newton was an enthusiastic and unashamed alchemist and he, too, was allegedly Grand Master of the Priory. As were Nicholas Flamel, Robert Boyle, Robert Fludd ... and Leonardo da Vinci? All of these men had the finest minds of their generations, some almost of all time; surely they, of all people, were not duped by a system of infantile hocus pocus?

The word alchemy is said to derive from the Arab words *al khem*, meaning 'the black land', which in turn refer to Egypt.[67] Legend has it that it was in Egypt that the 'Emerald Tablet' of Hermes Trismegistus was discovered in a cave, which bore the secrets of Hermetic wisdom for those with eyes to see.[68] (The most famous of these sayings is 'As above, so below', a possible variant of 'There is no God but God in Man'.) Certainly occultists have long believed that Hermeticism, the most ancient and powerful of magical systems, comes directly from ancient Egypt, and part of that work included alchemy.

The great Egyptian goddess Isis, often depicted as a black woman, is inextricably linked with alchemy and is closely associated with the Black Madonnas of Europe. Ean Begg, in his masterly book *The Cult of the Black Virgin*, writes: 'The ankh [the looped cross of Egypt] which Isis carries as supreme initiatrix may account for some of the oddly-shaped shaped sceptres carried by the Black Virgins who, like Isis, often favour the colour green. Their greenness and blackness points to the beginning of the opus whose secret, according to alchemists, is to be found in "the sex of Isis".'[69]

Isis, Black Madonnas and alchemy are preoccupations of the Priory of Sion. Ean Begg quotes their former Grand Master Pierre Plantard de St Clair: 'the Black Virgin . . . is Isis and her name is Notre Dame de Lumière'.[70] This may seem incongruous and confusing until it is realised that there is a specific association between the cult of the Black Virgin and that of Mary Magdalene, the central figure for the Priory. Ean Begg points out that fifty centres of the Magdalene cult also contain shrines to the Black Madonna. The figure of the Black Madonna plays little part in *The Holy Blood and The Holy Grail*, yet the authors must have researched the subject as in 1982 Michael Baigent and Richard Leigh wrote a series of articles about Black Madonnas for *The Unexplained*.[71] At Blois, when the Priory's Grand Masters are elected, the Black Madonna is singled out by them as especially sacred. Jean Cocteau, Grand Master of the Priory (1918–1963), perhaps oddly for one so renowned for his surrealism and world-weary cynicism, wrote part of the tourist leaflet for the Black Madonna shrine at St-Jean-Cap-Ferrat, Alpes-Maritimes.[72]

Black Madonnas, Isis, the Magdalene, alchemy, these tantalizing elements, the seemingly irrational connections and preoccupations that appear to belong to the Priory of Sion whirl around like piecemeal patterns in a kaleidoscope . . . sometimes one thinks it is all clear, a beautiful, meaningful and intricate pattern. Then the emphasis shifts and for a time all sense is blurred and it becomes nonsense. Then it shifts once more . . .

We have seen how the image of the hermaphrodite, symbol of the perfected Great Work, decorates not only many of Leonardo's notebooks, but also the outside of Chartres Cathedral. There is another connection, however, between that building and the Priory of Sion, and with Leonardo. Visitors will know that Chartres Cathedral is dedicated to *Notre Dame*, which is almost always taken to mean Mary the mother, the Virgin Mary. The great Parisian cathedral is also dedicated to *Notre Dame*, but in that case the honoured saint is actually Mary Magdalene, not the mother of Jesus. In fact, most of the churches in the area of Greater Paris that are dedicated in that fashion actually enshrine the Magdalene. We were intrigued by this, especially as many of these churches display statues of a young woman holding a baby – clearly, one might think, Mary and the baby Jesus. But perhaps there was once, when these churches were built, quite another cult behind them and their symbolism, one so arcane and 'heretical' that the average worshipper in them never even guessed at the secrets involved.

We have every reason to think that Chartres Cathedral was also secretly dedicated to the Magdalene, Jesus' alleged wife. Ean Begg alludes[73] to the symbolism of a Mary being 'the Ark of the Covenant' at Chartres; Graham Hancock in his *The Sign and the Seal* also cites a similar connection with stories about the Holy Grail: 'It followed that the "sacred blood" imagery associated with the Grail in popular culture was a gloss added by later authors . . . With a little more work on the subject I was able to satisfy myself that this process of "Christianization" had been sponsored by the Cistercian monastic order. And the Cistercians in their turn had been profoundly influenced and shaped by one man –

Saint Bernard of Clairvaux, who had joined the Order in the year 1112 and who was regarded by many scholars as the most significant religious figure of his era.

'This same Saint Bernard, I then discovered, had also played a formative role in the evolution and dissemination of the Gothic architectural formula in its early days (he had been at the height of his powers in 1134 when the soaring north tower of Chartres Cathedral had been built) . . . Moreover, long after his death in 1153, his sermons and ideas had continued to serve as prime sources of inspiration . . . for statuary and sculptures like those I had seen . . . at Chartres.'74

This same St Bernard, had, in fact, been closely connected with the rise of the powerful Knights Templar, cited by the authors of *The Holy Blood and the Holy Grail* as being 'the military arm' of the Priory of Sion, although they were soon to suffer a schism. Bernard's uncle, André de Montbard, was one of the Order's founders, and the saint's own rise to eminence closely paralleled theirs. De Montbard is also known to have been a likely – and possibly high-ranking – member of the Priory. Was Saint Bernard also one of their number? As Baigent, Leigh and Lincoln put it: 'Could the Order of Sion have actually stood behind both Saint Bernard and the Knights Templar? And could both have been acting in accordance with some carefully evolved policy?'75

As Ean Begg writes: 'The Templars, imprisoned and awaiting death in the Castle of Chinon . . . composed a prayer to Our Lady acknowledging Bernard to be the founder of her religion. In addition to the numerous hymns and sermons he addressed to her, he wrote about 280 sermons on the theme of the Song of Songs, the epithalamion of Solomon and the Queen of Sheba, whose versicle "I am black, but I am beautiful, O ye daughters of Jerusalem" is the recurring refrain of the Black Virgin cult.'76

Once again we have tantalizing fragments of the kaleidoscope: the Priory, the Templars, Isis, the Black Madonna – and by implication, Mary Magdalene – was she the real *Notre Dame* of Saint Bernard? And at Chartres Cathedral, brainchild of Saint Bernard, we have also seen that there is alchemical symbolism in the repeated motifs of the hermaphrodites. Clearly something has been going on for a very long time, something secret and possibly dark, that had successfully masqueraded as the cult of the Virgin Mary. We made yet another connection, found another thread in this immensely complex spider's web.

In the Priory's *Dossiers Secrets* there is the name of one of the most modern of their Grand Masters, Jean Cocteau, whose signature can be seen on many of their statutes. When we discovered that he had decorated the French church of Notre Dame de France just off Leicester Square in London we decided to investigate.

The original building had been flattened by a Nazi bomb, but it had been rebuilt after World War II with a foundation stone taken from the crypt of Chartres Cathedral. It is a round church – as are Templar churches – which is symbolic of the feminine. One of the Stations of the Cross, showing Jesus being taken down from the cross, seems to show a strip of cloth floating atop the crossbar; it conforms exactly to the shape of the 'crucified snake' symbolism employed by all alchemists from Nicholas Flamel onwards. But it was Cocteau's extraordinary mural that drew our attention – not for one visit only, but for many, because of its relevance to Priory symbolism.

It is found on the wall behind a side altar. It shows a Crucifixion scene, although you can only see the man on the cross from the knees downwards and below his feet is a large red rose: the Rosicrucian symbolism is obvious. The Priory believe that Jesus did not die on the cross: some of them go further, and suggest that a substitute, such as Simon of Cyrene, paid the price instead. Is it for that reason therefore that Cocteau depicts himself looking away, towards the observer, a slight frown of distaste – or even disgust – crinkling his forehead? There is also a young man, with just a sprinkling of hair on his chin, grimacing at the sight, his eyes rendered as fish-shaped. As the fish was an early Christian symbol, is the figure actually Jesus himself looking on, or is it his son, whom some Priory members believe was the Biblical character Barabbas?

There is a large black sun, like a spider. Some commentators have linked certain Priory beliefs with the goddess Arachne,[77] and a black sun is, yet again, an alchemical symbol. It has since been pointed out to us by our colleague Craig Oakley that a black sun is a negative image – something that is the reverse of the way it is usually perceived.

In the mural, two women are joined together by a giant, spreadeagled 'M' shape: the older one, presumably Mary the Mother, looks down, whereas the younger one is more distant and looks very obviously away. Is Cocteau saying that this is the Magdalene, the wife who was privy to this gross deception against her will?

Roman soldiers play dice by the foot of the cross: the numbers shown on the dice add up to fifty-eight, the sacred number of the Priory.[78]

The altar itself bears the spreadeagled M once more: M for the Magdalene in Cocteau's eyes. Take the symbolism all together, and link it with the foundation stone from Chartres. Is this church of Notre Dame really dedicated to the Magdalene? Is this a Priory outlet, no matter how far removed their beliefs may be from the majority of the people who innocently worship there?

So far we had found putative links between Leonardo and alchemy, and between another Grand Master, Cocteau, and the Priory. But we needed something more, something in Leonardo's own work that would reinforce all the hints, clues and rumours we had managed to unearth. And strangely, it was not difficult to find.

As we have seen, Cocteau painted himself looking away from the scene of the crucifixion; was this a Priory tradition, as some have suggested?[79] We looked at Leonardo's work and immediately found that he is generally taken to be the young man turning almost violently away from the 'Holy Family' in his unfinished 'Adoration of the Magi'.[80] Some have ingenuously suggested that this is because he did not feel worthy to face them: it is, given his secret background, much more likely to represent a complete aversion to the accepted Bible story.

It is also a work that is hardly a cosy, spiritual hymn to the Christian religion. The scene is set before a carob tree – symbol of John the Baptist – and the Magi may be seen bringing frankincense and myrrh to the baby Jesus, but there is no gold, for gold is not only a symbol of kingship, but also the alchemical symbol for the highest truth and perfection. As Leonardo wrote, gold is the 'most excellent of Nature's products, true son of the sun'.[81] While those who appear to be worshipping the elevated roots of the carob tree seem perfectly normal, those who apparently come to worship Jesus and his mother are hideous, gaunt, walking skeletons like the cadavers with whom Leonardo spent long candlelit nights with a scalpel in his hand. They claw and paw at the air around the insipid Virgin and child, while one man's hand appears to cut across the throat of a bystander in the manner of the Freemason's oath: to be reminded of it so graphically is to be called a traitor and to face execution. It is a gesture that is to be repeated in Leonardo's 'Last Supper', to which we now turn.

The only remaining part of the original church of Santa Maria delle Grazie at Milan, this fresco has come to be seen as the artist's expression of his Christian piety. It is in fact quite the reverse.

Many art historians agree that Leonardo painted himself as Saint Thaddeus, second from the observer's right. Certainly the model was a tall man: he is bent nearly double in order to meet the gaze of the last disciple at the table. In so doing, he is turned completely away from the centre figure, that of Jesus. Even though the fresco is badly aged, it is still possible to make out this character's features: shoulder-length hair parted in the centre, beard and moustache, long, knobbly nose with its idiosyncratic tip; just like the man on the Shroud. Look across to the other end of the table: there is a hand with a dagger in it, pointing straight at the stomach of the next disciple, yet not one art historian we have read has drawn our attention to it, and the artist who painted the only copy of this picture that has included this anomalous feature has had to alter the position of the next disciple – to make him more than a little of a contortionist – in order to make the gesture anatomically possible. As it stands, the hand belongs to nobody at the table.

It is strange that one of the most famous paintings in the world should be so little known, and certainly so little understood – but then that is probably just as well, for many who once loved it may now come to be repelled by it. The point of the Biblical Last Supper was, as all churchgoers learn, for Jesus to instigate the sacrament of wine and bread, saying 'this is my blood that is shed for you . . . this is my body . . .' Yet apart from a tiny token drop in the smallest imaginable glass on Leonardo's table, there is no wine. Certainly there is nothing Grail-like, no great – or indeed small – cup set out in front of the Redeemer, and you have to look very hard indeed to find the little that there is. Is Leonardo saying to those with eyes to see, that Jesus did not die on the Cross, that he did not shed his blood for us?

Look at the figure of Jesus with his red robe and blue cloak and look to his right where there is what appears at first glance to be a young man leaning away. This is generally taken to be John the Beloved – but in that case, should he not be leaning against Jesus' 'bosom' as in the Bible? Look yet more closely. This character is wearing the mirror image of Jesus' clothing: in this case a blue robe and red cloak, but otherwise the garments are identical. There is also a vague suggestion of a hairy chin: but as much as Jesus is large and very male, this character is elfin, and distinctly female. The hands are tiny, there is a gold necklace on show, and a dark smudge on the upper chest surely indicates breasts. This figure is connected to that of Jesus by a large, spreadeagled 'M' shape, just like that which connects the two Marys on Cocteau's mural. This is no John the Beloved: this is Mary Magdalene, to Leonardo at least, not only Jesus' wife but also a much holier figure than her husband. And a hand cuts across her throat, in that chilling Freemasonic gesture indicating a dire warning. Despite the delicate fringe of a beard, this is the one figure that no self-respecting Priory painter could possibly leave out of such a scene. It would have been unthinkable to do so. And the femininity of this character was even more blatant in the copy of this work, which mysteriously remains bricked up in London's Burlington House.

When Leonardo wrote 'Miserable mortals, open your eyes' he may have had in mind the symbolism with which he imbued all his work, some of which, as we have seen, is remarkably easy to grasp once it is perceived.

We thought that we knew what the Priory's beliefs and aspirations were, but we had merely scraped the surface.

We are open-minded but not credulous. While it is true that one can trace Priory symbolism through the works of its artists that in itself does not prove conclusively that the organization has the pedigree that it claims. While its existence is by no means essential for our hypothesis about the Shroud, it does provide Leonardo with a motive for faking it. Beguiling though all this symbolism was, we wanted to get back onto the more solid ground of documented history. Curiously, it was in Shroud literature itself that we were to discover not only hard evidence for the existence of the Priory, but also for the fact that it has long had an active interest in the chequered career of that relic.

— 6 —

THE SHROUD MAFIA

'History is an alliance of reality and lies. The reality of history becomes a lie. The unreality of the fable becomes the truth.'

Jean Cocteau

IF LEONARDO da Vinci had indeed created the Turin Shroud in 1492, one thing was certain: a Shroud that was supposedly the same one had existed since the middle of the previous century, so Leonardo's version must have been a substitute for the earlier one. Of course this raises two major questions. First, was there any evidence to show that the Shroud that was displayed before 1492 was in any significant way different from the one that was exhibited afterwards? Clearly, if records showed that they were identical then Giovanni's information was wrong. Secondly, was there any evidence from around 1492 of the substitution actually taking place, or at least of some skulduggery occurring in connection with the Shroud at that time?

To look for answers to our first question we worked our way through the Shroud literature for information on pre-1492 copies and descriptions of that alleged relic. In fact, there is virtually nothing there. There were no copies or depictions of the Shroud before the sixteenth century, testimony to the cloth's low status before honours began to be conferred on it towards the end of the 1400s. Other writers have realized that this almost total lack of information at least hints at the possibility of a switch having been made at some point. For example, in 1978 Magnus Magnusson asked: 'Has sufficient attention been given to the possibility that the forgery is much later [than the fourteenth century]?'[1]

Some commentators have considered the possibility that, as was rumoured at the time, the original Shroud was destroyed in the 1532 fire. Believers counter this by referring to the copy in the church of St Gommaire in the Belgian town of Lierre. The circumstances in which this copy were made are unknown, but it bears the date 1516, sixteen years before the fire. The image, they say, is shown much as it is today and, most specifically, the 'poker marks' are present. However, it is, in fact, not a particularly good copy. The blood flows in particular are inaccurate and some features appear which are not visible on the Shroud, such as toes. It appears to be painted from memory rather than from the Shroud itself. If the original had been destroyed in 1532, any replacement would have been bound to include damage such as the 'poker marks' (perhaps even using the Lierre copy to position them). We do not believe that the Turin Shroud is a 1532 substitution (all the puzzles about who created it and how would remain) but the Lierre evidence is certainly considerably less conclusive than the believers would have us think.

The Lierre version is the earliest (known) painted or drawn copy. Some Shroudies cite the pilgrim's badge that was found in the Seine in 1855 as an earlier copy. As we have seen, the medal has not been conclusively dated, but because it shows the coats of arms of the de Charny and de Vergy families it is assumed that it was made at the time of the first expositions at Lirey in 1357 or 1358, way back in the time of the first Geoffrey de Charny or his widow, Jeanne de Vergy.

These assumptions, however, may be wrong. There is nothing in the design or function of the medal itself that specifically reinforces this attempt at dating it. Such things were made and sold as souvenirs throughout the Middle Ages and well into the sixteenth century, and were it not for the coats of arms there would be no way of telling, even vaguely, what period it came from. In fact, it was not realized until 1960 that the medal showed the Lirey Shroud – before that it had been thought that it depicted its rival from Besançon.[2] This was made in the mid-sixteenth century and destroyed during the French Revolution, but it is known to have been a painting. Surviving copies show it to have been copied from the Turin Shroud, which was then at Chambéry. The vital difference between the two Shroud images is that the Besançon version showed only the front of Jesus – so the medallion found in the Seine, which shows both sides of the image, could not have been a copy of that one.[3]

The presence of the two coats of arms does not necessarily prove that the medal was struck at the time of the very first expositions at Lirey, since both Geoffrey de Charny's son, Geoffrey II, and his granddaughter Margaret were entitled to use them, being descended from both families. There is every likelihood that the medal had been made to commemorate a much later exposition: the coats of arms merely added the gravitas of the best possible pedigree. At this stage it is hard to tell. But, assuming that the medal does date from the fourteenth or early fifteenth century exhibitions, what does this tell us about the Shroud? Does it help to establish that this Shroud was the same one as today's?

The main problem is that the medallion – a sort of badge usually worn on the pilgrim's hat – is far too small for a proper comparison to be made. As these things were mass-produced to make a quick profit, accuracy was not of paramount importance. There is no question of being able to use the image on the medal to compare it to the fine detail on the Shroud, although it does show the same general characteristics – the double image with the hands crossed modestly over the loins – but further than that one cannot go. And being metal, it tells us nothing about the colour of the image. Amazingly, however, the cloth is depicted as being herringbone weave, but then a clever substitute would obviously be made on the same kind of cloth. Perhaps it would even be imprinted on the same piece, with the original image removed.

Some commentators[4] have suggested that the boldness of the medallion image indicates that the cloth it copies portrayed a more definite-looking Shroudman than the one we know today. Does the medallion show a different image altogether, or has today's Turin Shroud faded since the medal was made? It is much more likely that there was simply no point in creating anything other than a well-defined medal. Who would want one that you could hardly make out?

There is one feature, however, that is clearly visible on the medal that is not present on the Turin Shroud – a curious thick twisted band, like a rope, across the width of the cloth at the small of the figure's back. What this represents is anybody's guess. Also, there is one feature that is missing – the prominent footprint on the dorsal image – but perhaps we should remember that this can hardly be a work of precision.

Unfortunately, pre-1500 documents are little help either. Most of those that mention the Shroud are concerned with the various disputes in which the relic was embroiled, and do not bother to describe it. The earliest one, the 'D'Arcis Memorandum', does mention that the cloth shows a front and a back image, but gives no further detail. This is hardly proof one way or the other, as any halfway decent forgery would have the double image as well.

Evidence that suggests that the Shroud has altered in appearance over the centuries comes from the records of Cornelius Zantiflet, a Benedictine monk. He witnessed the expositions of Margaret de Charny at Liège in Belgium in 1449, when a commission set up by the local bishop concluded that it was a painting.[5] Zantiflet does not describe any details of the Shroud he saw, but, while agreeing with the findings of the Bishop's commission findings, he does compliment it as being 'admirably depicted'. We must remember that we can only appreciate the full glory of the image in photographic negative: in his day what is today's Turin Shroud would have seemed pale and lack-lustre to the naked eye. By no stretch of the imagination could it have been called 'an admirable depiction' of the crucified Jesus.

Zantiflet, like Bishop D'Arcis fifty years before, was also in no doubt that he had seen a painted image. In fact, everybody who expressed an opinion about 'the' Shroud before the second half of the fifteeth century states that it was a painting. Even so, there is no real evidence one way or the other to show whether the Shroud that was exhibited after 1492 was – or was not – identical to the one that was shown before. Certainly there is nothing to demolish the idea of a substitution having been made, and there is enough doubt to have allowed several leading researchers to speculate that such a switch had in fact happened.

So uncertain is 'the' Shroud's pre-1500 history that Ian Wilson – as recently as January 1994 – after years of championing the 'orthodox' version of its early whereabouts, still felt able to pose this question: 'Was it possible that instead of ever being owned by the de Charnys, the true Shroud had been in Cyprus and has been brought into the Savoy family by a Cypriot princess?'[6] This refers to a northern Cypriot legend that the Shroud had been kept at a monastery at Lapithos until it was given to the Savoys – the princess being presumably Anne de Lusignan, of Cyprus' ruling house. Wilson took this rumour seriously enough to allow a Dutch television company to finance his trip there: unfortunately the monastery is a barracks these days and they took exception to his knocking at their gate. There were a tense few moments as he and his wife looked down the barrel of a gun, before being unceremoniously turned away.

Some years earlier, in his 1986 book *The Evidence of the Shroud*, Wilson had acknowledged the possibility of a substitution in Leonardo's lifetime. When discussing Noemi Gabrielli's suggestion that Leonardo or one of his school was responsible for such an eventuality, he writes: 'The theory does of course demand that someone from the Savoy family must secretly have commissioned Leonardo for the task, but this is by no means unthinkable in the notoriously unscrupulous times of the Renaissance.'[7] While he personally rejected the idea it was impossible for him to produce solid evidence to refute it.

This brings us neatly to the second of our two major questions, namely: is there any positive evidence of a substitution around the crucial year of 1492? Obviously, when dealing with a conspiracy that would involve people at the highest level, it would be unlikely that any direct documentary evidence would survive – certainly not in the public domain – even if any had existed at the time. But it should be possible to find suggestions of such a plot in the highways and byways of history: in the provocative links between the major players in this drama and in the patterns of the events they shaped.

Of all times, the early 1490s was the most likely time for the Shrouds to be switched. Between the supposed transfer of the relic from Margaret de Charny in 1453 and a display by Duchess Bianca of Savoy on Good Friday 1494, there are no records of it having been displayed or even seen – a gap of just over 40 years.[8] Some suggest that it was not displayed because in 1471 work began on rebuilding the Savoy's church at Chambéry specifically to house the Shroud, and this was not finished until 1502 (when the relic was installed there with great pomp). But the fact remains that the Shroud was exhibited elsewhere in 1494, so this can hardly have been the reason for the delay.

We referred above to the 'supposed' transfer of 1453 because it is by no means certain that the Shroud was given to the Savoys at that time, despite the frequent assertions of the believers. The date is inferred from the gift of a castle and lands to Margaret de Charny in that year in exchange for 'valuable services'.[9] It is usually understood that this is a reference that includes handing over the Shroud, but it ignores the fact that Margaret's family were related to the House of Savoy and that her late husband had served it in various capacities throughout his lifetime. In fact, four years later the canons of Lirey were still involved in legal proceedings against Margaret for the return of the Shroud, which they claimed as their own property – and in 1459, her half-brother was negotiating between her and the canons over the question of compensation.[10] This is an extremely odd – not to mention futile – thing to have done if she no longer actually owned the Shroud! In fact, the first documented evidence of the Savoys' ownership comes a full five years afterwards, in 1464 when Louis of Savoy paid the required compensation (fifty gold francs).[11] So the Shroud could have come into his hands at any time up until that point.

The year 1464 is significant because it was then that the first serious claims of its authenticity were made by churchmen. Before then it had attracted little interest and a fair amount of actual hostility. The new claims were made by a Franciscan, Francesco della Rovere, who subsequently rose to become Pope Sixtus IV, in his treatise *On The Blood of Christ*,[12] although there is no evidence that he ever actually saw the Shroud for himself. In his treatise the relic is mentioned only briefly, but since its supposed authenticity supports his theological arguments it is given his whole-hearted approval. However, his role in changing the fortunes of the Shroud did yield some highly provocative clues. A conspiracy was beginning to emerge.

At this time the papacy – never a stranger to intrigue, corruption and outright decadence – was going through one of its most colourful periods.[13] Several factions, grouped around rich and influential families, were engaged in plots and counter-plots to gain or keep control of this most powerful position. Sixtus – the builder of the Sistine Chapel, which is named after him – was of one such family, the della Roveres, and even by fifteenth-century standards he still manages to emerge as one of the most corrupt, ruthless and ambitious popes ever to have held office. The instigator of several wars within Italy, he has been said to have 'embodied the utmost concentration of human wickedness'.[14] He had several illegitimate sons ('papal nephews' as they were officially known), one quite probably by his own sister, and introduced a number of novel ways of raising funds for the Holy Office, including licensing the brothels of Rome. It was Sixtus who instituted the Spanish Inquisition and appointed the dreaded Torquemada as its Grand Inquisitor – altogether not what one would hope to expect from the first champion of the Holy Shroud.

When Sixtus died in 1484 there was the usual undignified scuffle over the succession. The della Roveres managed to retain control, but it was deemed expedient to do so through a puppet rather than a member of the family. Sixtus' nephew (a genuine relative, apparently) masterminded the election of Giovanni Battista Cibò as Pope Innocent VIII. He was one of the weakest and most ineffectual of all the fifteenth-century popes (British writer Colin Wilson sums him up as a 'belligerent nonentity'), but he still managed to keep a string of mistresses in the Vatican and introduce one major innovation: he was the first pope to acknowledge his bastards publicly, a precedent followed by his successors. Another of his acts was to have such long-ranging effects, both on the everyday life and the psychological and spiritual health of millions, that its echoes are still felt to this day: he endorsed the *Malleus Maleficarum* (*Hammer of the Witches*), the infamous textbook of witch-hunting by Kramer and Sprenger. A terribly dull read, it was nevertheless to spread the ultimate superstitious paranoia throughout Europe and was to cost the lives of millions of innocent people – mainly women – before sanity reasserted itself.

Innocent was Pope in 1492 (dying in August of that year) and, according to our information, he was the authority behind Leonardo's Shroud forgery. On his deathbed, Innocent was attended by physicians who attempted to prolong his life by the direct transfusion of blood from three youths, who all died as a result. After his death, the della Rovere faction were outbribed and lost control of the papacy to the Borgias, in the person of the notorious Alexander VI (Rodrigo Borgia, who reigned as Pope 1492–1503), father of Lucrezia and Cesare (who employed Leonardo as military engineer between 1502 and 1503). During this time no further honours were granted to the Shroud, even though the rebuilding of Chambéry church was finished and the relic had already been installed there.

After the incumbency of Alexander's successor, Pius III, who was Pope during 1503, the della Roveres made a comeback. Giuliano della Rovere became Pope Julius II until his death in 1513. Within a few months of taking office in 1506 he began to promote the Shroud, granting the church at Chambéry the title Sainte Chapelle – a rare privilege, as this had only been given once before to St Louis' famous chapel of relics in Paris – and assigning the Shroud its own feast day (4 May).[16] A clear pattern emerges: when the della Roveres were in power, the Shroud's cause is advanced, and when they are not in control, little papal attention is given to it.

We also found that there were close ties between Innocent VIII and Lorenzo de Medici who (even though Leonardo was by then working at the Sforza court in Milan) was still the Maestro's patron. (Artists were regarded as diplomatic 'gifts' from one ruler to another, but were still subject to their original masters, which sometimes gave rise to acrimonious disputes as cities demanded 'their' celebrities back.) Lorenzo worked hard to build diplomatic bonds with Innocent, even marrying his favourite daughter, Maddelena, to the Pope's dissolute and unpleasant bastard son, Fransceschotto Cibò.[17]

Leonardo's patrons in later life had dynastic connections with the House of Savoy. During his troubled period in Rome around 1515, when Lorenzo de Medici's son was Pope Leo X, Leonardo's protector and patron was another of Lorenzo's sons, Giuliano, who was, incidentally, obsessed with alchemy. This young man married a daughter of the Duke of Savoy.[18] Leonardo's last patron, Francis I of France, was the son of Louise of Savoy, and he married one of his own daughters to Duke Emmanuel Philibert, who brought the Shroud to Turin.

Giovanni said that Leonardo faked the Shroud in 1492: so this is precisely the right time, being just two years before the Shroud emerged from its forty-year period of obscurity. Moreover, Leonardo himself was in exactly the right place at the right time. The Duchy of Milan shared a long border with Savoy, and Vercelli – the place where the Shroud was 'returned' to public gaze in 1494 – was virtually on the border of the two duchies. It is less than 65 km from the city of Milan where Leonardo was working at the time.

We know that at some time in the late 1480s or early 1490s (the exact year is not known) he took a trip to Savoy. His visit is mentioned in his notebooks dating from the last years of the 1490s, in which he reminisces about a waterfall and lake that he saw there.[19] The reason for his trip is not recorded. The lake in question, however, is near Geneva, which is less than 80 km from Chambéry, capital of Savoy, where the Lirey Shroud was – it is believed – then kept.

A final, but very significant, piece of evidence lies in the fate of Leonardo's notebooks. Several people have asked us, if he was such a compulsive note-maker, why did he not jot down anything that refers to the Shroud? Apart from the necessity for the utmost secrecy, it is quite possible that he might well have jotted down some aspects of his preliminary research – for example, the photographic method and his relevant anatomical experiments. A third of all his known notebooks have, however, been lost over time, but the fate of some of them is known.

Leonardo left all of them to his faithful companion, Francesco Melzi, who kept them carefully. But they began to be dispersed under Melzi's son, who did not prize them so highly. In the 1570s just one of the notebooks was bought by an agent acting for none other than the Duke of Savoy, Charles Emmanuel. The book was put in the Savoys' library, and since then nothing has been heard of it.[20] Why should that family have been so keen to own that particular book – and then be so careless as to lose it? David Sox, among others, has suggested that the extensive archives of the House of Savoy might include some guilty secret about the Shroud. Umberto II, the last Savoy to own it, seems to have believed it to be authentic, but his estranged wife, Maria José, thought the opposite. She lived in Geneva, and used the Savoys' archives to write a history of the family. It has never been published, but according to those who have read the manuscript the Shroud receives a single mention in a footnote, where it is dismissed as a forgery. As Sox writes: 'One cannot help but wonder what led her to this conclusion.'[21] Perhaps Leonardo's 'lost' notebook had something to do with her unequivocal pronouncement about the Shroud. In considering these circumstances even Ian Wilson admits, 'While there are no known documents suggesting the Savoys had secret dealings with Leonardo, the idea is by no means impossible'.[22]

There were two other events that took place during Leonardo's lifetime which provide circumstantial evidence to show that at least some key people knew about his role in faking the Shroud. The great German artist Albrecht Dürer (1471–1528), travelled to Italy in the late 1490s and in the first decade of the 1500s to learn the technique of the Italian masters. Described by Kenneth Clark as 'the artist most like Leonardo', Dürer was a great admirer of the Maestro and consciously emulated him – some of his works are direct copies of those of his hero.

It is highly significant that Dürer made a special visit to see the Turin Shroud and made a long and detailed study of it.[23] In the light of our discoveries about Leonardo and the Shroud, it is also interesting that in 1500 Dürer should have done something that, certainly in his day, would have been an unthinkable blasphemy – he painted himself as Jesus.

This picture is often taken to be an imaginary portrait of Christ, and was featured as such on the cover of an SPCK book in 1993. For the same reason it was also used to dress the set of Castle Dracula in Francis Ford Coppola's 1992 film *Bram Stoker's Dracula*, although it was very subtly altered to include physical characteristics of actor Gary Oldman as he looked in the lead role.

Another of Leonardo's great admirers was the French king, Francis I, who the Maestro stayed with in the years immediately before his death. Just six months after Leonardo arrived at his court, Francis made a trip to Chambéry to see the Shroud.

Having established to our satisfaction that there is at least circumstantial evidence of a conspiracy to substitute Leonardo's Shroud for the cloth originally acquired by the Savoys, it seemed logical to try to trace the conspiracy back to its inception. Did the Savoys of the fifteenth century begin to panic that the relic they owned was no longer convincing to the public of the increasingly discerning Renaissance? Was the Lirey cloth just another fraud to trick gullible pilgrims? And is today's Turin Shroud connected with the events of 1492? To answer these questions, we had to look more closely at the characters involved in the Lirey affair, namely the first recorded owner of the relic, Geoffrey de Charny the elder, his son Geoffrey and granddaughter Margaret and their respective spouses.

Like many conspiracy stories of that era, it appeared to begin with the Knights Templar: in this case with Geoffrey's supposed link with them. Ian Wilson had, as we have seen, invoked the Templars to provide a link between the Mandylion's disappearance from Constantinople in 1204 and its supposed reappearance as the Lirey Shroud in the late 1350s. He based this idea on the fact that Geoffrey was linked to one of the highest ranking Templars executed in 1314 – his uncle, also called Geoffrey de Charny.[24]

This was no coincidence. Geoffrey of Lirey was known to have been a prime mover in establishing a new chivalric order that was a clear attempt to revive the Templars. Since their overthrow there had been many such new orders that sought to maintain their ideals (and pass on their secrets). Some, such as the Knights of Christ in Portugal and the Order of Montesa in Spain, consisted of Templar survivors regrouping under new titles. Others, such as England's Order of the Garter, were established to ensure that at least their ceremonies survived. In one form or another, the Order of the Temple maintained a potent hold on the hearts and minds of those who yearned for high ideals: it was not going to sink into the mists of history without a struggle.

At around the same time that he founded the church of Notre Dame de Lirey, Geoffrey founded a new order, whose ideals, rule and ceremonies were clearly based on the Templar model: the Order of the Star, which was founded in January 1352.[25] It was not to survive long – Geoffrey and most of the other founding knights died at the battle of Poitiers four-and-a-half years later. (A purely ceremonial version was revived almost immediately, but did not last beyond the seventeenth century.)

So Geoffrey de Charny, first recorded owner of what is supposed to

have been the Turin Shroud, clearly had Templar sympathies, if only
because of his family ties. But it still requires a huge leap of fact
to deduce from all this that the Shroud had originally belonged to
the Templars, or that they originally came to own it after the sack
of Constantinople. The major drawback here is that the Templars
were not actually present at that event. Wilson and other Mandylion
enthusiasts, notably Noel Currer-Briggs, have to make some quite wild
assumptions to account for the Templars – allegedly – coming to own
the Shroud.

It strikes us as odd that the core of their argument is their identification
of the Shroud with Baphomet, a demonic idol in the shape of a
man's head that the Templars confessed to worship. It was supposed
reverence for this head that was enough to have them executed
for heresy. Wilson, however, believes that Baphomet was really the
Shroud folded – as in its alleged incarnation as the Mandylion –
so that only the head showed.[26] The allegations of devil worship
were, he suggests, simply their enemies' deliberate attempts to discredit them. But this theory does not hold up. Wilson claims that
the secret of the Mandylion (that it was in fact the Shroud) was
discovered while it was in Constantinople.[27] But if it was known
to be a full-length image, why did the Templars fold it up again
and worship just the face? Either its true dimensions were unknown,
in which case it could hardly have been Robert de Clari's *sydoine*,
or they were known, in which case it could not have been the
Templar idol.

When the Templars were interrogated they made it clear that whatever
else Baphomet was or was not, it was certainly a three-dimensional
object; probably some kind of severed head, not a flat image.[28] Their
confessions included a variety of descriptions of this thing: that it
was the head of a bearded man being the most common, or a skull,
or a head-shaped reliquary. Isolated references were made to it as a
painting, but only ever as being on 'a beam or wall', never on cloth.
A few referred to the head as that of a cat, or a multiple image
made up of two or three cats. Out of all those descriptions there
is nothing at all that is reminiscent of what we know as the Turin
Shroud.

There being few, if any, other candidates to provide the necessary
missing link for the Shroud's early history, we believe that the Templar
connection is manipulated, distorted and forced by those who have
come to rely upon it. Noel Currer-Briggs,[29] for example, notes one
Knight's confession that described the idol as being 'a head with
four feet'. He suggests that this is in fact a good description of
the Shroud, if you imagine it being hung over a rod at the middle

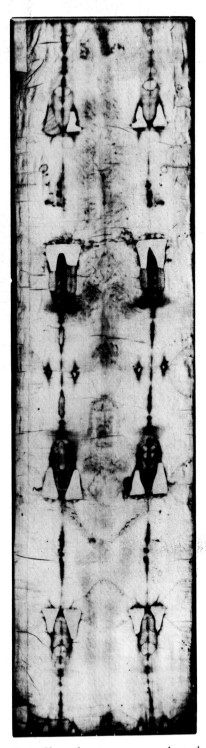 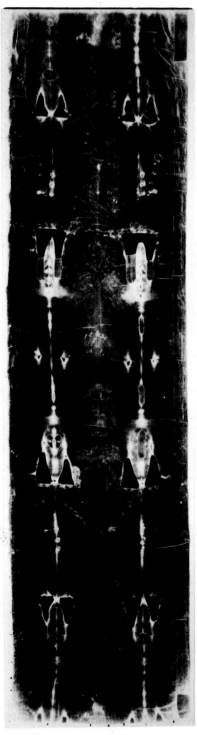

The Turin Shroud as it appears to the naked eye. The image is that of the front and back of a crucified male body, 'hinged' at the head.

The back and front of the Shroud in photographic negative, revealing a startling clarity of detail. This in itself has been taken as proof of its miraculous origin.

Andy Haveland-Robinson's computer wizardry produced this contour map of the Shroud head for us. Displaying areas of different brightness as different heights it reveals that not only does the head appear to be totally separate from the body, but also that there is an almost complete absence of the much-vaunted 3-D information.

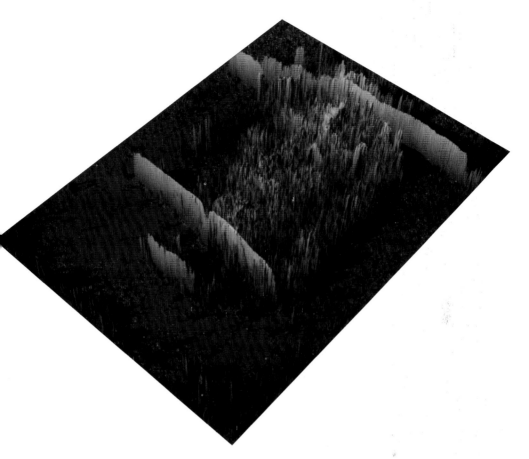

Another of Andy's computer-enhanced images, using a more extreme scale, also does not contain the 3-D information claimed by other researchers, and shows the abrupt termination of the head image at the neck in starker detail, with a clear space between head and body.

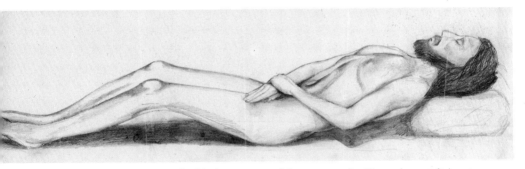

Sketch by Keith Prince showing the likely position of the man in the Shroud according to the foreshortening of the image, based on a drawing by American artist Isabel Piczek. This requires the cloth to have been stretched flat over and under the body. The foreshortening, however, is explained more effectively by the idea that the image was projected.

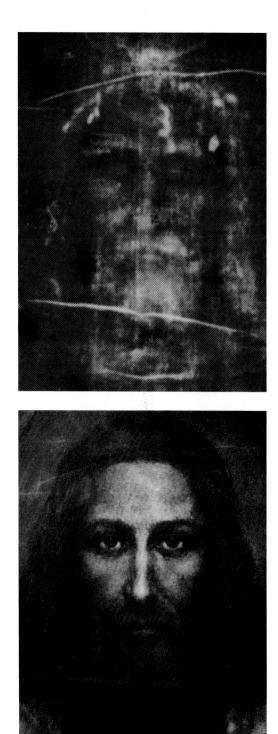

Compare the face of the man on the Shroud, both in negative and in Aggemian's 1935 portrait *(bottom)* taken from the cloth, with that of Leonardo's as it appears in the three best-known portraits reproduced on the following page. The similarities are striking.

(Top left) The profile portrait of Leonardo from the Royal Library at Windsor.

(Top right) The posthumous portrait of Leonardo held in the Uffizi Gallery, Florence.

(Bottom left) The self-portrait (c. 1514), in the Biblioteca Reale, Turin.

Experts from the different disciplines of Computer Graphics and Psychiatry have used morphing to show that the *Mona Lisa* is a mirror image of Leonardo's face. Did the artist also put his own image on the Turin Shroud?

Leonardo's sketch *Witch with a Magic Mirror* shows a male face (very like his own) on the front of the head and a female face on the back. This classic occult symbol provides a definite link between Leonardo and the alchemical underground.

In his *Last Supper* Leonardo painted himself as the disciple on the second from the right: note how he is turned away from Jesus. The 'young man' on Jesus' right is joined to him by a giant spread-eagled 'M' shape. Is this meant to be seen as the Magdalene? Where is the all-important wine, symbol of the sacramental blood?

Triangular Lodge, Rushton, Northamptonshire. Our research shows that the lower ground floor acts like a camera obscura. Perhaps the photographic technique was one of the best-kept secrets of alchemy.

The Salon Rose-Croix poster, 1894, showing Dante (left) as Hugues de Payen, founder of the Knights Templar and Leonardo as Joseph of Arimathea, Keeper of the Grail. Leonardo's esoteric involvement has been well known in certain circles for many years.

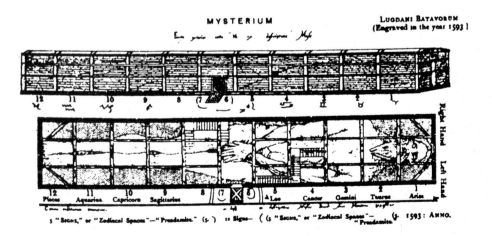

This 'Rosicrucian Ark of Noah', dating from 1593, shows a Shroud-like figure with astrological associations.

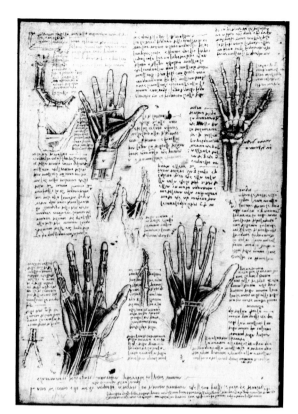

Leonardo's studies of the hand. His anatomical research provided him with opportunities to experiment with the techniques of crucifixion.

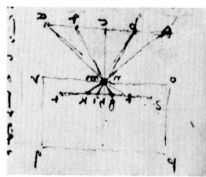

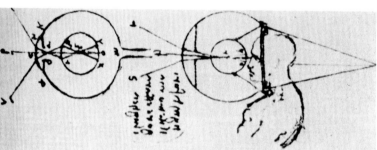

Leonardo's camera obscura *(above)*, and his 'Model of Sight' *(left)*. Does the secret of the Turin Shroud lie in his obsession with optics, lenses and light?

This sketch of a bicycle by one of Leonardo's apprentices is presumed to be a copy of a sketch by the Maestro. Its equal-sized wheels and chain mechanism would not be brought together in the same machine until 1900.

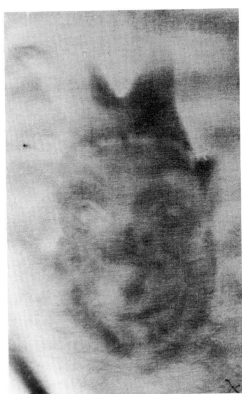

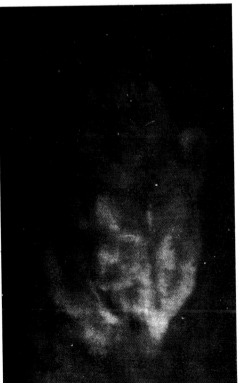

(*Top left*) 'Bok', the gargoyle head we first used in our experiments.

(*Top right*) Our image of 'Bok' seen in positive, created using chemicals, light and a very basic camera obscura.

(*Bottom left*) The 'Bok' image in negative.

(*Top left*) Keith Prince cuts the cloth.

(*Top right*) The light-sensitive mixture (egg-white and chromium salt solution) is made up. It is left for a couple of hours to bind.

(*Bottom left*) A coating of the mixture is applied to the cloth, which is left to dry.

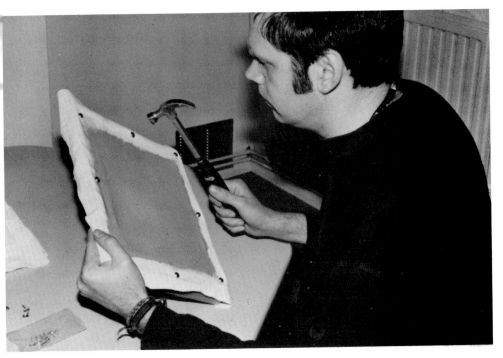

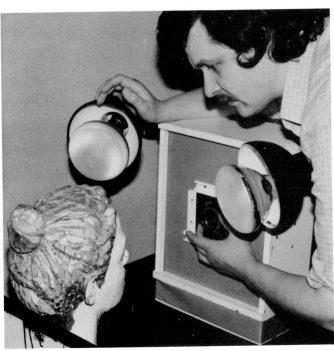

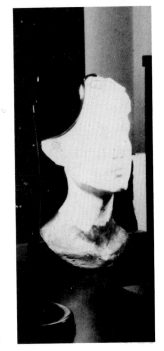

(Top) The cloth is stretched over a wooden frame.

(Bottom left) Clive Prince positions the model in front of the camera obscura.

(Bottom right) The UV lamps are turned on and the exposure left for 6-12 hours. The hot Italian sun would have sufficed for Leonardo.

(Above) The frame is removed from the camera. The image parts have now hardened and are insoluble in water whereas the rest is still soluble.

(Left) Washing in cold water removes the mixture from the unexposed parts, leaving only the image.

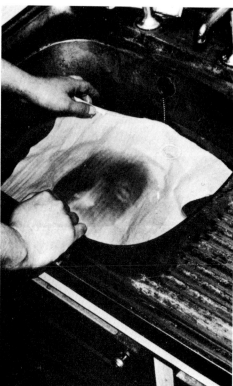

Lynn Picknett exposes the cloth to heat, and the egg-white scorches the underlying fabric, as with invisible ink.

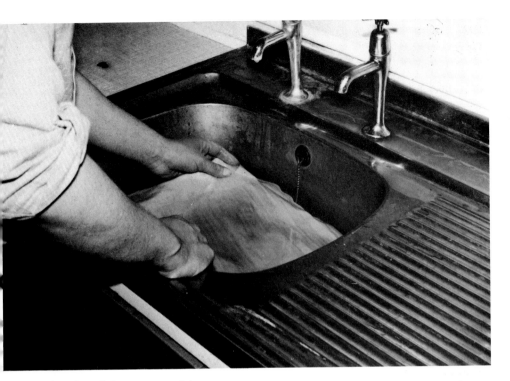

A second wash with hot water and detergent removes all trace of the mixture, leaving only the scorched image.

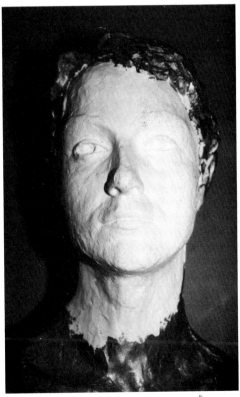

The end result.

The plaster bust we used in our experiments.

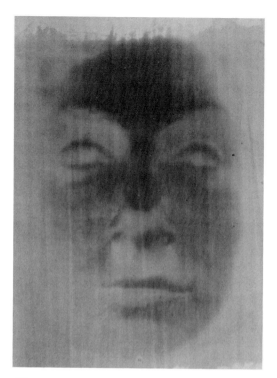

The positive image of the bust.

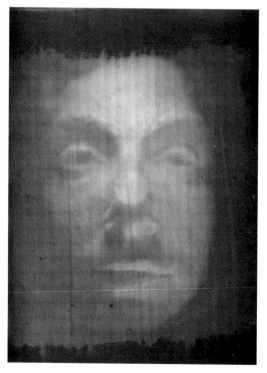

The negative image of the bust. Note how much more lifelike it looks, just like the Shroud image seen in negative.

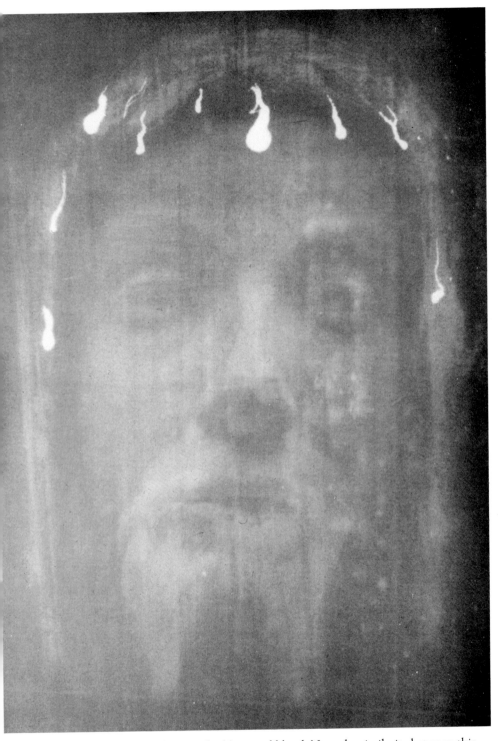

Negative image of the bust with retouched hair and blood. Note the similarity between this and the image on the Shroud.

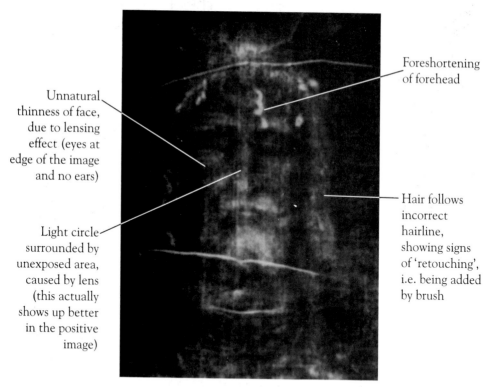

Unnatural thinness of face, due to lensing effect (eyes at edge of the image and no ears)

Foreshortening of forehead

Light circle surrounded by unexposed area, caused by lens (this actually shows up better in the positive image)

Hair follows incorrect hairline, showing signs of 'retouching', i.e. being added by brush

Features of head image revealing use of lens.

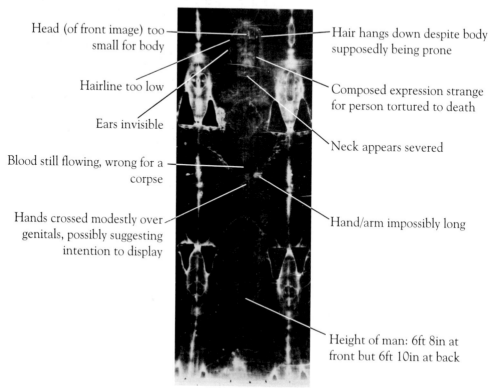

Head (of front image) too small for body

Hair hangs down despite body supposedly being prone

Hairline too low

Composed expression strange for person tortured to death

Ears invisible

Neck appears severed

Blood still flowing, wrong for a corpse

Hands crossed modestly over genitals, possibly suggesting intention to display

Hand/arm impossibly long

Height of man: 6ft 8in at front but 6ft 10in at back

Anomalies of the Shroud image.

and falling so that the legs of both front and back images can be seen: hence the 'four feet'. But why were the body and hands not described? And, once again, if they had the Shroud why did not one of the Knights, especially in the persuasive grip of atrocious torture, actually say so? Why, indeed, was there any necessity to display it in such a perverse fashion? Why not just hang it up full length so it could be appreciated properly? And we have tried, but failed, to find any similarities between the Shroud image and that of even the largest cat!

In *The Jesus Conspiracy*, Elmar Gruber points out in particular the selectivity of Ian Wilson's use of descriptions of the head idol taken from Templar confessions, demonstrating that Wilson omits parts of the full texts which do not fit the Shroud comparison.[30]

Currer-Briggs disagrees with Wilson about the Shroud having been the Mandylion, while accepting that the cloth had reached Constantinople by an unexplained method. He maintains that it had always been known to be a full-length image, which makes the Templar worship of it as a head only all the more mystifying.

Equally mystifying to us is the amount of space given in Shroud literature to a wooden panel bearing the painted image of a man's head that was found hidden in the ceiling of a cottage at Templecombe, Devon, in the 1940s.[31] Since, as its name suggests, Templecombe was a Templar holding, and because the painting bears a very slight resemblance to the Shroud face – it depicts a bearded man with long hair – it is taken as evidence for the 'head idol' theory, on the assumption that it must have been copied from the Shroud by the Templars. There is, however, absolutely no evidence that the painting ever belonged to them. Why it was hidden in that fashion is anyone's guess, but it could hardly have been put there by the Templars as the cottage was only built centuries after they had been dispossessed of their property in that area. Also the image is extraordinarily unlike the Shroud face: its eyes are wide open and its mouth is gaping. There are no traces of blood, which would have been an essential part of the image had it been copied from the Shroud, and it is a natural colour, without the brownish stain-like quality of the alleged relic. In our view, this is the best 'evidence' that Currer-Briggs, Wilson and others can offer to back up their theory that the Templars were once custodians of the Shroud.

It may not be appropriate, however, to dismiss the connection between the de Charnys of Lirey and the Templars too hastily. Taken with other evidence the connection is highly suggestive of some kind of historical conspiracy involving the people who owned the Shroud in the fourteenth and fifteenth centuries. Our own research has revealed that there were dark secrets that drew together those whose interests would be best served by Shroud forgeries.

BSTS member Noel Currer-Briggs, a distinguished genealogist who has worked for *Debrett's* and *Burke's Peerage*, accidentally pointed us in the right direction in his book *The Shroud and the Grail* (1987), which he had researched because of his fascination with the idea that there may be some connection between the Shroud and the Grail romances of the late twelfth and early thirteenth centuries. He thinks that the Shroud is literally the Holy Grail (or rather, the Grail was the reliquary in which the Shroud was kept).[32]

He notes that the Grail romances arose at the time when Western Europeans were beginning to re-establish links with the Byzantine Empire. News of Constantinople's treasures had become a talking point. He also points out that the first Grail stories do not actually describe the relic: it could have been anything. In the most persistent legends it was the cup that had been used by Jesus at the Last Supper and which contained his blood, or in some versions, his sweat, and which was later taken by Joseph of Arimathea to Europe. Currer-Briggs believes that the early Grail romances were actually describing the Shroud, which 'contained' the blood and sweat that had soaked into it. Later writers assumed that it must have been a cup or some such similar vessel – and so, he suggests, a great myth was born. The carbon dating, however, proves that the cloth was not in existence at the time the early Grail legends were being written. As a genealogist, Currer-Briggs is on a much firmer footing when he attempts to show links between the French Crusaders involved in the sack of Constantinople and the later Shroud story; events which hint at the real purpose behind the foundation of what he calls the 'Shroud Mafia' (a term that seems, to us, perhaps more appropriate in describing the relic's most recent enthusiasts, see Appendix).

The families involved all hail from France, mostly from the regions of Burgundy and Champagne, and, as might be expected, they include the de Charnys. The family is also known as Mont St Jean, after a village close to Charny. Also involved in the 'Shroud Mafia' of this date were the Vergys, into which Geoffrey married, and two closely-linked families from Champagne, the Joinvilles and the Briennes.

In the early thirteenth century the House of Brienne had held the title of King of Jerusalem, a title which, according to the Priory of Sion, indicated that they were supposedly of the Merovingian descendants of Jesus and Mary Magdalene, and which eventually came down to Anne de Lusignan, wife of Louis, Duke of Savoy. Besides the Savoys, Currer-Briggs also lists in his 'Shroud Mafia' the families of de la Roche, Courtenay, Montferrat and d'Anjou.

He discovered that:

- The two families that have owned the (or a) Shroud, the de Charnys and Savoys, besides the la Roche and Vergy houses, into which the de Charnys married, had close links before, during and after the time when the Lirey Shroud appeared. The most significant link was the fact that the de Charnys were related to the House of Savoy, to whom the Shroud was passed. (Making it all the more likely that Margaret de Charny did not, as believed, actually sell the relic to the Savoys. She may simply have given it to them, to 'keep it in the family'.)

  The extent of the intermarriage among those two families was remarkable, even for those times. Margaret de Charny and both her husbands were directly descended from Guillaume de Vergy (her great-grandfather). Both she and her second husband, Humbert de la Roche-Villersexel, were direct descendants of Otto de la Roche (of whom more later). Her first husband, Jean de Beauffrémont, had maternal grandparents who were both direct descendants of Jean de Joinville, another significant player in this complex and subterranean game.

  In those days it was common to reinforce dynastic links through marriage, but with these families the connections were repeated to an unusual extent – which points to a common purpose and, presumably, aims.

- The same families all had close connections with the leadership of the Templars, especially during the final dramatic years of the Order's official existence. For example, not only was Geoffrey de Charny the nephew of the Preceptor or overseer of Normandy, but was also second cousin to Jacques de Molay's predecessor as Grand Master, Guillaume de Beaujeu, who was one of the Mont St Jean family. (Actually, there was a short-lived Grand Master between the two.) The Templar Geoffrey de Charny was officially received into the Order by Amaury de la Roche, Templar Master of France, who came from the same family as Margaret de Charny's second husband.[33]

  As the home of the Order, the Champagne and Burgundy regions had always welcomed the Templars, but even so the close ties between these families and the Order's leadership are still remarkable.

  Both Geoffrey de Charny and his wife, Jeanne de Vergy, had grandfathers who were seneschals (roughly the equivalent of an English sheriff) of Champagne and Burgundy respectively. His grandfather was Jean de Joinville, who is best known as the author of the *Life of Saint Louis*, a work that extolled the piety of his friend and patron, Louis IX, the polar opposite of Philip IV, who had instigated the vicious Templar purge. Jean was seneschal of Champagne, while Jeanne's grandfather, Jean de Vergy, was seneschal of the Duchy of Burgundy.

It was the seneschals who, two weeks before the Templar arrests, received Philip's secret orders to round up all the Templars within their districts. Of all the Templars in France, it was those in Burgundy who most successfully managed to evade capture, including the Commander of the Paris Temple, Gérard de Villiers, the only senior member to escape. He was a kinsman of both the seneschals mentioned above. Apart from him, only sixteen French knights escaped, two because they were out of the country at the time. And, writes Currer-Briggs: 'Of the remainder, most were Burgundians and kinsmen of each other or of the de Charny, de Joinville and de Vergy families'.[34]

- A century before the demise of the Templars, and a century and a half before the appearance of the Lirey Shroud, the same families had also held key positions in the Fourth Crusade, in which the *sydoine* disappeared.

The leader of the Crusade was Boniface, Marquis de Montferrat, whose House was closely connected to that of Savoy through frequent intermarriage. In time, the Montferrat title was absorbed by the House of Savoy and became one of the minor titles of the dukedom (as did the title of Lord of Mont St Jean). One of Boniface's closest confederates was Otto de la Roche, ancestor of Margaret de Charny's husband.

Obviously there is a need for caution here, for virtually every French noble in Geoffrey de Charny's day would have had ancestors who had taken part in the predominantly French Fourth Crusade. But as Currer-Briggs admits: '. . . the de Charnys and the Savoys who owned the authentic [sic] Shroud in the fourteenth and fifteenth centuries were not only related to each other, but shared common ancestors in three, if not four, of the principal men and women who had the handling of it in 1204. One is bound to ask, therefore, if there were a long-standing Mafia-like conspiracy to obtain it by fair means or foul . . .?'[35]

This led Currer-Briggs to the following theoretical reconstruction: the 'Shroud Mafia' group of families, believing that they had some claim to the relic and knowing it was among the treasures in Constantinople, conspired to capture it and bring it back to Europe where it could be secretly kept by them. Over the next seventy years it was transferred among the families, including those who were Templars and Templar sympathisers, where it became an object of worship. It was saved from the

Templar Treasury in Paris by Gérard de Villiers, who had been warned of the impending arrests by his kinsmen in Burgundy, and eventually, after the decimation of the Order, it passed into the safe-keeping of Geoffrey de Charny and his widow, Jeanne de Vergy, who instituted the public expositions. Even after this it was kept 'in the family' when the last of the de Charnys, Margaret, married Humbert de la Roche-Villersexel and eventually passed the Shroud on to the Savoys.

These connections may seem persuasive, but there are a number of difficulties with them:

- The carbon dating indicates that the Shroud did not exist at the time of the Fourth Crusade (1204).
- It would mean that the Crusade had been deliberately engineered for the specific purpose of obtaining the Shroud. This is extremely unlikely, as the Crusader attack on the city only came about after a series of complex and unpredictable events.[36]

The Crusaders had agreed, in return for support for their mission to the Holy Land, to help the deposed Emperor Isaac II's son regain Constantinople. It was only after one of their own – Baldwin of Flanders – was hailed as the new Emperor that the Shroud was taken by Boniface de Montferrat, according to Currer-Briggs. He suggests that it was through Margaret-Mary of Hungary, widow of Boniface, that the Shroud returned to Europe.

There was certainly some kind of hidden agenda for the Crusaders, but it was not one that involved the Shroud.[37] They hoped that, in return for help in regaining his Empire, the Emperor would bring the Eastern Orthodox Church over to Rome, thus healing Christianity's greatest schism so far. When he was killed, however, the only way their objective could be achieved was by installing a European – one of the Crusaders – as Emperor. It all made perfect sense; it was simple politics.

There was no reason for the 'Shroud Mafia' families even to think they had any claim to the Shroud. Currer-Briggs' suggestion that they were so inspired by the Grail story that they sought a Quest of their own is unconvincing, to say the least. Then there is the problem of why, if they had the Shroud, were they so keen to keep it secret for years, then suddenly display it for no apparent reason? None of it fits. Something else was their prime motivation, something much deeper and some would say darker.

Two books, Michael Baigent and Richard Leigh's *The Temple and the Lodge* (1989) and John Robinson's *Born in Blood* (1990), have shown, to us conclusively, that the Templars survived the official dissolution of their Order, and that they still exist in parts of the world to this day. Both books claim that it was the Templars who were the early Freemasons. Apart from this, it is a matter of fact that, outside France, many Templars simply transferred their allegiance to other orders. Some, such as the Portuguese Knights of Christ were created specifically as a haven for the fugitive Templars, while others, such as the Teutonic Knights of Germany, were already in existence but welcomed former Templars with open arms. If the Shroud had been, as claimed, such a sacred object to the Templars, why did they not simply give it to one of these orders instead of handing it over to Geoffrey de Charny?

The genealogical links discovered by Currer-Briggs seem to indicate that the 'Shroud Mafia' were up to something, but certainly before Lirey it could hardly have been anything connected with the Shroud. However, if one takes into account other, considerably more controversial evidence, then a highly provocative pattern does indeed begin to take shape. We are looking, once again, at the evidence for a secret society that was active well before the Fourth Crusade and well after the appearance of the Lirey Shroud – evidence that is found in *The Holy Blood and the Holy Grail*.

Baigent, Leigh and Lincoln found evidence that the Priory of Sion (then known as the Order of Sion) was behind the founding of the Templars in 1118, and that until at least 1188 the two organizations were effectively the same.[38]

Whatever the Templars got up to later on, there was definitely something mysterious about their origins. The official story of the Order's foundation, accepted unquestioningly by historians, makes little sense, and several writers have suggested that this story was a cover for other activities.

The official version[39] states that in 1118, after the recovery of Jerusalem by the First Crusade, nine French knights, led by Hugues de Payens and Godfrey de St Omer, travelled there and pledged themselves to keep the pilgrims' routes safe. For several years they seem neither to have done anything nor to have gained any new members, before returning in triumph to Europe in 1127. Shortly afterwards at the Council of Troyes, the Order was officially recognized with Hugues de Payens as its first Grand Master, and given its own Rule, which was – significantly – drawn up by St Bernard of Clairvaux. From this date it underwent the enormous expansion that led to it becoming, in a remarkably short time, one of the wealthiest and most influential institutions of the Middle Ages.

This story is patently nonsense. How could just nine knights police all the highways and byways of Palestine? There was, anyway, another military organization doing precisely that, the Knights Hospitallers of St John. And as the authors of *The Holy Blood and the Holy Grail* point out,[40] the Templars' cover story dates from at least fifty years after the events it describes, whereas the names of de Payens and his eight companions are conspicuous by their absence from contemporary chronicles, which otherwise eagerly recorded every event in the Holy Land at this time.

So what were those nine knights really up to? Most recently, British writer Graham Hancock has argued convincingly that they were engaged in a search for the Ark of the Covenant, which they believed to be buried under the Temple Mount in Jerusalem – where they lived, and where they are known to have carried out excavations.[41] Baigent, Leigh and Lincoln came to a similar conclusion, but believe them to have discovered some kind of document relating to the Priory of Sion mystery. But there is evidence that the Knights of Christ (as the Templars were known before the Council of Troyes) existed four, perhaps even ten, years before 1118.[42] There are equally clear signs of conspiracy concerning the Council and its official recognition of the Order.

Baigent, Leigh and Lincoln uncovered evidence of a conspiracy surrounding the Order of Sion (sometimes referred to as the Order of Our Lady of Sion), which involved a number of families from Champagne. This, they claim, was behind the founding of the Templars. The prime mover in these events was Hugues, Count of Champagne, who was instrumental in founding the Order, and who eventually joined the Templars himself in 1125. Some historians believe that Hugues was related to Hugues de Payens – the records are sketchy – but he certainly was his feudal lord.

The Templars and the Cistercian orders – one military, the other spiritual – grew and expanded together. The Cistercian order was founded in 1098 and St Bernard became its third leader, but it was not a significant movement at its start. One of the original nine knights was André de Montbard, who was St Bernard's uncle. It was Hugues of Champagne who donated the site of Clairvaux to Bernard, where he built his abbey and from whence he expanded his 'empire'. He became the official 'sponsor' of the Templars, and it was his influence that ensured papal recognition at the Council at Troyes, this being the capital of Hugues' land. It was here that the Templar Rule was drawn up by Bernard, based on that of the Cistericians, and it was from here that they were granted their livery of white mantle, later to be emblazoned with the distinctive red cross pattée (an equal-armed cross with the arms tapering towards the centre). It was a disciple of Bernard's, Pope Innocent II, (formerly a monk at Clairvaux) who freed the Templars from all allegiance to anyone except the Pope himself.

According to Baigent, Leigh and Lincoln, the Order of Sion was founded in the 1090s by Godfroi de Bouillon, one of the leaders of the First Crusade who had recaptured Jerusalem. They claim that it was this

Order that lay behind Hugues of Champagne and the founding of the Templars. They record that: 'In 1104 the Count of Champagne had met in conclave with certain high-ranking nobles, at least one of whom had just returned from Jerusalem . . . Also present was the liege lord of André de Montbard.'[43]

Immediately after this conclave Hugues travelled to the Holy Land, where he remained until 1108. He returned there briefly in 1114, then went back to Champagne and donated the Clairvaux site to St Bernard. Four years later – according to the official story – his vassal and possible relation, Hugues de Payens, with André de Montbard and seven companions, set out on their mission and formed the embryonic Knights Templar. In 1125 Hugues of Champagne himself joined the new Order.

It was the conclave of 1104 that had set the train of events in motion, a group that consisted of the representatives of certain families, and, as the authors of *The Holy Blood and the Holy Grail* note, 'Among these present at this conclave were representatives of certain families – Brienne, Joinville and Chaumont – who . . . figured significantly in our story'.

As we looked at all these facts, it appeared that something very odd seemed to be happening here. Were members of Currer-Briggs' 'Shroud Mafia' to be prime movers in our story, too? We soon realised that he had not cast his net wide enough. Those families were involved in other secret dealings surrounding the formation of the Knights Templar – but had nothing to do with the Turin Shroud.

It also struck us as significant that the families involved in the origins of the Templars should have been involved in the equally mysterious events surrounding its end. We were also surprised to find how often the Priory of Sion appeared in our story: from 'Giovanni' in the twentieth century, to Leonardo as Grand Master in the fifteenth, and now back once more to the turn of the twelfth century.

Some critics deny the existence of the Priory, but we felt that the facts bear out the existence of an age-old conspiracy. Perhaps fear forces some to seek refuge in derision; we decided to look further.

Yet more of a pattern, an intertwining of families, began to emerge. Guillaume de Champlitte, part of the 'clique' surrounding Boniface de Montferrat during the Fourth Crusade – and married into the Mont St Jean/Charny family – was descended from Hugues, Count of Champagne, prime mover in the establishment of the Templars. When he finally joined them himself in 1125, Hugues handed his lands and titles over to his nephew, Theobald. Guillaume de Champlitte was Theobald's great-grandson.[45] Moreover, the leader of the Fourth Crusade was originally to have been the then Count of Champagne, a later Theobald and a closer relative of Hugues'. Theobald died while the Crusade was in its planning stages, and Boniface de Montferrat replaced him.

We have also seen that this Boniface married Mary-Margaret, widow of the former Emperor of Constantinople. It was a short marriage, as he was killed in 1207 in Greece. Within three months she married her third husband, Nicholas de St Omer, who was from the same family as one of the original nine Knights Templars, Godfrey de St Omer, who was second in importance to Hugues de Payens himself.[46] Mary-Margaret made another unfortunate choice as Nicholas died in 1212.

While looking back at the founding Templars we should also note that a Joinville – André, uncle of Jean de Joinville – became Templar Preceptor of Payens, a prestigious post, being connected to the lands given by the first Grand Master of the Order.[47]

Currer-Briggs notes that his 'Shroud Mafia' are all 'families descended from or linked with Fulk of Anjou' who died in 1143[48], another potent link between the Knights Templar and the particular interests of the Priory of Sion. This Fulk (or Fulques) was so closely associated with the early Templars that, according to *The Holy Blood and the Holy Grail*, he 'became, so to speak, an "honorary" or "part-time Templar".'[49] His father had been Templar number ten, joining the order in 1120. By marrying the niece of Godfroi de Bouillon, Fulk also became King of Jerusalem in 1131. One of his grandchildren, Princess Sybilla of Jerusalem, married twice, first to one of Boniface of Montferrat's brothers and then to Guy de Lusignan – from whom was descended Anne de Lusignan, who by marrying Louis of Savoy brought the title of Jerusalem to the House of Savoy.

This title brings us back, yet once again, to the Priory of Sion. We have seen that they claim to exist in order to restore the Merovingian bloodline to a position of power – allegedly that of Jesus' and Mary Magdalene's descendants. While we believe this to be a smokescreen, it is clear that they want people to believe in the importance of that bloodline.

By the time Anne de Lusignan married the Duke of Savoy, the title of King of Jerusalem was meaningless, if still prestigious. Yet to the Priory of Sion it retained a symbolic potency, and it would always become important once more when and if the kingdom of Jerusalem was ever restored. The Priory are proud of the genealogies they have drawn up that link the Lusignan family with the bloodline as far back as the mid-tenth century[50] – but why?

The 'Shroud Mafia' group seem particularly anxious to keep the title of King of Jerusalem among them. Fulk's son Amalric of Jerusalem who died in 1174, had two daughters (by different wives), but no male heirs, so he left it to the Pope, the Holy Roman Emperor and the Kings of France and

England to decide which one of them should succeed him. The daughters were Isabella and Sybilla, who had earlier both married the brothers of Boniface de Montferrat, thereby ensuring that the title was kept in the family. But one brother, William, had died and his widow, Sybilla, married Guy de Lusignan. While the succession was being debated, Conrad of Montferrat, husband of Isabella, was murdered. Within two days a marriage was arranged for her with Henry, Count of Champagne, and within eight days they were married. While the speed of events might suggest that Henry himself was behind the murder, an equally plausible explanation might be that this was simply crisis management – Henry could well have been acting swiftly to prevent the title from slipping away from the conspirators in case of a decision being made in Isabella's favour. Henry was a descendant of Hugues de Champagne, the man behind the founding of the Templars, and also second cousin to Guillaume de Champlitte. In fact, the decision was finally made in favour of Sybilla, thus giving the title to Guy de Lusignan, but when Henry died Isabella married Guy's brother, Amalric de Lusignan, who inherited the title on Guy's death.

The title to Jerusalem was one of the most fraught successions in history, which may seem very strange as there was no land to go with it! It was often bequeathed outside the direct line of descent, so eventually there were two lines claiming to be the rightful heirs. At one stage it was with the House of Brienne, but its claim was lost in 1264 to the House of Lusignan when the Pope decided (improperly, according to the rules of succession) in their favour. Another rival claim derived from the marriage of the Holy Roman Emperor (of the von Hohenstaufen family) into that of Brienne, but in 1268 the last of this line died out and the Lusignans became – for the time being – undisputed heirs. Another claim, that of René d'Anjou, came from the time when an ancestor, Charles, bought the title from yet another rival claimant.

Against this complex background it is worth noting that the House of Savoy, too, had Merovingian connections, although they were chiefly territorial rather than by blood. The House of Savoy ruled the ancient kingdom of Burgundy[51] (not to be confused with the Duchy of Burgundy, which was annexed by France in the tenth century). This 'forgotten' kingdom is one of the most remarkable in European history, since it retained its borders more or less intact for almost a thousand years, from the fifth to the fifteenth centuries. In his book *Phoenix Frustrated: The Lost Kingdom of Burgundy* (1986), Christopher Cope traced the many attempts that have been made over the centuries to restore this land to its status as a kingdom. (Older filmgoers may remember that there was at least a fictional attempt to do so in that splendid Ealing comedy *Passport to Pimlico*: where a small part of London was discovered to belong to Burgundy. The highspot of the newly-declared Burgundians' European life was the abolition of British licensing laws.)

Originally the homeland of the Burgundian tribe, it was captured by the Merovingians, who ruled the rival Frankish kingdom, under Sigismund in 534. The Merovingians, however, preserved Burgundy as a separate kingdom, and, contrary to their usual rules of succession, it was not divided among the king's sons at his death, but kept intact until the end of the dynasty in 751.[52] After that it was subject to the Holy Roman Emperors, but continued to be recognized as a separate kingdom. Besides his imperial title, the Emperor could also call himself 'King of Burgundy'.[53]

The Savoy family were Burgundian nobles who, around 1000, were known as the Counts of Maurienne – the first recorded member of whom was the delightfully-named Humbert Whitehands. By the end of the thirteenth century they controlled all of Burgundy. As they rose in power the Savoys were keen to make much of their links with this period of Burgundy's history, especially by acquiring the sacred regalia of St Maurice, the martyred legionnaire who was Burgundy's patron saint.[54] This consisted of his lance, signet ring and spear, the latter being the now-famous 'Spear of Destiny', which is kept in Vienna. The Order of St Maurice was founded by the Dukes of Savoy, each being its Grand Master in turn, and members guarded the Turin Shroud during expositions until the end of the monarchy in 1946. So, in a sense, the marriage of Louis of Savoy and Anne de Lusignan represented the reunion between the Merovingian bloodline and part of its former empire. It is unfortunate, however, that Fate chose such an unsuitable couple for such a lofty event.

There is yet another connection with the Priory of Sion in the title King of Jerusalem. At the time that Anne de Lusignan married Louis of Savoy the title was also claimed by René d'Anjou, although only because a late thirteenth-century ancestor had bought the inheritance from one of the rival claimants. Through his patronage of art, literature and the advancement of knowledge René is one of the most important figures of the formative years of the Renaissance. And, significantly, he is also claimed by the Priory of Sion as their ninth Grand Master, holding the title from 1418 until 1480.[55] He was therefore head of the Order at the time that the House of Savoy acquired the Lirey Shroud.

It was directly as a result of René's influence that Cosimo de Medici sent agents out to look for ancient texts (see Chapter 5), which resulted in the revival of Neoplatonic and Hermetic thought, which in turn played such an important part in Leonardo's life.[56] And René's viceroy in Naples was one Arano Cibò, father of Pope Innocent VIII, the pope who, according to Giovanni, had commissioned Leonardo's Shroud forgery.[57]

There is also a potent geographical link between the Shroud and the Priory of Sion. Throughout *The Holy Blood and the Holy Grail* the story continually returns to the area surrounding the enigmatic village of Rennes-le-Château in Languedoc, the centre of the mystery. The sacred land of Rhedae to the Celts, this was later an important centre of the Merovingian Empire, and was subsequently known as the Razès. It was also the centre of the Cathar faith, the so-called 'Albigensian Heresy'.[58] After the loss of the Holy Land the Templars attempted to create their own state in this very same area, and the ruins of many Templar castles can still be seen around Rennes-le-Château. So it struck us as something more than a mere coincidence that, according to documents preserved in the French National Archive,[59] Geoffrey de Charny (of Lirey Shroud fame), though living in the north of France, held lands in precisely this region, covering Toulouse and Carcasonne – and including the 'holy place' of Rennes-le-Château itself.

Our research has convinced us that Currer-Briggs' 'Shroud Mafia' and the network of families connected by Baigent, Leigh and Lincoln to the Priory of Sion were one and the same.

This means that these families were involved in a much wider-ranging conspiracy than simply stealing and gloating over a lucrative relic, and one that went much further back in time even than the Fourth Crusade, back to the founding of the Templars themselves. Currer-Briggs, we discovered, was essentially right about a conspiracy having existed, but his mistake lies in thinking that because of the involvement of these people with the Shroud, the relic was their only concern.

When seen in this light, as a calculated enterprise that stretched over centuries, a pattern can be discerned in the actions of the Charny and Savoy families. In fact, they made three attempts to foist a fake Shroud on Christendom. First, at Lirey in the late 1350s, which was foiled not so much by the intrusion of the Bishop of Poitiers but by the death of Geoffrey de Charny himself and the uncertainly caused by the war with England. Secondly, there was the attempt by his son, Geoffrey de Charny the younger in 1389, which was stalled by the scepticism of Bishop D'Arcis. (The obvious behind-the-scenes activity surrounding these expositions has caused Ian Wilson to remark: 'there is something more to the affair than meets the eye'.) And last – but emphatically not least – was the third attempt in 1492 in the shape of Leonardo's Turin Shroud.

GETTING THE MEASURE
OF SHROUDMAN

'Why is his head too small?'
Abigail Nevill

HAVING DELVED and delved again into the historical background of the Turin Shroud, we then posed ourselves another question. Was there anything about the image itself that effectively gave away the fact that it was 'made by hands', and even which told whose hands had made it? Was it possible to prove that the face of the man on the Shroud was, in fact, that of its creator, Leonardo da Vinci? Most open-minded people we had asked for their opinions had said it looked like him, but we wondered if there was any way of comparing Leonardo's face and the Shroud objectively? Perhaps we ought to be trying to use the kind of techniques the police use to determine someone's identity.

We decided to examine the Shroud closely. We believe that it is composed of three images – the face, the body from the neck down at the front, and all of the head and back. Was it possible to prove that this was the case? And could we show conclusively that a photographic image was used? We already knew that the face was a bad fit, which supports the idea that the whole image is a composite, and this was an obvious place to start, but we hoped that something in the actual image would yield clues.

Clearly we needed expert help from someone with a background in image analysis, and who had the equipment with which we could examine the image on the Shroud in minute detail and under different conditions. The best way to achieve this was by using computerized image enhancement; with the image converted into digital form it could easily be manipulated so it would give up at least some of its secrets.

One expert who offered us help at an early stage of our research was Mark Bennett, a Canadian living in the UK who we had known for some time. The editor of the futuristic magazine *Black Ice*, he was eager to discuss the whole subject of Leonardo and his relationship with the Shroud (of which he was more than a little persuaded), and he found us the now-rare 1970s Italian television series *Leonardo*, which proved useful in many ways. Mark also produced some interesting digital enhancements of the Shroud image for us, before the pressures of editing an independent magazine took over his time. He did, however, introduce us to a television company who were producing a pilot for a proposed companion series to the magazine, *White Light*, and we were delighted to take part in it to discuss our work and show our replications to the camera.

Steve Pear, a friend with a great deal of knowledge of the rapidly expanding networking culture, put out an appeal on an electronic bulletin board, 'E-mail', asking for help from computer graphics experts who might be interested in our work. Within a day, one of the best in the field was intrigued enough to reply. Andy Haveland-Robinson, a north London desktop publisher and consultant in 2-D and 3-D computer graphics, rapidly became an integral part of this work, devoting many long hours to our work with great insight and inspiration.

Today's revolution in information technology is, perhaps, something akin to the great leaps forward in knowledge during the Renaissance. Our new technology has finally managed to bring scientific and creative minds together: computer graphics and animation techniques have created new art forms that effectively remove the barriers between logic and imagination – just as Renaissance thinkers saw no distinction between science and magic. And just as the Renaissance was supported by a revolution in communication, the spread of printing, our Renaissance is underpinned by the growth of communication networks, enabling millions of people and archives the world over to be reached instantaneously from our own homes.

If this is indeed a new Renaissance, then Andy Haveland-Robinson is a good example of a new Renaissance man. Apart from his successful desktop publishing business, he also designs computer animations for pop videos, and has a wide range of other interests, such as music. Our first meeting with him in summer 1993, when he demonstrated some of his amazing computer animations, left us spellbound and convinced that we had found the person we needed. We have to say, however, that Andy always remained strictly objective, and was by no means a total convert, although he would say, after many hours of scrutinizing the Shroud image, 'I think Leonardo was involved in this somewhere'.

We had hoped that there would be some way of using computer imaging to establish beyond doubt that the face of the man on the Shroud was that of Leonardo, by matching up the image with portraits of the Maestro – in the same way that Lillian Schwartz had shown that 'The Mona Lisa' is Leonardo's self-portait.[1] However, this was not possible. The fact is that there is not enough information about Leonardo's appearance to make hard-and-fast comparisons. All likely techniques, whether computer-based or forensic, need certain basic reference points and some way of calculating the scale of different images in order to compare them. Surviving portraits of Leonardo do not have this information.

In short, the best equipment for measuring the similarity between two pictures is the human eye and brain. A computer, unless given extremely precise data, can never hope to match them.

The pictures have to be accurate. Comparisons often involve tiny measurements – such as the distance between the inner corners of the eye, something that does not change with age or fluctuations in weight – and even minute errors in the picture will throw the comparison out. Obviously all (or almost all) representations of Leonardo are painted, so there is never any guarantee of accuracy, especially in the fine detail.

The only portrait that we could be sure was accurate enough was his only surviving self-portrait (disregarding the pictures in which he painted himself, such as 'The Adoration of the Magi' and 'The Last Supper'), a drawing in red chalk. He did this when he was in his sixties, but looking considerably older and more than ever like an Old Testament prophet. It now hangs in Turin, in the Royal Library. (It is a source of some amusement to us that Serge Bramly's biography of Leonardo opens with the words: 'Not far from the Turin Cathedral, which houses the famous but now disputed Shroud, there is, in the Biblioteca Reale, the least contested self-portrait of Leonardo da Vinci.' Bramly goes on to draw parallels between the reverence with which both images are kept – 'Like the Shroud, this self-portrait is rarely exhibited in public: ravaged by time, it is stored away from the harmful effects of air and light.')[2]

We know that this portrait is accurate because it was used successfully by Lillian Schwartz to match up with 'The Mona Lisa'. However, it dates from many years after his creation of the Shroud, when he was forty, and although there is still a resemblance to Shroudman, it is not precise enough for our purposes. The cheeks are sunken with age and the mouth has changed, probably because he had lost several teeth over the years. But the biggest problem of all is that the angle of the face is different from that of Shroudman: here Leonardo half turns to the viewer.

There is only a handful of portraits of Leonardo that date from his lifetime. Later pictures, such as the engraving in Vasari's *Lives of the Artists* first published in 1550, although based on earlier portraits, are not at all reliable. The second well-known depiction shows Leonardo nearer to the right age, but in complete profile, making comparison with the Shroud impossible. This is now in the Royal Library in Windsor (with a copy in the Ambrosiana Library in Milan), and was probably painted by a pupil, possibly Francesco Melzi. Raphael painted Leonardo as Plato in 'The School of Athens' but, although the two artists had met, it could not have been painted from life as Leonardo was living in France at the time. A painting in the Uffizi Gallery, which has perhaps the most striking resemblance to the face of the man on the Shroud, was long thought to be a self-portrait, but was shown in the 1930s to be a seventeenth-century work. It was certainly based on a lost self-portrait, but it is invalid for purposes of comparison. (Incidentally, this portrait was painted over a depiction of Mary Magdalene.)

What we needed was a portrait of Leonardo at the age of forty, looking straight out at the observer. Of course, annoyingly, there is one – Agemmian's 1935 portrait of the man on the Shroud – but we could hardly use that for comparison! If there had been lots of surviving portraits, even from several different angles, we could have combined them to make a three-dimensional model that could have been rotated to face the screen. Sadly and frustratingly, we could not even begin to do this.

The few existing portraits show many signs of inaccuracy. The Windsor portrait is widely believed to have been altered in order to flatter the Maestro: his nose – in life a splendid example of nasal domination, being more like a ski-jump than anything else – has dwindled to less alarming proportions, thanks to the instant plastic surgery of a crafty paintbrush. It is also possible that the Turin self-portrait has been altered over the years.[3]

With Andy we looked at all the possible candidates in case there really was some way of making an objective comparison. We even considered the possibility of using 'The Mona Lisa', but in the end we had to accept that we simply could not do it. As Andy put it: 'The tolerance with people's features is quite small and with different angles of view of Leonardo and lack of scale information the result would be inconclusive. Without a full-frontal picture of his face, it can't be done.' There is also the possibility that the process of projection has distorted his features.

With that avenue closed to us, we turned instead to a study of the image itself, looking for tell-tale discrepancies that might support our theory or throw some light on Leonardo's method. To us, the single most important anomaly is the 'severed head' effect. As Abigail Nevill had pointed out so shrewdly, the head is 'on wrong' and is too small for the body. Not only is it in the wrong position in relation to the body, but there is also a clear gap between the end of the neck and the beginning of the chest – the head appears almost to be floating in a sea of darkness. The space itself might – assuming the Shroud's authenticity – be explained by the lie of the cloth, but the unnatural positioning of the head cannot, nor can the fact that the neck ends so abruptly in a transverse line, neatly squared off. Some photographs even show a sharp white line (in the negative) at the base of the neck, but this could be a fold in the cloth, as it does not appear in all pictures. However, even without this the head appears very clearly to be cut off at the base of the neck, even in the infrared and ultraviolet photographs taken by STURP and in the '3-D' pictures produced by John Jackson and Eric Jumper. Andy's computer-enhanced images also reveal this anomaly quite dramatically, showing the image falling away completely at the neck-line, with not the faintest trace of an image beneath it. This is a significant breakthrough; at last we have proved the head is separate.

At the very start of our research, we had asked two Shroud experts, Ian Wilson and Ian Dickinson – both believers – how they accounted for the 'severed head' effect, and got two diametrically opposed answers. Wilson[4] said he could not see anything wrong with the position of the head at all, while Dickinson[5] said there was an anomaly, but that he could explain it. (When he first met one of us, at the exhibition at Bath, he said, 'I've been over this image with a fine-tooth comb and there is something very peculiar about it: the head appears to be dislocated.') He says that the cloth was folded under the chin when the image had been created. When the Shroud was straightened out, the fold made the head appear as if it had been displaced upwards and caused the neck image to be abruptly terminated by a horizontal line. However, we had already noted the complete absence of any similar distortion due to folding and draping anywhere else on the image: if Dickinson was right we should be able to see other such anomalies elsewhere on the cloth, particularly on the face. They are not there.

The odd positioning and squaring off of the head cannot be explained by any of the other theories of how the image was formed. However, it makes perfect sense if the image is a composite – that is, Leonardo's own face and someone else's body. The line under the neck is the cut-off point. This would also explain the small size of the head.

We needed to measure the differences in size between the body and head objectively, which meant looking closely at the physique of the man on the Shroud. What we finally came up with – by applying the 'Emperor's new clothes' approach we had learned from young Abigail – was very unexpected.

To the naked eye, the head is too small for the body. But could we demonstrate this anomaly? We set out to compare the ratio of head to body.

I (Clive) and my brother Keith – who as a trained artist is familiar with the proportions of the human figure – set out to do some calculations. The usual ratio between head and total height is 1:8 (that is, the head goes into the total height eight times). This is an average, with individual variations ranging from about 1:7.5 and, very rarely, going as low as 1:8.5. The smaller ratio tends to happen in people of smaller build – the shorter you are, the larger your head is in comparison with your body.

To find out the head/body ratio of the Shroudman, we obviously needed to know his height, something which has proved to be a vexed question for Shroudies. In part this is due to the faintness of the image and the way it appears to fade into the background at the edges, making precise measurement difficult. There is also disagreement about the way the body is positioned, which is important in that attempts to work out the height needed to allow for any foreshortening due to the positioning of the limbs. Those who believe that the image was formed by direct contact with a body also have to take into account any distortion caused by the way the cloth was draped. (Although, as we have seen, the cloth must have been laid flat.) A great setback here is the way the shoulders have disappeared under the patches: this was especially frustrating for us, as it would have been much easier to judge how badly positioned the head is if the shoulders were visible.

By far the most extensive work on the position of the man on the Shroud has been done by Isabel Piczek, a leading American religious artist who is very much in demand for her striking murals, which grace many American churches and cathedrals. She approached the problem from the point of view of a professional artist, someone trained in depicting the human figure and very experienced with the problems of foreshortening. Although a believer in the Shroud's authenticity, and therefore given to over-enthusiastic acceptance of some of the odder theories around (her own is that the image was the result of 'time reversal'), her work here is convincing and well-argued, and does indeed present the most acceptable reconstruction.

Piczek looked at the way the limbs are foreshortened and the varying intensity of the image – for example the way the backs of the knees are less clear than the calves and the buttocks – and found that the whole image is absolutely consistent with the attitude of crucifixion. She assumes this is because rigor mortis had set in by the time the body was placed in the Shroud. There is, however, no reason why an anatomically-aware artist could not have depicted the body in this way to reinforce the identification with Jesus, or why Leonardo could not have arranged his model in such a position. This explains why we can see the footprint, since the knees are drawn up so that the feet are placed flat on the cloth – perhaps with one foot slightly over the other because of the way the body had been nailed – which is borne out by the foreshortening of the legs on both front and back images.

Piczek's work also confirms that there is no distortion due to the cloth being draped over and around the body, which agrees with our conclusion that the cloth had to have been flat when the image was created. But something else, something that was to us much more significant, also emerged from her work.

During a visit to London in November 1992, she presented her findings to a meeting of the BSTS,[6] which we attended with some friends. Her talk showed convincingly that her reconstruction fitted the body as we see it on the Shroud, and included slides of her work showing how models had demonstrated her theories. It was only during question time that one fact she had failed to mention came to light, in reply to a question from our colleague Tony Pritchett. He asked what conclusions she had reached about the positioning of the head, something that she had conspicuously avoided mentioning. Piczek replied that she had had problems in determining how the head had been placed, since she was unable to find a model who could get their head into the same position as Shroudman while maintaining the correct position of the rest of their body. In fact, she said 'the head appeared separated'. This was, to us, impressive confirmation by an expert of Abigail's innocent observation in Bath. Put simply: the head just does not fit.

It is also clear just by looking at the image that the face is brighter (in negative) and much sharper than the rest of the image – that is, the rest of the front and the whole of the back. This is also apparent from the '3-D' pictures created by the VP-8 Image Analyzer, in which the face stands out more clearly than the rest of the image. Although, as we shall see shortly, we have grave doubts about the validity of all the claims made for that particular series of tests, this does not affect the fact that the Image Analyzer found the face to be more intense than the rest of the image. This cannot be explained (as some have tried to do) by saying that the face is more angular. If the intensity of the image is due to its proximity to the body, then those parts that were supposedly touching the cloth – the tip of the nose, the chest, the backs of the hands, the knees – should all be equally intense. But instead we find that the face as a whole is much better defined, another indication that it was created separately and, perhaps, with more care.

Still trying to puzzle out the head/body ratio, and the need to discover Shroudman's true height, we soon realized that Isabel Piczek's work was the best basis on which to work. One might think that measuring his height would be a simple matter, even allowing for a few inches at either end, but no. When we came to look at the literature for clues, we simply could not believe our eyes.

The most common height given for Shroudman is about 180 cm, although this is always hedged around with some qualifications about the problems of making a precise measurement given the vagaries of the image. In fact, estimates of the man's height have varied so enormously as to be farcical.

Giulio Ricci,[7] a staunch (some would say fanatical) believer, calculated that the man was only 162.5 cm, allowing for the distortion caused by the (non-existent) draping and, curiously, the 'expansion of the cloth' over time. As a believer, he had obviously calculated that this expansion had taken place over a period of 2000 years – an assumption that is hardly scientific. At the other extreme, Lorenzo Ferri (a professor at the University of Rome) and anatomist Luigi Gedda independently arrived at an estimate of 188 cm.[8] For those readers who, like ourselves, still have difficulty with metric measurements let us give these in feet and inches, as they are too important here not to be clearly understood. Ricci's estimate was 5ft 4in; Ferri and Gedda's was 6ft 2in, but the most common estimate is 5ft 11in. Such wide discrepancies led us to do our own sums.

The problem is, as the real thing is locked away, that we always see the Shroud image in miniature. If it were on permanent display, perhaps one of the Shroud's most telling anomalies would be more widely known and questioned.

Keith and I realized that we first had to know the actual length of the image as it appears on the cloth, from the top of the head to the tips of the toes. From that (making allowances for the foreshortening found by Isabel Piczek) we should be able to arrive at a reasonably good estimate of the man's height. Absolute precision is impossible, but we should be able to get a good enough estimate for our purposes. As we believe the head of the front image to have been created separately, it would be particularly interesting to see if the front image were exactly the same height as the back. We bought a photograph of the entire Shroud from the Holy Shroud Guild (of New York), measured it and, knowing the dimensions of the Shroud itself, scaled up our results accordingly.

Our calculations put the height of the man on the Shroud – at the front – at 203cm. Not surprisingly, we blinked and repeated our calculations several times. This had been no mistake: the front image is indeed around the 203cm mark. So what is the height of Shroudman at the back? Curiouser and curiouser – he is 208cm! Put in imperial measurements we calculate that the front image is 6ft 8in and the back 6ft 10in. Strangely enough, if you look closely enough at the Shroud literature you will find these calculations in there somewhere, but they are hardly picked out in banner headlines.[9]

Not only is the image absurdly, impossibly, big, but the image – supposedly of the same man and made at the same time – is 5cm (two inches) taller at the back than the front! (The tips of the toes are missing from the front Shroud image, as the cloth stops slightly short, but this would not make a whole 5cm difference.)

Believers have never made much of the overall length of the body, although they all know it. If they mention it at all they argue that the drape of the cloth over the body's contours would distort the measurements, making the image appear much taller than the actual body. But from the work of Isabel Piczek, herself a believer, as well as the evidence of our own eyes we know that there is simply no such distortion. The cloth could only produce the foreshortened – but otherwise entirely natural – image if it were flat.

A possible explanation is that the crucifixion position shown by Piczek's work (with the knees drawn up and the feet flat on the floor) extends the image by the length of the feet, adding several inches onto the height. Ricci, for example, argues that measurements should be taken only as far as the heels. This is true, but then we also have to allow for the length lost by the raising of the knees, which foreshortens the image and makes the legs appear too short. In order to discover just how much difference the raising of the knees does make to the overall length of the human body as seen from directly in front, Keith and I measured ourselves lying completely flat with knees raised to the level found by Isabel Piczek, while allowing our feet to be flat on the floor. By doing this we found the optimum position for such raising of the knees. With the feet placed flat the knees are drawn up much too far and the image would be ridiculously foreshortened, but it is possible to reach a good compromise with the backs of the knees about 25–27 cm from the ground.

In fact, the overall length of the body – from the top of the head to the heels when lying flat and to the tip of the toes with the knees raised – hardly changes at all. The extra length given by the feet is exactly offset by the foreshortening caused by drawing the knees up. Of course individuals will always vary, but even at the most generous estimate the figure could only be extended by as much as 5cm through this explanation.

Although we had discounted Ian Dickinson's idea that the head appears to be displaced upwards by the folding of the cloth under the chin, we decided to check to see if it could account for the extra height. But no – the back image actually confirms our measurement and goes even further, being 5cm longer than the front. We could only conclude that if the length of the image is 203cm, then the smallest possible man whose image it was must have been 198cm that is, 6ft 6in.

Now we understood the real reason for all the endless discussion about draping, folds and expansion of the cloth. It was flim-flammery to obscure an unpalatable fact, one that edges the Shroud into farce. Surely, if Jesus had been a giant, it would have been mentioned in the New Testament? But its pages are as innocent of such a fact as they are about a miraculously-imprinted Shroud.

This anomaly is hardly a problem for those who believe that the image is painted – or for us, who suggest it is in fact projected. When projecting images from life (as we were to discover) it is very easy to make them a little too small or a little too big. Moving the object that is being projected just an inch or two towards the focusing mechanism results in a disproportionately enlarged image. And the reason why there is a discrepancy between the front and back images is because the head does not actually belong to the body.

From Rodney Hoare's A Piece of Cloth we learned another seldom-mentioned fact – that the back of the head is slightly wider than the front.[10] Of course, Hoare has a ready explanation. The head must have been on some kind of a pillow, he says, placed under the Shroud and pushing it around the sides of the head to allow them to appear on the image. Hence the back of the head appears to be wider. But there is none of the distortion one might expect to find.

Now that we had an estimate of Shroudman's height, Keith and I could work out the head/body ratio. Measuring the head and comparing it to the estimated height gave a ratio of 1:8.7 for the front image, well outside the normal range. Knowing exactly where to take the measurement, given the faintness of the image's outline, is difficult, but we had built in a generous margin of error. Comparing the size of the image of the head at the front with the height we had calculated for the whole of the back image – again erring on the side of caution – produced a minimum ratio of 1:9, possibly as much as 1:94. So we had proved that the head really is too small for the body. Laboriously we had finally confirmed Abigail's insight. And, as Isabel Piczek had confirmed that the rest of the body is in good proportion, it supports our theory that the head is a completely separate image. This fact also makes it seem unlikely that the Shroud is painted, as the image as a whole is quite brilliant, and what good artist in his right mind would get the head so wrong? Incidentally, from the average ratios the face of Shroudman belongs to someone of between 178cm and 183cm (5ft 10in and 6ft). Leonardo was known to be tall, although his exact height is not recorded. But it would be wrong to jump to conclusions: there is still the fact that a projected image could come out at more or less any length.

Our work on the physique of the man on the Shroud had made us aware of other discrepancies and anomalies, some of which were to prove very important when we came to replicate Leonardo's method, others which deserve a passing mention.

We had observed quite early in our studies something that has been commented on by sceptics but largely ignored by believers: the convenient placing of the hands, crossed over the genitals. It seems an unusual way to lay out a corpse, and preserving the man's modesty seems to indicate that the cloth was intended for display with the hands arranged in order to avoid offending the sensibilities of the faithful. Perhaps, however, the position of the hands was also chosen to avoid another dilemma. As it was supposed to be Jesus, accuracy would demand that he would be circumcised (as medieval and Renaissance Christians knew only too well, there being several Holy Foreskins doing the rounds in their day), yet, as Peter de Rosa points out in the prologue to his *Vicars of Christ*, Christians would not have been comfortable with this reminder of the Jewishness of their Lord. So the artistic convention grew up of depicting the crucified Jesus with a loincloth, which de Rosa calls 'the biggest cover-up in history'.[11] We are particularly amused to note that many copies of the Turin Shroud add a loincloth.

It is also impossible to place the hands of a corpse in such a position without either tying them together or supporting the elbows. Predictably, believers have argued that there were supports, in the form of bundles of cloth under the elbows. (If all the pillows and bundles of cloth that are cited to explain away anomalies had actually been used, not to mention the accompanying blocks of spices, the entombment of Jesus must have presented one of the oddest spectacles in history. It would have resembled the first day of the sales in Harrods' linen department.)

If, on the other hand, the image was faked, it would have been easy to keep the hands in the required position while also keeping the means of doing so invisible. The easiest way would be to tie the thumbs together.[12]

There is also the matter of the hairline and the hair. If the man had been lying down, as is generally believed, the hair would not frame the face in the way it does, but would fall backwards away from the face. The hairline itself is completely unnatural, and there is a curious blank strip between the sides of the face and the hair. Then there is the bizarre fact that Shroudman has no ears. The face is too narrow: the outside corners of his eyes are virtually at the edge of his face. This man has neither ears nor temples.

But the oddest aspect of the face is the size of the forehead. Any artist will tell you that as a rule the eyes are just about the centre of the face, midway between chin and crown. (The centre line is, in fact, just below the eyes.) However, on the Shroud image the eyes are much too high because the forehead appears to be foreshortened. We began by thinking that it must have been due to the way Leonardo overlaid the image of his face, but it was only later – as we will describe in the next chapter – that the full significance of the size of the forehead became apparent.

By far the most often-quoted of the oddities about the Shroud is the '3-D information' it allegedly contains. This means that there is a precise relationship between the intensity of the image (darkness as seen by the naked eye, brightness as seen in negative) and the distance of the body from the cloth. That relationship can be used to construct a three-dimensional picture of the man on the Shroud by showing the lighter areas as higher, as in a contour map. This was demonstrated most graphically by the VP-8 Image Analyzer pictures in the mid-1970s.

The three-dimensional information contained in the Shroud was, we were led to believe, an odd and extremely unusual property of the Shroud image. Neither paintings nor photographs, unless they are taken under very specific conditions, behave in such a way. Other image-creation theories cannot account for it, except, perhaps, the ridiculous 'nuclear flash' theory championed by Jackson, which (as we have seen) can easily be dismissed on several grounds, some of them pure common sense. The 3-D information is different for the face and the body. If the Image Analyzer is adjusted to show the face in natural relief, the body (front and back) hardly stands out at all. If the body image is adjusted in this way, the features of the face stand out far too prominently. This supports our idea that the two images were created separately.

We realized, however, that if it were a photographic image it would be unlikely to exhibit the '3-D effect'. The Image Analyzer works with light and shade, assuming that darker areas are further away from the camera than the light areas, and that there is a direct relationship between the intensity of the image and the distance. Normal photographs are invariably lit more on one side than the other, so that the two sides of a face, though equally distant from the camera, are of different brightnesses. Only when the light source is shining from the same direction as the camera will you get a 3-D effect. A spotlight mounted above a camera might do the trick, but it is still unlikely because the difference in the amount of light reflected would probably be too subtle, the variations too small to make a reliable attempt to work out the distance from camera to object. A rough estimate would be possible, but not the precision of the VP-8 images.

In our attempt to replicate the Shroud image, described in the next chapter, we realized that Leonardo would have used the sun as his source of light. So it would have been impossible to measure the difference in the amounts of light reflecting from different parts of the face and body.

Initially we had speculated that there might be a way of lighting the scene so as to cause a 3-D effect accidentally, which might then give us some clues as to how it had been lit. The effect could have been a coincidental by-product of the exposure times. The sun would have moved during an exposure time that must have been several hours long, so the two sides of the face would have been lit at different times, whereas the high points – the nose and brows – would have been illuminated constantly, causing them to become more fully exposed.

We asked Andy to look into ways of reproducing the VP-8 pictures using modern software. Using the Holy Shroud Guild's photographs of the full image and close-ups of the face, Andy scanned the images, converting the picture into 'dots', each one being assigned a value according to its brightness. Andy explained: 'The picture was scanned in at 300 dots per inch on a flat bed colour scanner in monochrome, then converted to a grey scale image.' The resulting data was stored in digital form, which meant it could be used by many different programs to manipulate it in various ways. Different brightnesses could be converted into colours, or displayed as a contour map. It could even be converted into sound and played as music (Andy has produced some beautiful abstract pictures by displaying sounds as shapes and colours). Individual parts of the picture could be blown up on screen to look at the most minute detail, or parts of the image could be cut out and moved to compare to other parts. For example, Andy easily managed to take half of the front image of Shroudman and match it up against the half of the rear image, showing graphically – and very effectively – that the back is indeed longer than the front.

To reproduce the 3-D pictures created by John Jackson and Eric Jumper with the Image Analyzer, Andy took the digitized data and ran it through programs that converted it to a height map. In his own words: 'The image was rendered as a height field using a public domain ray tracing package. Because of the graininess of the original image – there were speckles etc – the 3-D image would have had large spikes, which would confuse things.

'The spurious spikes needed to be removed and this was done using a paint-box package called Photostyler to apply a Gaussian filter to smooth out the "noise" and leave a trend. The results were re-rendered.

'This revealed a more meaningful image but the results were still disappointing if looking for 3-D "proof". I tried different angles of view and applied different textures to the object.'

Using this technique the image could be 'tilted' so that (as with the VP-8 pictures) any intensity-distance relationship could be displayed as a three-dimensional picture. The result was – to say the least – surprising. Andy was unable to reproduce the 3-D information found by the VP-8.

There was a slight three-dimensionality, but no more than one would expect from an evenly-lit photograph. Most striking was the fact that there was no appreciable difference between the brightness of the bridge of the nose and the brows, making it impossible for the image analysis software to distinguish between them in terms of height. The images, using several different scales to exaggerate any slight difference in the intensity, always showed the same result: a flat face, with nose and brows all the same height. Andy tried various methods to eliminate any errors in his findings, but found that 'the results were still inconclusive'.

We were disconcerted. We double-checked our method, but could find nothing wrong with anything we or Andy had done. Slowly the significance of what we had discovered began to dawn on us: could it really be true that the much-vaunted '3-D information', the one allegedly unique factor in the Shroud image that has puzzled believers and non-believers alike for many years, simply does not exist?

We wondered if Andy's equipment might be inferior to the VP-8, so we turned once again to the Shroud literature to trace the rise of the 3-D information as one of the Shroud's most potent selling points. It seemed to rest entirely on those twenty-year-old experiments by Jackson and Jumper. No-one apart from us seemed to have tried to replicate their work, which is especially surprising given the advances in computing power since their day.

Jackson and Jumper, because of their founding of STURP, are two of the enduring stars of the Shroud world. However, despite their scientific credentials they are and always have been firm believers in the Shroud's authenticity, even before they embarked on their studies of it. Although STURP is known as a scientifically-based body, less attention is given to the fact that both men are on the Executive Council of the Holy Shroud Guild[13], an organization that was founded on the premise that the Shroud is authentic and that it has an important message for us all. Their own scientific papers,[14] presented at the 1977 Albuquerque Conference, reveal their preconceptions – they refer to the Shroud image throughout as being that of 'Jesus' body'. According to *The Jesus Conspiracy* by Kersten and Gruber, at the international symposium in Paris in 1989 'he [Jackson] declared that he could only explain the formation of the image by a miracle.'[15]

Jackson and Jumper had worked on the three-dimensionality for some time before the VP-8 was brought in, using manual techniques. They were following up a suggestion of Paul Vignon's at the start of the century. We had long realized that these experiments were open to all kinds of flaws, but, like everyone else, we were won over by the computer-enhanced pictures they produced a year later. Their initial experiments have been comprehensively attacked – especially on their protocol and the collection and analysis of data – by Joe Nickell in his *Inquest on the Shroud of Turin*.[16] To begin with he notes that 'the whole methodology of three-dimensional reconstruction is dependent on circular reasoning, and begs the question of whether or not the Shroud ever enveloped a real human form'. Jackson and Jumper started from the assumption that it had.

They had found somebody they considered to be the same build and height of the man on the Shroud – but as this person was not 203cm at the front and 5cm taller at the back we wonder just how they arrived at their conclusion – and covered him with a cloth on which they had traced the Shroud image. There is obviously something self-fulfilling about this, as for a start, they found someone who would fit their traced image. But then they had to make assumptions about the way the cloth was draped over the body, in which case they also had to find a model who fitted their assumptions. Their model was laid flat on his back, in what was then considered to be the correct position for the man in the Shroud – flat on his back with the cloth folded up at the feet. We now know from Isabel Piczek's work that this is wrong. The volunteer's knees should have been raised and his feet flat on the floor. They also made much of the fact that there was only 'one way to cover the body correctly'. But then, if they had chosen another position for the legs and feet and a volunteer of a different build, they would have discovered that there was only one possible way to cover him.

They then measured the distances between different parts of the model's body and the cloth, down the centre of the image only. Separately, they measured the intensity of the Shroud image down the centre line using an instrument called a microdensitometer. They then plotted on a graph the two sets of figures, and claimed that the two matched up. This method allows for a great many errors. Their judgement of the height and build of the model and their assumptions about the way the cloth was draped over the body could easily have been incorrect. They took their measurements of cloth-body distance manually from photographs taken from the side (with the model covered and uncovered). The microdensitometer readings were only valid for the middle strip of the image, so how would they know if the same effects hold true for the rest of it?

Most serious is their 'smoothing out' of the two sets of data on the graph. They actually show a wide scatter, perhaps due to an error in measurement, but Jackson and Jumper drew a curve through the points to make an average. In his description of the results Ian Wilson writes that their graph reveals 'a perfect curve, demonstrating beyond question that there was a positive and precise relationship'.[17] Joe Nickell, however, reports that the correlation is initially 'only fair' and that the curve was added using the experimenters' own judgement: 'Any number of different curves could equally be chosen to average the data scatter and replace it with a smooth function.' Further adjustments are made, and then – most damning of all – the data is 'iteratively modified so that a more human-looking figure can be obtained'. In other words it is possible to question the reliability of Jackson and Jumper's findings. The final result, according to Nickell, is that their method 'allows some of the Shroud-image characteristics to be superimposed on the relief of the human model. Hence the resultant "statue" is actually some blend of the shroud image and the human model.'

However, it was the VP-8 work, with which Nickell did not deal, that seemed to be more unassailable, primarily because it does not depend on plotting graphs but presents an easily-understood picture. The story, as given in the believers' literature – for example, in Ian Wilson's *Evidence of the Shroud* (1986),[18] is that one day John Jackson visited radiographer Bill Mottern at the Sandia Scientific Laboratories in Albuquerque. Mottern happened to be experimenting with the VP-8 Image Analyzer, a piece of equipment that had been developed for NASA, but which was now beginning to find wider industrial applications. He casually suggested that they put one of the slides of the Shroud that Jackson had with him into the machine. Quite spontaneously, without any special adjustments to the Analyzer, the 3-D images, now so familiar from Shroud literature, appeared on the screen. The moment has gone down in Shroud history as almost rivalling that when Secondo Pia first viewed the negative effect.

Common sense, however, suggests that there has to have been more to it than that. It is a matter of scale, of calibration. The Image Analyzer simply determines the relative intensity of different points on an image. To display it in a form recognizable to us it needs to know the distance represented by a given change in intensity, ie the scale. Andy demonstrated this graphically by showing us different views of the Shroud face using different distance/intensity scales. The difference between a light point and a dark point might represent say, 15cm, or 5cm, or 1cm. There is no way that any machine, no matter how sophisticated, can work this out for itself. It has to be told the scale by the operator. In fact, he can try out different scales until he finds one that suits his particular purpose. In the case of the Shroud image, you keep adjusting the scale until you get the most recognizable picture of a human body.

This in itself does not mean that the Shroud image has no 3-D information, but it does show that there must be more to the tale of the spontaneous appearance of the image without giving the Analyzer the required scale. This would be little short of a miracle in itself. In any case, Andy's results using the computer only confirm something that is obvious to the unaided eye – or should be, if we were not beguiled by the technological wizardry of the VP-8 machine. The basis of the VP-8 work is that the brighter any area of the image is, the higher it stands out on the computer-generated picture. What are the brightest parts of the Shroud face? A glance at photographs shows clearly that they are the moustache and beard. Yet in the VP-8 pictures of the face these are *lower* than the tip of the nose, which is not as bright! More 'iterative modification' of the image, one wonders?

Other members of STURP have been more cautious about the claims of Jackson and Jumper in relation to the 3-D information. In a report summarizing STURP's work, Lawrence Schwalbe plays it down, blaming the press for misrepresenting and sensationalizing the claims, and concluding that Jackson and Jumper's studies 'have not as yet suggested a particular image formation mechanism nor do they even imply that a three-dimensional object was necessary to produce the image . . . no direct conclusions about the Shroud's authenticity can be inferred'.[19]

Without more details of the Jackson and Jumper scenario it is hard to say why Andy – using pictures and equipment at least as good as those used by Jackson – failed to see what they saw back in the 1970s. But we see no reason to doubt Andy's results. And, given the criticisms levelled at Jackson and Jumper's earlier experiments with the microdensitometer, we feel that their VP-8 work must also remain suspect. Andy's conclusion was characteristically objective and cautious: 'My findings don't necessarily support your hypothesis, but it does support your idea that the head is completely separate and may have been faked using a photographic technique.'

Others have made three-dimensional models of the Shroud image, but they used only the eye of the artist – people have no need of computer-enhanced images in order to see how two-dimensional pictures will look in three dimensions. To prove the point, one of the best-known models was made in the 1960s by a British fashion photographer, Leo Vala, by projecting a slide of the Shroud face onto a block of clay and fashioning the clay, estimating the depth caused by the shadows. But this technique could be used equally well on paintings – in fact, Vala made a prototype using 'The Mona Lisa'.[20]

When we began our collaboration with Andy, we, like all other Shroudies, believed that the Shroud exhibits amazing, inexplicable and unique 3-D information. Though we were persuaded that Leonardo had created the image, we could not see how he had managed to produce that particular effect and felt that attempting to replicate it would be a real stumbling block in our experimental work. Now we faced no such problem, for the much-vaunted 3-D information simply does not exist. Whatever the precise circumstances that lay behind the announcements of Jackson and Jumper, we feel that – intentionally or unintentionally – that tale seriously misrepresented the qualities of the Shroud image and in doing so has misled a generation of researchers and millions of ordinary people.

What lay ahead for us was still no walkover, however. We set ourselves the task of replicating Leonardo's pioneering photographic technique, and in so doing we had to achieve what no one else has done – we had to recreate the method used to create the image on the Turin Shroud. We took a deep breath, and began.

— 8 —

POSITIVE DEVELOPMENTS

'Every body fills the surrounding air with images of itself, and every image appears in its entirety and in all its parts. The air is full of an infinity of straight lines and rays which cut across each other without displacing each other and which reproduce on whatever they encounter the true form of their cause.'

Leonardo da Vinci[1]

ALTHOUGH THE idea that the Shroud image was some kind of photograph went a long way towards explaining many of its most intriguing features, it was still difficult not to be sceptical. Could even a genius of Leonardo's stature have developed a photographic process some 350 years before its known invention? Even if he had the knowledge, were Renaissance materials adequate for the task? If he had invented such a process, why did he keep it a secret?

The last question is the easiest to answer. Even leaving aside his 'forbidden' magical and hermetical practices, Leonardo was obsessively secretive. Sometimes this can be ascribed to the natural caution of the innovator in an age before the advent of patent law, but sometimes far more complex reasons come into play – for example, he refused to set down details of his submarine in his notebooks, realizing that if such an invention fell into the wrong hands it could result in the death of hundreds of innocent passengers.[2] In the case of photography, however, there are good reasons for believing that he regarded them as part and parcel of his magical practice.

Today we are so familiar with the whole idea of photography that it is almost impossible for us to put ourselves in the place of someone encountering it for the first time. To the average Renaissance Italian the act of capturing an image from life would have been regarded as a totally magical act. Try convincing the Church, which was highly suspicious of any innovation, that this was a perfectly natural process. Try convincing those whose picture you had taken that you had not also stolen something vital from them, perhaps even their very soul.

Even educated men would have taken this view, and it is likely that Leonardo himself would have regarded basic photography as something magical. This is not mere speculation. It is a fact that during the Middle Ages and Renaissance experiments with optics and light were kept strictly secret, and were firmly in the province of the magical adept, the alchemist and the occultist.

Leonardo had a passion for light and optics, probably devoting more time to researching this area than any other. He had remarkably advanced ideas about the nature of light and vision.[3] In the fifteenth century the prevailing view was that the eyes see by projecting some kind of beam. Leonardo, however, understood that the eye is simply a receiver for light rays that are reflected from the surface of objects: he likened light to the ripples that spread out from a stone dropped in water. He realized that light travels in waves, and that it therefore had a speed – there are even indications that he tried to calculate it. (Remarkably, similar attempts had also been made by Roger Bacon, the highly-respected English polymath) in the thirteenth century.) He dissected eyeballs and discovered that they contain a lens, understanding that they work on the same principle as what we know as a camera – a principle with which he was already familiar. He also designed devices that would reproduce the workings of the eye artificially.

The Maestro experimented extensively with lenses, particularly in order to overcome the problem of chromatic aberration – the blurring of the edges of an image which was such a drawback with all early lenses. Mirrors, which can be used to focus like a lens, were a source of endless fascination for him. He also performed some experiments investigating the behaviour of light: for example, he discovered the 'inverse square rule' – that is, the amount of light received from a source diminishes in proportion to the distance it has to travel. He invented a device, the photometer, for measuring the brightness of an object – something not rediscovered until the late eighteenth century by Count Rumford, one of the pioneer photographers.[4] Leonardo's research was precisely what would have been necessary before embarking on an attempt at photography.

Underlying all this work – with lenses, mirrors, the workings of the eye, even in his innovations in painting techniques – was his fascination with light itself. Reading through the notebooks in which he describes his quest to understand light, the way it carries images, and the many ways in which reflected images can be captured, we were left in no doubt that someone with his obsessions and abilities would have at least considered the possibility that images can be caught and captured permanently. He certainly would have tried.

Evidence that Leonardo was obsessed by the thought of capturing images from life comes from the great historian of photography, Josef Maria Eder. In his classic *History of Photography*, written in the 1940s, he discusses methods used by the forerunners of true photography to take images from life rather than reproducing them by painting or drawing. One simple method, known as 'nature printing', consisted of pressing painted objects, such as a leaf, onto suitably prepared paper. Interestingly, this method was invented by Leonardo and included in his writings dating from around 1490 (and which are preserved in the *Codex Atlanticus*).[5] He recommended using paper coated with lamp-black and 'sweet oil', onto which was pressed a leaf coloured in white lead. This produced a negative image of the leaf.

Leonardo was not the only one to dream that images could be captured for ever. As long ago as the first century AD the Roman poet Statius had written of the recording of people's images on silver- or gold-plated mirrors. Such ideas surfaced many times over the centuries, and could have fired Leonardo's imagination and acted as a springboard for all his most advanced inventions.

Giovanni had told us that Leonardo used photography, an idea that at first seemed completely wild, but as our research progressed it came to seem increasingly likely. Others had obviously mused on the question too: a Leonardophile acquaintance once remarked to one of us, without knowing the reason for our interest in the Maestro, that if Leonardo were alive today he would be a photographer. If making photographs were possible at some level in Leonardo's day, then one could rest assured that he would have done it. Having said that, however, problems arose immediately. Surely, we thought, capturing a projected image depends on synthetic chemicals that can only be produced in post-Industrial Revolution factories and with lenses of high modern quality? Even a genius cannot create without the materials. After all, Leonardo also predicted the telephone,[6] but in his day there was no question of actually producing a working model!

The obvious way to test this idea was to attempt to replicate a Leonardo-style 'photograph', using materials and equipment that would have been available to him, or at least within the reach of the technology of his day. If we were successful, it would go a very long way towards proving our theory, as the Shroudies frequently claim that reproducing anything like the Shroud image is impossible even using modern technology. Even *The Times* in its leader the day after the carbon dating results were announced stated: 'modern science can discredit it but cannot make its duplicate.'[7]

Just making visually satisfactory duplicates, without even attempting to replicate a likely method, has been found difficult by artists. For example, designer John Weston, who was commissioned to make two copies for use in the the film *Silent Witness*, had to experiment for several weeks before finding a satisfactory method that just used paint. Each copy took him five weeks to paint.[8]

At the start of this enterprise, nearly five years ago, we were hampered by the fact that neither of us had anything other than the sketchiest knowledge of photography, let alone of optics and chemistry. Fortunately, we were able to call upon the talents of Keith Prince, who is not only a gifted artist who has studied photography and has an excellent working knowledge of its basic principles, but also has a sound grasp of physics and chemistry. In the course of our researches, we were constantly indebted to his near-photographic memory, his ability to make imaginative connections, plus his skill in knocking up the most complex apparatus out of odds and ends in double-quick time.

If we were to replicate Leonardo's putative method for creating the Turin Shroud, we had to begin by freeing ourselves from the preconceptions of modern photography. These days we are used to the idea of complex lenses, and film that reacts to light in hundredths of a second, creating images that need various chemical treatments – developing, fixing and printing – before they become usable. We were looking for something much simpler. It made sense, therefore, to look at the origins of photography, and see what the known pioneers had used, in the hope of finding some clues to Leonardo's method.

Photography was the result of the coming together of two main inventions – the camera, which collects the image, and the film which records it. The first had been around for centuries in the shape of the camera obscura – literally a 'dark chamber' – or the pin-hole camera. Originally it was actually a darkened room with a small hole in one wall, but later versions were portable and contained a lens to add greater clarity to the image. In fact, many of the landscape painters of the seventeenth century used this device, setting up portable camera obscuras that projected images of the required scene onto canvas or paper, where it was painted – almost like 'painting by numbers'! As time passed, the camera obscura was refined by adding better lenses and reducing it from the original room-size to a small box, the precursor of the modern camera. It inspired those who used it to look for a way to fix the image permanently.

The principle of the camera obscura has been known for centuries, if only as a curiosity. When light shines through a small hole into a dark chamber, pictures of things outside – upside down and in mirror image – are projected onto the opposite wall. Aristotle wrote of it in the fourth century BC, as did the Arab philosopher Ibn al Haitam in the eleventh century, and it is known that a description of a camera obscura was given in 1279 by an English alchemist, John Peckham.[9] But the credit for the first scientifically accurate description of such a device was for many years given to Giovanni Battista della Porta, a Neopolitan who published a description of it in 1552.[10] He retained this claim to fame for almost 300 years, and even today some textbooks still accord him this honour. It was only towards the end of the nineteenth century that Leonardo da Vinci's long-neglected notebooks were deciphered and translated: they showed quite unequivocally that he had beaten Della Porta to it by fifty years. The *Codex Atlanticus* contains a diagram that shows the workings of the camera obscura (which Leonardo called the *oculus artificialis*, the artificial eye), with the explanation: 'If the façade of a building, or a place, or a landscape is illuminated by the sun and a small hole drilled in a building facing this, which is not directly lighted by the sun, then all objects illuminated by the sun will send their images through this aperture and will appear, upside down, on the wall facing the hole.'[11]

In another notebook he wrote: 'You will catch these pictures on a piece of white paper, which is placed vertically in the room not far from that opening . . . the paper should be very thin and must be viewed from the back.'[12] Elsewhere he notes that thin white cloth will do as well for the screen. (Della Porta's camera used a linen screen.)

Returning briefly to the question of the secrecy that surrounded many of these experiments, it is instructive to take a hard look at what happened to the early experimenters in this field. Della Porta, for example, was a Hermeticist and alchemist – he founded a secret group, the Academy of Secrets, which was disbanded by the Pope, and the description of his work with projected images appears in a treatise entitled *Natural Magic*. Della Porta makes it clear that he is consciously revealing something secret, prefacing his description with the words: 'Now I want to announce something about which I have kept silent until now and which I believed that I must keep a secret.' He does not even claim it as his own, and we do not know how long this knowledge had been kept under wraps, or the identity of those from whom he acquired it. One thing is certain: his circumspection was absolutely justified. On giving a public demonstration of the camera obscura, in which he projected the image of a group of actors on to the wall of a house, he was promptly arrested and charged with sorcery – from which he extricated himself only with the greatest difficulty.[13]

Obviously completely unchastened by this experience, della Porta later gave the first public moving picture show, using animated drawings.

In the 1640s a scientific Jesuit, Athanasius Kircher, invented the magic lantern (an early type of slide projection that projected pictures painted on glass). His demonstration of this device also raised suspicions that he was a sorcerer and necromancer. (Kircher, despite his calling, was in fact a devoted student of alchemy, Hermeticism and the Cabala.)[14]

Leonardo's work with optics and the camera obscura caused him to be accused of necromancy. His first known experiments into this area took place in Pavia in the late 1480s and are linked by Maurice Rowden in his biography of the artist with the beginnings of Leonardo's reputation as a sorcerer: 'In Pavia he worked on his camera obscura, to demonstrate his theory that all vision is determined by the angle at which light falls on the eye: the upside-down image thrown on the wall from the camera's pinpoint of light was a more graphic argument than words, and it was little wonder that he got the reputation of being a sorcerer and alchemist.'[15] We have at least adequate proof that research into optics and light was an intrinsic part of Renaissance occultism, and that only a fool in those days made his work in this area public knowledge.

So, the principle of the camera (the shortened term was first used by the astronomer Johannes Kepler (1571–1630), who developed a portable camera obscura) was well known, and Leonardo was an important figure in its development. Photography as such came about when chemically fixed images were created.

In Leonardo's time it had long been known that it was theoretically possible to capture an image. Everyday observations bore this out, for example many substances are affected by exposure to light; paper and cloth yellows, the colour of vegetable tissue deepens and so on. The search was on for some means of speeding up such a reaction and then fixing the image. Many of the great inventors and industrialists of the seventeenth and eighteenth centuries put their minds to this task.[16]

In the eighteenth century, fast-reacting substances, notably the silver salts, were discovered and used to make pictures – stencilled letters that would appear as if by magic on chemically-treated materials. In 1802 Thomas Wedgwood, son of the famous potter Josiah, working with Sir Humphrey Davy (1778–1851), made the first successful attempt to produce an image on paper which had been treated with silver nitrate. These were silhouettes, using a camera obscura to focus the image. The great problem was that such images were not permanent, because they were created by a chemical that reacts to light, so that when the paper was removed from the camera light reacted with the area that was formerly the silhouette, and the image disappeared. The next step was to find a way of 'fixing' the image.

What is generally regarded as the first permanent photograph was taken by a Frenchman, Nicéphore de Niépce (?–1833), in Provence in 1826, using bitumen as the light-sensitive material. It was not, however, a practical method. It was Louis Daguerre (1789–1851) who in 1839 announced his success in fixing a silver iodide image using common salt. He also discovered the principle of the latent image – that is, the fact that some chemicals react to light very quickly but do not show a visible image until they are 'developed' by a further chemical treatment. By 1841 Daguerre had refined his method, chiefly through using better lenses – so that his exposure times, which originally had been about ten or fifteen minutes, went right down to around fifteen seconds. In the same year that Daguerre announced his invention, Fox Talbot (1800–1877) invented the first paper negative process. From then on many people added to the advances that led to modern photography.

However, it was the prehistory of photography that interested us – the discoveries that led up to its early days, and in particular the light-sensitive chemicals that might have been around before the Industrial Revolution. We were to find that, yet again, the pioneering photographers built on the work of the alchemists.

In an early attempt to debunk our theory, BSTS Chairman Rodney Hoare – who used to teach photography – objected that it was impossible for the Shroud image to be a photograph as it was 'inconceivable [Leonardo] could have discovered the effect of light on silver salts'.[17] In our view this is incorrect on two counts. First, silver salts are not the only light-sensitive materials, and secondly, their action was quite definitely known before Leonardo's time. There is an enigmatic reference in Pliny the elder's *Natural History*, which was written in the 1st century AD, that has been taken to reveal his knowledge of the darkening of silver chloride on exposure to light (and this work was very well known to Leonardo).[18] Be that as it may, it is absolutely certain that this property of silver salts was known to alchemists from at least the twelfth century, who were the first to produce and investigate many of the salts that were important in later photography.[19]

The great eighth-century alchemist Jabir-ibn-Hayyan, commonly known as Geber, is reputed to have used silver nitrate, although the earliest known copy of *De Inventiones Veritatis*, a work ascribed to him in which this is mentioned, dates from only the mid-1500s. Albertus Magnus (1193–1280) knew that silver nitrate turned black with exposure to light. Other alchemists who were known to have worked with silver salts are Angelo Sala and Johann Glauber in the 1600s. Robert Boyle (allegedly one of the Priory's Grand Masters) experimented with the effects of light on silver chloride. The response to light of iron salts was also known by them.

Another vitally important process to nineteenth-century photographers, the production of silver chloride from a solution of silver nitrate using sodium chloride, was known to alchemists from at least the early 1400s. In fact, the eminent twentieth-century historian Josef Maria Eder devotes a full chapter of his classic *History of Photography* (1945) to this work of the alchemists – which of course represents only the tip of the iceberg about what they were really up to – and states that 'it is these ideas from which sprang the science of photochemistry'.[20]

Perhaps most significant of all was the discovery that has been hailed as 'the beginning of photography'[21] – the first scientific description of the light sensitivity of silver salts, by Johann Heinrich Schulze in 1727. It is surely no surprise to discover that he made this breakthrough while trying to replicate an alchemical experiment originally made in the seventeenth-century by Balduin. Schulze himself impressed his peers by making stencilled writing appear in salt sediment in bottles of water, but the image soon faded. *The Focal Encyclopaedia of Photography* (1993) reports that 'photography was eventually built on Schulze's discoveries'.[22] Eder is more emphatic: 'Schulze must be declared without doubt the inventor of photography with silver salts.'[23]

It struck us as immensely significant that the two elements that would later be brought together in photography – the means of projecting the image and the light-sensitive chemicals – had been known and investigated by alchemists for centuries beforehand.

We discovered yet another connection during the course of some quite different research in the summer of 1993. The historic fifteenth-century manor house of Rushton Hall in Northamptonshire has attracted much interest recently because of a series of mysteries that surround it and its original owners, the Tresham family. Today it is a home for children with visual and other handicaps that is run by the Royal National Institute for the Blind – for which Clive then worked – so it was natural for us to know about it, and to take an interest in it.

Thomas Tresham (1545–1605), one of the last of the family to own the house (it was confiscated after his grandson was involved in the Gunpowder Plot of 1605), was an architect who left several enigmatic symbolic works for posterity, the most puzzling of which being the Triangular Lodge, now outside the grounds of the Hall and in the care of English Heritage. This three-sided, sharply angled building rears up before one's startled gaze for three floors and is literally covered with symbolic carvings and inscriptions. The standard explanation is that they are connected with Thomas' Catholic beliefs (in Elizabethan times all Catholics were regarded with deep suspicion, so perhaps he could hardly have flaunted his faith in any more obvious ways). But they are much easier to explain in terms of alchemical symbols, which is almost certainly what they are.

We had heard that one of the Lodge's phenomena is connected with small triangular windows set at ground level, which give on to the lower floor, which is partly below ground. On sunny days, the shadows of people outside the Lodge are cast onto a blank wall opposite, but they are turned upside down. We visited the Lodge on such a day with our fellow researcher and good friend Craig Oakley and tried out this effect for ourselves. We soon realized that it was, in fact, not the person's shadow that was being inverted, but a faint image of the person. In effect, the whole lower floor of the Triangular Lodge is a camera obscura. Admittedly the windows are so large that the image is indistinct and shadowy, but perhaps Thomas and his fellow alchemists had a way of refining the image. This discovery made us muse all the way back home that perhaps one of the major secrets of alchemy (in the past) was photography itself.

At this point, and without intimate knowledge of alchemy ourselves, many things had to be guesswork or intelligent assumption. We knew though, that apart from silver salts, other materials had been known for years to be sensitive to light. The great Roman architect Vitrivius (first century BC – early first century AD) knew that cinnabar (mercuric sulphide) reacts to light, as he warns in his *De Architectura* not to use it on outdoor decorations. And his works were very highly regarded by Renaissance architects, including Leonardo.

It was known even earlier that the purple dye with which Roman Imperial robes were coloured only turned this colour when exposed to light. It was extracted from snails, and was yellow when first taken. But apart from the process of dyeing, nothing was done with this knowledge until the seventeenth century, when it was one of the first substances used in attempts to capture images.

Leonardo would, therefore, have been well acquainted with some chemicals that react to light. But we thought it was unlikely that he used silver salts for the Shroud, because they create a grey or black image, not a brownish one. Iron salts were a possibility, but the problem remained: how did Leonardo fix the image?

We needed to find a method that would have been within his reach, and it seemed that the obvious next step was to try it for ourselves, for only then would we learn the hard way just what his difficulties were. So throughout 1993 I (Clive) and my brother Keith devoted as much of our free time as we could to this task.

The first thing we did was to construct our own camera obscura. It was easily done using a wooden box, about 50cm square, laid on its side and with a small hole drilled in its base. With the lid removed and replaced with a paper or cloth screen – as recommended by Leonardo – and a sheet thrown over the screen end so that it could be viewed in darkness, we took it in turns to look at each other as lit by a spotlight. Even though we were used to the sophisticated images of television and cinema, there was still something oddly magical about this effect.

When the spotlight was turned full onto our faces, a pale image appeared on the screen. There was undeniably something of the ethereal, ghostly character of the Shroud image. With a very transparent screen there was an almost holographic effect, with a pale and apparently disembodied living head appearing as if it were actually inside the box. Although it was a simple experiment, just to get a feel for the camera obscura, there was indeed something impressive about the ability to create such an image so easily.

It was hard not to imagine Leonardo having done something similar, and with his passion for light and the representation of life, being thunderstruck at the results. But that was the easy bit. The hard part was finding a way to imprint the image onto the screen.

We knew the general characteristics of the image we were trying to create. It had to be in negative. It had to come out brown or sepia and look like a scorch mark. It had to be unacceptably faint and unremarkable to the naked eye – in other words not very impressive as compared with even early nineteenth-century experiments in photography.

The problem broke itself down into component pieces. First we needed a light source that would illuminate the object. Secondly, we needed a means of focusing the image onto the cloth. And then we needed a way of fixing the image so that it recreated the characteristics mentioned above.

The light source was easy. Although Leonardo had various techniques for creating bright lights, including one capable of 'lighting up a room as though full of flames',[24] he would obviously have made use of the most powerful and reliable source known to him – the sun. Undoubtedly he would have supplemented it, as we did, with arrangements of mirrors to reflect yet more light onto the subject. This proved to be much more of a problem for us than it would have been for Leonardo. He had the golden light and long summer days of Renaissance Italy, whereas we had the unpredictable English summer sun to contend with. (Somehow even the best light Reading could offer paled into insignificance beside that of a typical Milanese day.) It was clear that however it had been done, the exposure time had to be lengthy. Niépce's first photograph – of the courtyard of his Provençal farmhouse – took eight hours to register, which produced the interesting effect of the the sun apparently lighting up both sides of the courtyard at the same time. Although we were uncertain at that early stage exactly what chemical we would use, we did know that exposures of several hours would be needed, and as our work proceeded on a trial-and-error basis, we needed as much light as possible.

Unfortunately, the summer of 1993 was not the best on record. The many other demands of research on our time (not to mention the need to earn a living), meant that we had little time to devote to these experiments. In the end, as autumn approached and the days shortened, we reluctantly decided that we would have to use artificial means of lighting the object: we invested in some industrial ultraviolet lamps (Osram Ultra-Vitalux, which are used in industry for testing materials under tropical conditions). In the main, it is the UV part of the spectrum that the substances we were using reacted to.

As the experiments intensified, the car was banished from my garage at my house in Reading – coincidentally not far from where Fox Talbot (1800–1877) made his photographic discoveries – as we turned it into a makeshift studio.

Early on we had to decide what to use as the model, and how far to try to take the replication. Because of the trial-and-error nature of our work, we realized that it would be implausible to try for a full-length image, as on the Shroud, for several practical reasons. One was simply lack of space. Using a camera obscura to project a life-sized image follows a simple rule: the exact distance between the object and the screen depends on the size of the aperture, but the rule is that the object must be the same distance from the hole as the screen is from the hole on the other side. Apart from the difficulty in finding a life-sized model, to get the full image on the right scale you would need a room-sized camera obscura and at least twenty feet of floor space. Without full-time access to a large studio or workshop it just was not possible to get the desired effect. Once again, Leonardo had the advantage over us.

So we decided to concentrate on producing an image of just a head. Since we knew that this would have been created separately in any case, it was quite legitimate to do so, and producing a life-sized head would require much less floor space. Once we had the method right we could then extend it to a full body image.

The fact that the image is a composite – Leonardo's head added to two separate images of the body of a crucified man, on the front from the neck down only – would have presented no difficulty at all, either as a concept or in its execution. Leonardo would simply have needed to mask off the relevant parts of the Shroud, or even more simply, avoid applying any of the light sensitive chemicals to the head area until after the body image had been captured. (We may never know the identity of the body model, or the circumstances in which he was crucified.)

For the majority of our experiments we used as a subject a plaster gargoyle head, dubbed 'Bok' after a similar character in a *Dr Who* story, which is about 20 cm high from his chin to the tip of his horns. This was for our convenience, since the exact exposure time was unknown, and neither of us fancied sitting motionless for hours at a time. This, of course, did raise questions about what precisely Leonardo had used. If he used himself as the model for the head then, even given his well-recorded capacity for standing motionless staring into space, it seemed unlikely that he would have been able to sit still for hours – perhaps days. Of course, with meticulous positioning and the use of a frame that would place his head in exactly the same position, it would be possible to carry out several sittings, but if the exposure time were more than say, four or five hours, it would be more practical for him to have used a sculpted or plaster-cast life-mask of himself. (Leonardo was adept at taking death-masks and would have had no problem with this.) Although it would be more pleasing to think the Shroud image was one of the Maestro's own person, it is more likely that we are looking at a photograph of a model or mask of his face.

The problems involved in keeping still for so long would hardly have affected the model for the body, as the man was very likely dead, but problems of a different nature arise. Unless very skilfully embalmed, the body would have begun to decompose rapidly, especially if it were constantly exposed to the full heat of the sun, and the resulting image would show signs of this. However, it is possible that the exposure time was just short enough to avoid this eventuality. Even so, a sculpted or, more likely, a cast model could easily have been used for the body image as well – taking casts from bodies was, after all, one of the skills Leonardo had learned from his apprenticeship under Verocchio. However, we believe that he had access to chemicals that would react in a day or, at the most, two.

The model, whether human or artificial, would have needed to be as reflective as possible. In our case we managed this by painting Bok with white gloss paint, and Leonardo would have had something similar on his model. If he used his own face and another body he would have painted both of them with white make-up: he was an old hand at everything connected with theatricals as he had been the producer of several spectaculars for the court of Ludovico Sforza, the Duke of Milan and Leonardo's patron between 1482 and 1499.

We had to decide on a method of focusing. The first cameras obscura used only an aperture. The problem here is that there is a trade-off between the brightness and clarity of the image: the larger the hole the more light gets through, so the image is brighter, but less distinct. Although the first recorded use of a lens in a camera obscura was not until 1568, there is no reason why Leonardo could not have anticipated it – indeed, given his fascination with lenses it would be surprising if he had not tried it. There was nothing special about the 1568 lens – it was simply taken from a pair of spectacles. However, there remained the question of its quality, which was impossible to guess at this stage. Early lenses, we knew, had been dogged by problems of chromatic aberration – the fragmenting of light at the edges in much the same way as in a prism. There were also problems with the 'depth of field', familiar to photographers today, where only parts of the image are in sharp focus. Pin-hole cameras do not have this problem, as everything in the field of view is equally sharp, no matter how near or how distant. However, Leonardo ground his own lenses, and given his expertise in so many areas he could easily have had good quality lenses. At that stage, though, we could not be sure of this.

Another possibility was the use of a concave mirror, or perhaps a series of mirrors. Before lenses were generally good enough, focusing was often done by such mirrors. Giovanni Battista della Porta used a concave mirror placed opposite the aperture of his camera obscura to project the image onto a paper screen above the hole, which allowed him to use a bigger aperture and create a brighter image without its losing clarity. Leonardo is known to have employed a great number of parabolic mirrors in a mysterious series of experiments in Rome in the early 1500s, the object of which has been the subject of keen speculation ever since.[25] Whatever he was doing was instrumental in getting him accused of sorcery and making his stay in Rome more than a little uncomfortable. For us, though, such mirrors were almost impossible to find, since they have very little relevance now that high quality lenses can be easily manufactured.

The problems of lighting and focusing were small compared to discovering which light-sensitive substance Leonardo had used. It would not have been too hard for him to have overcome the first two problems – ironically, it was probably easier for him than for us. But somewhere there had to be a relatively simple substance that could fit the bill. The pioneer photographers tried out a great many. But as they have all been superseded and have only curiosity value now, it was difficult to find any information on them. We hunted through old textbooks and books on early photography looking for clues about the materials that were discarded as more complex and faster-reacting industrial chemicals became available.

The earliest experiments, as we have seen, used either naturally-occurring substances or chemicals that could be manufactured using the tools of the alchemical trade – which were quite comprehensive, and, with the exception of electrical power, up to the standard of a modern school's chemistry department. They had the apparatus for heating, distilling, combining chemicals, extracting them from metal ore, and so on.

Niépce's first photograph, for example, had been taken using simple bitumen or asphalt. Specifically, he used Bitumen of Judea, which comes from the Dead Sea. All bitumen is light-sensitive to some extent, but the chemical make-up differs according to the area where it is found – Bitumen of Judea has a particularly good reaction to light. Niépce coated a metal plate in it and exposed it in the camera. Wherever light fell, the bitumen hardened. The unhardened parts (ie those which had remained in the dark) were then washed away using lavender oil or alcohol. A negative image remains, which can be used to produce positive prints on paper.

Here was a naturally occurring substance that could have been used by Leonardo. However, it could not have been responsible for the Shroud image, as the bitumen would have flaked off with the folding and rolling of the cloth over the years.

We had always been struck by a possibility that has been overlooked by Shroud researchers, one that would account for the scorch-like appearance of the image. The easiest way of producing a picture that looks similar is to do it in invisible ink: lemon juice is the classic example, or the readily available source used by spies during World Wars I and II – urine. Invisible when applied, messages written in it appear when the paper is heated. This is because the 'ink' burns at a lower temperature than the paper, and as it does so it reduces the carbon in the paper beneath. The result is exactly that seen in the Shroud: the image is visible, not because of anything added to the cloth, but because the cloth has been oxidized and dehydrated – degraded in a way suggestive of accelerated ageing. (Heating, ageing and attack by acid all result in the same changes to the structure of the fabric.) Early on we made some simple paintings in lemon juice just to see what would happen, and found that one of the Shroud's most puzzling characteristics could easily be reproduced – providing the material was not over-heated. As we have seen, the image does not penetrate the cloth, and we could produce this effect by scorching only the top fibres of one side of the cloth.

Of course, the Shroud image was far too big and detailed to have been painted in invisible ink, but it could have been block printed using the same substance. However, even prints would hardly produce the Shroud's photographic accuracy. But then Keith realized that Niépce's method had raised another intriguing possibility – that the image was photographed onto another cloth that had been coated in bitumen. The unexposed areas – the shadows on the subject – could then be washed out, leaving a hardened and slightly raised image, which could then be used as the printing 'block'.

Ingeniously simple though it was, unfortunately we were unable to try it out, as it is no longer possible to find Bitumen of Judea in the UK, the only variety we knew to be suitable. We did try out the general method using a modern photo-stencil chemical which is used in silk-screen printing, and found that it was possible to get good images. The basic method was feasible, but we needed to know just how quickly it reacted in the set-up we had constructed. Niépce's eight-hour exposure used lenses to focus a small, bright image, whereas we were trying to create a life-sized image, preferably without a lens. The photo-stencil emulsion obviously reacts much faster than bitumen, but we had no way of telling how much faster, so the experiment was invalid.

At this stage we were looking for workable techniques rather than specific chemicals, as it seemed more likely that Leonardo's process had not been the equivalent of simple snapshot photographs, with the cloth impregnated with a light sensitive chemical, whether or not it needed subsequent developing and fixing. If the image was merely created by daubing on chemicals, they would long since have been detected. Time and time again we came back to silver salts, since they had been known about in Leonardo's day, but they would be easily detectable, and in any case, the image would have disappeared long ago, just as Wedgwood's did.

It was then that, ploughing through an early twentieth-century dictionary of photography, we came across a process – or rather a series of processes – that had been used in the early days of photography, but had long since been superseded by more convenient methods. These processes did not depend on the film changing colour at all, but instead used a property of certain chemicals which, when mixed with an organic substance (derived from plants or animals), would react to light in such a way as to make the organic parts insoluble in water.[26] (Oddly enough, the exact chemical reactions involved in this process are still not fully understood.) The sensitizing chemicals most often employed are chromium salts, chiefly potassium bichromate or ammonia bichromate. Many common substances were used as the organic component: gelatin (made from boiling the skin and bones of animals), gum arabic (extracted from the acacia plant[27]) and albumen (egg-white), collectively known as colloids.

What caught our interest at first was the fact that each of the organic substances named were in common use by artists from medieval times onwards. Egg-white was a staple ingredient of paints, and gelatin[28] and gum arabic had widespread uses; so we tracked down exactly how they were used by the early photographers.

The main shortcoming of these substances was that, although they produced the required reaction, the image was not very distinct. A simple way of overcoming this was to mix in some powdered pigment: the mixture reacts by becoming insoluble where light hits it. In a similar way to Niépce's bitumen process, the unexposed parts, where the shadows fall, can then be washed away, this time using water rather than oil. The photographer is left with an image of the exposed parts – but now, because of the added pigment, it is clearly visible. An alternative was to add ink after washing, which would stick to the exposed areas. This method was much favoured at one time because it produced highly detailed and graded images, but because it is the light areas that have trapped the pigment, it can only produce a negative image. For this reason, the process came to be chiefly used to produce prints from photographic negatives taken by other methods.

This process was an especially simple one. Provided the right sensitizer could be found, it was within the reach of Leonardo's technology. However, there was one drawback: it uses pigments to make the image visible, and we were already convinced that there was no pigment in the Shroud image. Could Walter McCrone be right after all – had he really discovered pigment on the cloth? One of the pigments favoured by nineteenth-century advocates of the method was Venetian red – the one McCrone claimed he had found. But all the arguments that we have already given against pigment being responsible for the image were still valid. Also, although pictures produced in this way do not need to be fixed in the same way as do other photographs, there is still some unwanted chemical reaction when they are displayed, so they have to be treated to stop the image changing. There would have been a definite 'sheen' and the image would have cracked over time.

At this point I thought again about the 'invisible ink' idea that seemed to be telling us something significant about the final form of the Shroud image. And then I realized that the two concepts could easily be put together because the organic parts of the colloid mixture would act as an invisible ink if the cloth were heated. No pigment was necessary. Heating the cloth, so that the colloid mixture scorched it, was a simple but effective way of 'fixing' the image. Moreover, after scorching, the mixture could be washed out using some form of cleaning agent which would remove every trace of the original mixture while leaving the scorch marks. (Or perhaps not every last trace: albumen was detected on the Shroud image by STURP. However, not much can be said about this, since it is a common substance and fits neatly into other theories – it is a common ingredient in paint, and is present in the bodily fluids of a badly injured man.) The basic reaction between sensitizer and organic material would also take place with the cellulose in the linen itself.

Keith and I set out to try out this idea. After all, although it worked in theory, it may show an entirely un-Shroud-like image in practice. We obtained some ammonium bichromate solution for use as the sensitizer. Out of solution this is an orange-red crystal. Egg-white was the easiest source of the organic part of the mixture (although gum arabic was also tried with similar results). There was still an irritating amount of trial-and-error, since we were using the technique in a way that had not been tried before, and there were many questions still to be answered. We needed to find the correct strength of mixture, how long it would take to react in the camera (with and without lens) and so on.

We must say straightaway that there is no evidence that this particular solution was used in Leonardo's day, still less by the Maestro himself. It is, however, not impossible that it was. We were more concerned to find a method that worked, chiefly because there are so many possible substances that might fit the bill, that finding and testing them all would take far more time than we had available.

There are numerous natural substances that are light-sensitive but which have no value in modern photography. The classic study was carried out at the turn of the nineteenth century by Jean Senebier, who catalogued a huge number of such materials: various extracts of woods, many resins, alcoholic tinctures made from the petals of plants, solutions of cochineal, henna root, the juice of aloe leaves, and many others. In the inorganic world, iron salts, copper salts and mercury salts are all light-sensitive – and all were known to the alchemists. Chlorphyll from plants and mustard oil can be used as sensitizers, as can various acids and some dyes derived from sodium salts.

Several chromium salts, but chiefly ammonia and potassium bichromate, were used in the kind of processes we were interested in, and are the best for the kind of method we were exploring. These were not officially discovered until the close of the eighteenth century, but there is no reason why Leonardo would not have been able to produce them.

The salts we worked with are derived from ferrochromite ores, in which chromium (which is never found in its pure form in nature) is combined with iron and other impurities. Chromium is the twentieth most abundant element on Earth. As far as science acknowledges, the production of chromium from the ore did not happen until 1798, when it was discovered by the French chemist Vauqueline in red lead ore from Siberia. The material did not achieve commercial viability until the discovery of vast reserves of the ore in Siberia and South Africa. However, it is by no means rare in Europe, being found in reasonable quantities in Scandanavia, the Balkans, France and, in smaller deposits, in Italy.

The production of chromium salts from the raw ore is very easy, needing no more sophisticated equipment than a kiln. Sodium bichromate is produced by roasting the ore with soda ash and lime, the potassium salt by using potash in place of soda ash. Simple chemical reactions of the residue with common acids result in the production of ammonium bichromate, the chemical we were using.[29] Apart from the ore itself, all of the other materials and all of the necessary equipment were in common use (but not especially advanced) in Leonardo's day. It is not impossible that alchemists had discovered and experimented with chromium salts, although they would never have been in plentiful supply. The fact that there is no record of it having been discovered before 1798 is not too much of a problem – remember that history dates the discovery of the light-sensitivity of silver salts from 1727, whereas we have shown that alchemists knew of this at least 300 years earlier.

It is likely that there are other substances that would do the job just as well, although this has not been explored by post-nineteenth century science. For example, within a couple of years of their discovery, the bichromate salts were being used in the tanning industry, since it makes use of exactly the same property as the one we were interested in. The salt solution reacts with the organic material of the hide to make it waterproof, which is essentially what we were hoping to do. It is reasonable to assume that whatever materials were supplanted in the industry by the advent of bichromate salts – chiefly chemicals extracted from the barks of various trees – acted in the same way.

Leonardo's skill as a chemist should not be underestimated. Apart from his alchemical pursuits, chemistry was part of the day-to-day business of all Renaissance artists. They needed to know their chemistry in order to prepare paints, varnishes and so on, and they searched for new chemicals with which to produce more effective materials. Leonardo, particularly, excelled in this field. He even invented a kind of plastic (which he called 'vetre parrichulato' – plastic glass), a synthetic resin that he hoped to market for manufacturing chess pieces and ornaments. He kept the recipe secret, even in his notebooks. (This may not have been unconnected with his photographic work. The mixtures we worked with, when left in a bowl or jar and exposed to daylight for several days, invariably hardened into a plastic-like lump, which could easily have been shaped in moulds.[30])

Having assembled all our equipment and chemicals, we followed this method. We made the mixture with egg-white and sensitizer. For some reason fresh eggs work best, and the reaction is also speeded up if the egg-white is beaten before the bichromate is added. We tried various strengths, but we got the best results with around 10ml of solution per egg (if you add too much sensitizer the reaction is inhibited). We then left the mixture in warm conditions for two hours for the sensitizer and egg to bind together properly. (Some attempts failed because it was left in the cold.) After this, the mixture, which is a vivid yellow colour, can be painted onto the screen and left to dry. We used cotton rather than linen because it was cheaper, but the reaction would be no different with linen. When dry, the screen was stretched over a wooden frame which we then put inside the camera obscura.

For the camera we used our original wooden box, with the addition of a hood of light-proof photographer's cloth over the screen end. Our one concession to modern methods was to add an aperture mechanism taken from an antique camera, which allowed us to vary the size of the aperture easily. Both outdoors in the sun and indoors using the ultraviolet lamps we used arrangements of mirrors to reflect as much light on to the subject as possible.

Our first experiments were carried out using sunlight and no lens in the camera. Although a coated cloth left in the sun reacted within minutes, it did not register in the camera after being left there for a day, even with a series of mirrors reflecting more light onto Bok, such was the decrease in light. We tried different combinations, but days passed with nothing to show for it.

We convinced ourselves that we were on the right track by using a different technique. To show that it was possible to create an image by light using this mixture, Keith painted, in black paint, a copy of the Shroud face on a sheet of glass. By channelling the sun's rays through this, rather like a slide projector, onto a square of treated cloth, we did get a satisfying negative image. When the areas that had not hardened – ie where the black paint had masked the sun's rays – were washed out in cold water and the cloth heated, as expected, the egg-white then browned, scorching the fabric (and filling the house with a sulphurous smell!). Hot water, with a little detergent, removed the rest of the mixture, leaving a negative, scorched image of the original painting. It was scorched on one side only, just like the Shroud.

Although this experiment did not confirm our whole theory, we felt we had achieved a small triumph, by at least finding a quick and easy way of making Shroud replicas. For example, if John Weston had used such a technique for *The Silent Witness* replica, painting a black negative version of the Shroud image on a large sheet of glass (or even using a full-sized transparency of the real thing) and laying it over a cloth coated in the way described, he could have completed his replica in a fraction of the time.

On one occasion, after a full day's exposure, traces of an image began to appear, but the mixture had not reacted enough to survive the washing. We realised that we would need at least some advice from an expert photographer. Lynn got in touch with Amanda Nevill at the Royal Photographic Society in Bath, and on 13 October 1993 – the fifth anniversary of the release of the carbon dating results, and of course, Templar Day – we travelled down there to meet Amanda and Michael Austin, a professor of holography and a past president

of the RPS. In a sense, we were returning to where our story had
started.

When we outlined the basis of our method we were relieved to find
that Michael was not as sceptical as we had feared. Surprisingly, it
was not the chemical side he objected to – he readily accepted that
it was possible that some such sensitizing chemical might have been
available in Leonardo's day. He even offered the suggestion that, since
the chromate salt we were using is primarily used in the tanning industry,
the method could have arisen from there, since both parts of the mixture
– the sensitizer and the animal by-products such as gelatin – would have
been available together. His objection was about the optics involved.
Using an unlensed camera obscura, he acknowledged, the amount of
light hitting the screen would be so reduced that exposure times of
weeks would be needed, especially for the full body image, since much
of the light reflecting from the body would fall off over the gap between
the body and the camera. He would not say categorically that such a
thing was impossible, mainly because nobody had ever worked on such
a scale. (From the earliest days photographers worked in miniature,
life-sized photographs being hopelessly impractical.)

Michael also made some interesting observations about the Shroud
image. He was particularly intrigued by the fact that the hair and beard
are more or less the same colour and tone of the rest of the face and body,
which, he pointed out, violates the negative effect. Shroud researchers
had noted this before, but we had not given it much thought. If the
man on the Shroud were anything other than white-haired the hair
ought to be darker on the negative photographs. But if anything it is
lighter, especially the moustache and beard. Yet after all, the hair of
the man used for the full back image may have been white, and as for
the front, Leonardo was known to have gone white quite suddenly and
fairly early, although whether this was around the age of forty when he
faked the Shroud is not recorded. In any case Leonardo, realizing that
dark hair would be less reflective and may not show up at all, would
have powdered the hair. Of course, if he were using sculpted or cast
models the problem would not have arisen in the first place.

Michael also pointed out that although the face itself is realistic, the
hair of the front image looks very much as though it were painted on.
We looked – and realized that he was on to something. We have already
discussed the bizarre foreshortening of the forehead and the unreality of
the hairline: the hair here appears to be hanging straight down, which
is inconsistent with a figure laid on its back.

We came away from Bath with a lot to think about. We realized
that we were going to have to use lenses in our camera obscura, and
we also puzzled over just what the enigma of the hair was telling us.

Obviously the hair had not come out on the photographic image. We did not realize why this should be so, and just what its significance was, until later. At the time we surmised that, because the hair was darker – either on the human model or because it had been painted darker – it had not shown up. If you take a picture of a dark-haired person against a black background – as in the Shroud image – the hair is difficult to make out. On the faint Shroud image it would have been completely invisible, and the same would apply to the beard and moustache. They would have had to be added later.

The chemical mixture, as well as being applied as a coat of 'emulsion' to the linen, could just as well be applied by brush for retouching, and then treated in the same way as the rest of the image: exposed to the sun and then heated to scorch the underlying cloth before being completely washed out. This would explain why the hair looks unnatural and painted, and why the beard is much lighter in the negative pictures than it should be: as the painted-on parts would have been exposed directly to the sun rather than being projected through the camera, it would have been easy to overexpose these areas. We were, however, to discover that this reasoning was only partly correct.

In our next series of experiments with the camera obscura after returning from Bath, we used lenses. An assortment were taken from a slide projector and bits of old cameras and tried out. Modern mechanisms in cameras and projectors have a complex series of lenses to shrink or magnify the image and to correct chromatic aberration, but we still wanted to keep the system as simple as possible.

All this was eating into our time: it meant yet more trial and error to find the right lens or lenses through which to project the image. But at least we knew that using a lens removed the restriction of the lenseless camera: that the model always had to be the same distance from the aperture as the screen on the opposite side. We tried all sorts of combinations: different lenses caused different problems with the depth of field – sometimes the tip of Bok's nose would be sharp and detailed and his face a blur, but correcting the face would make the nose a blur. Again, we were handicapped by the limited resources we had to work with.

Eventually we found a lens that projected a good, life-sized image of Bok onto the screen. Although it was much brighter than the non-lens image, it still was not absolutely sharp – but neither is the Shroud image. Also, in order to get the correct-sized image Bok had to be less than 30cm away from the lens, and there was a 'fish-eye' effect that we were less than happy about, but it was the best that could be managed. With our new set-up we had another try at capturing the image. This time after an eight-hour exposure we were able to see that an image had been caught. It was slightly distorted but at long, long last, it was also quite distinct!

After carefully washing out the unexposed areas, we were left with a picture of Bok in the chemical mixture. Now we had to see how it would appear when scorched. We held the cloth in front of a fire, making sure that it was evenly heated. The chemicals charred before the cloth began to show any signs at all of exposure to heat. After heating it for as long as we dared, we washed the cloth in boiling water. All traces of the salt/egg-white substance were removed, and we were left with an image of Bok – life-sized (in fact, rather smaller, as we had miscalculated on the first attempt), in negative, and scorched lightly onto the top fibres of the cloth only! We photographed it and found that not only is the contrast enhanced by the emulsion in the positive print (as happens with the Shroud) but also the negative showed a much more detailed, recognizable image of the gargoyle. Over the next few weeks we produced several more versions, correcting various errors – although, to our annoyance, it was not possible to eliminate completely the fish-eye distortion.

We found that the scorching of the cloth was not completely satisfactory using just egg-white or gum arabic in the mixture, as it required a high temperature to burn, which sometimes affected the untreated cloth. However, we realized that a simple improvement – on much the same lines as the early photographers who added pigment to the mixture – was to mix in some other substance that scorched more readily at a lower temperature. Lemon juice produced some pleasing results, although there was a tendency for it to curdle with the rest of the mixture. Indelicate though it may seem, we got the most Shroud-like results with urine. (Which, both human and animal, was a staple ingredient for many Renaissance painters, including Leonardo.)

It was all very exciting, but it was only a starting point. Although Bok had done us sterling service, we still had to produce a larger image of a human head to make our point. Bok himself was only roughly half the size of the average head, and being a caricature of a human face exaggerated the distortion at the centre of the lens.

Neither of us fancied remaining motionless for hours under those ultraviolet lamps – at close range they were stronger than a sun-ray lamp and guaranteed to bestow a deep tan in half an hour – so we acquired a life-sized bust of a girl. As it was silver-grey, we painted the face white, but left the hair untouched, as this would give it a natural-looking contrast. We set up the experiment and left it for around ten hours to ensure that we got a good exposure. This length of time actually produces a bolder image than the Shroud, and the lamps produce less ultraviolet than comes from the sun, so a shorter exposure time is possible. However, since some of our attempts with

Bok had failed because we had not left it long enough – wasting most of a valuable day – we wanted to be sure of getting a result. In any case, we were not too worried about the exposure time, as we simply do not know exactly what chemical Leonardo used. The two lamps we used, allowing for the distance between subject and treated cloth and the reflectivity of the former, produced at most 20 per cent of the power of sunlight at the height of a British summer.[31]

As this was the first time we had used a human figure, we immediately noticed two features of the image that had not shown up with Bok (a smaller and more distorted figure to start with). The fish-eye effect was still there, which slightly widens the centre of the face, but not to the point that it looks in any way unnatural or unrecognizable. What was more striking was the effect using a human head had on the outlines of the face. First, the forehead was much foreshortened, making the distance from the eyes to the top of the head absurdly small. Secondly, the distortion had the effect of making the sides of the face much too straight, squaring it and making the edges fade into the background. The ears, although prominent on the model, did not show up at all on the image projected onto the screen. The man on the Shroud does not, apparently, have ears; his face is squared off, with blank strips on both sides, and his forehead is foreshortened. No theory, whether based on real contact with a body or on artistic forgery, has ever been able to account for these bizarre characteristics. We think ours has: QED.

These features were noticeable when viewing the image from the back of the cloth when we started the experiment. Was there anything else that would be revealed when the final image appeared? There was. At first it caused us some irritation, until its full significance finally dawned. When the image was 'developed' by the washing and heating, it left us – as with Bok – with a perfectly graded, if faint, scorched image, visible on one side of the cloth only. However, prolonged exposure through the lens had resulted in a circular patch in the centre of the image, a sort of photograph of the lens itself. Around the circle, which had formed where slightly more light had fallen, there was a faint area of unexposed cloth, a kind of 'corona'.

At first we were put out about this, and were actually concerned that it might not be possible to eradicate it even by using different lenses. However, there was a chance that Leonardo had had the same problem, so we looked at one of our many pictures of the face of the man on the Shroud (Lynn's living room is decorated from floor to ceiling with these pictures). To our absolute astonishment – and utter delight – there, over the bridge of the nose, the exact geometric centre of the face, was precisely this same feature. It had, strangely, gone completely unremarked by any Shroud researcher. But there it was: a distinct circle of light, surrounded on two sides by a dark corona where the lens had stopped the light from falling.

Mindful of many things – coins over the eyes and so on – which have allegedly been seen on the Shroud over the years, we checked other pictures of it, taken at different times, from Secondo Pia's to STURP's, in both negative and positive. In all of them this circle is undeniably there, distinct even on positive photographs. We checked with other people, and they could see it too. It was unmistakeable. It was precisely in the place where a lens would have been focused: the exact centre of the face.

Taken together with the foreshortening – the reduction of the forehead and the straightening of the sides of the face, making the ears disappear – we saw that at long last we had proof positive that the face of the man on the Shroud had been created using a lens. Nothing else explains these features. It also supplies a reason for the 'retouching' of the hair, which was done, we realised, only partly because of its dark colour. In our version, the hair on the top of the head has all but vanished with the foreshortening and, although our model has her hair pulled back, and not hanging down the sides of her face, the fact that her ears had disappeared shows that the same thing had happened with the Shroud image. Leonardo would therefore have had to add hair artificially, using the same substance as in the camera, but being forced to follow an unnatural hairline. The 'retouching' of the hair and beard, using the same chemical mixture, which was then exposed to the lamps, scorched, then washed out, proved to be relatively easy and blends in well with the photographic image (see illustration). The best effect, we found, was obtained by applying the mixture with our fingers – a brush tended to overload the cloth with mixture which then soaked through. Then we turned our attention to adding the 'bloodflows': because of their anatomical accuracy on the Shroud it has always been thought they would be difficult to fake. In fact, they were surprisingly easy. The trick is to make them *backwards*. Place a drop of 'blood' on the cloth (we used theatrical blood), then use a cocktail stick to trace out a thin line to the point where the 'wound' welled up.

Although there are still many questions to be answered – the two greatest being the exact substances Leonardo used and the problems he encountered in creating a composite image – to us these discoveries are enough to prove our thesis. Obviously we do not have the resources to double check our work against STURP data. We cannot discover what spectrographic analysis[32] of our image would reveal, for example. STURP noted spectrographic differences between the image and the scorching caused by the Chambéry fire: these could easily be explained as by the substance being burned to create the original image, as in our experiments. Do traces of the original chemicals used by Leonardo remain on the cloth and were they detected without their significance being realized? For example, we remember that STURP detected a level of iron on the cloth in both image and non-image areas, which might be significant as some iron salts can be used in the same way as the chrome salts that we used. There is no way in which we can address these points.

We must stress that our experiments have been extremely limited, both where time and materials are concerned – in fact, professional photographers would no doubt laugh at our amateurishness. But we have proved that Giovanni's information was correct, and that many of the most cherished beliefs of the pro-authenticity lobby are not. Our mystery man's clues have proved more than useful in this work, which implies that he was, at least in this, telling the truth. Perhaps it really is the case that not only did Leonardo create the Shroud, but also that he did so using this technique. All we can do now is refine the method, hopefully with input from others who may be interested (this would make an excellent project for students). But so far this is enough to prove our point. Before 1993 nobody had succeeded in creating an image bearing so many of the characteristics of the Shroud image, including its puzzling anomalies. But now we have.

CONSPIRACIES AND CONCLUSIONS

Many are those who trade in tricks and simulated miracles, duping the foolish multitude; and if nobody unmasked their subterfuges, they would impose them on everyone.'

Leonardo da Vinci[1]

THE IMAGE ON the Turin Shroud is not that of Jesus. He was not, as it appears on the cloth, beheaded. The circumstantial evidence for the theory that the image is a self-portrait by Leonardo is enormous and compelling.

Certain aspects of the Shroud's story are highly provocative. It has always been believed that the Shroud exhibited astonishing and unique '3-D information' – indeed, when we came to write the first draft of this book we also accepted it. But our own later research, outlined in the last chapter revealed that although it was the basis for Jackson and Jumper's famous V-P 8 image of the Shroudman, and the statue made from it, this alleged 3-D information is virtually non-existent.

At first we had to conclude that our co-researcher, Andy Haveland-Robinson, simply had better equipment than that of Jackson and Jumper all those years ago. But he pointed out that they used a NASA computer for this work, and surely that was, even in 1976, the equivalent of what he owned now.

Also, neither the unusual height of the image nor the discrepancy in length between the back and front images were reflected in Jackson and Jumper's 3-D recreation. It is undoubtedly significant that Jackson and Jumper are leading lights in the Holy Shroud Guild of New York. (Such is the esteem in which John Jackson is still held in the Shroudie world that his wife's theory – that the Shroud was the tablecloth at the Last Supper – was given a lot of space by the BSTS in recent publications. But even they had to admit that this claim was unlikely to be true: first-century Jews did not use tablecloths.)[2]

Joe Nickell makes the point in *Inquest on the Shroud of Turin* that it is very unusual to find modern scientists who are deeply religious, yet of the forty scientists who made up the STURP team no fewer than thirty-nine fitted that description![3] We have seen how they treated the one dissenting voice – that of Walter McCrone. How much of what we have taken to be objective research was in fact contaminated by the tunnel vision of personal belief? While there was almost certainly no conspiracy among STURP scientists to misrepresent the facts as such, it is impossible to know whether the anomalies that suggested that the image could not be that of Jesus were minimized. At this stage we will never know, but the facts are certainly suggestive.

As our work has already been publicly misrepresented (see Appendix), it is worth restating the main points of our argument before we go on to examine the implications of the story we have uncovered. First, let us consider the reasons against the Turin Shroud being genuine:

1. A miraculously imprinted burial cloth is not mentioned in the New Testament.
2. The early Christians never mentioned such a thing.
3. A 'Holy Shroud' appeared in 1350 without any provenance, exactly at a time when alleged holy relics were providing rich pickings for their manufacturers and exhibiters.
4. The image has many anomalies, including the hands folded over the genitals. This could well be because the cloth was destined to be publicly displayed in an age when modesty forbade full frontal exhibitions. The New Testament tells us that the disciples had no time to lay out the body because of the imminence of the Sabbath, yet it is impossible to arrange the hands of a corpse like this without tying them, and these hands were not tied, otherwise the marks would have shown up in photographic negative like the scourge marks etc.
5. Not one of the theories put forward to account for the creation of the image actually works. All of them are open to serious logical objections.
6. The face is too small for the body.
7. The image is 203 cm at the front and 208 cm at the back: two separate heights, both of which are far too tall. Although there are several objections to these measurements – for example, the consideration that one knee was raised and that the cloth

itself would have distorted over the years – nothing explains the extraordinary height of Shroudman. As usual, one must take into account the fact that much of the evaluation of the Shroud so far has been undertaken by those with a pro-authenticity axe to grind. As we know, however, the cloth was flat when the image was formed, which would make the man impossibly big whether his knees were raised or not. There is no possible explanation for this unless one considers that it is, as we claim, a composite projected image, the front being made up of the image of two people, while the back is a single image.

8. The head image is completely separate from that of the body at the front, as we have demonstrated conclusively using the most sophisticated computer enhancement techniques. As far as we know, Jesus was not beheaded either before or after death, so whoever the image on the Shroud belongs to, it is not him.

9. The 1988 carbon dating tests indicated that the cloth dated from between 1260 and 1390. While there were inconsistencies involved in the collating of the results, it is unlikely that the kind of conspiracy invoked by the believers was involved. Even if the carbon dating results were totally fabricated, the lack of positive evidence for an historic Shroud is enough in itself to relegate it to the ranks of clever fakes.

10. The much-vaunted Palestinian pollen allegedly found on the cloth by Max Frei, who later authenticated the Hitler diaries, was never checked by any other authority. Pollen was, it was claimed, found on the cloth from all the major places where Ian Wilson believed that the Shroud had been, in the centuries before 1350. STURP, however, said there was very little pollen of any sort on the cloth. Frei, who was accompanied by Ian Wilson on his trip to find control samples of pollen and whose trip was financed by David Rolfe (later a convert to Christianity because of the Shroud), never looked for pollen that may have originated from any other place. For all we know it bore samples of pollen found only in the Bristol area. Besides, Frei's findings do not in themselves constitute proof of the Shroud's authenticity for another reason: a great deal of cloth was brought into medieval Europe from Palestine by the Crusaders, so the cloth used by a faker could still bear the pollen Frei claimed to have found on it.

11. It has been claimed that the Mandylion of pre-1350 Constantinople was in fact the Shroud folded in four (tetradiplon), with only the face on display. If this were so then it does provide an otherwise missing historical link for the relic which is necessary to the believers' story. While it is true that the Byzantines had something that they called a

tetradiplon, the Mandylion cannot have been the Shroud, for several commonsensical reasons. For a start, the Shroud, although thin, is huge, and to fold it up so only the face was showing would mean that the bulk of the cloth would be behind it: a roomy box and not just a frame would have been necessary to contain it. The cloth would have yellowed due to its lengthy exposure to the air, while the rest of it would remain unaffected: this is not so. Finally, if the Byzantines really had possessed the Holy Shroud of Jesus, showing all his sacred wounds, why would they want to hide most of it? Images of Jesus' face abounded, but no one else had the full-length image and evidence of his crucifixion. To answer this last question Ian Wilson suggests that the Byzantines did not know what it was that they possessed, but if they had such a bulky item why did they never investigate the hidden part? If they thought they merely owned a painting of a face, why did they actually refer to it as being doubled in four – a phrase unknown in any other context than this? All the evidence points to their owning something else entirely, something that was considerably larger than a painting of a face, but, equally, something that certainly was not what we know as the Turin Shroud.

12. Wilson has suggested that the Shroud, doubled in four, was the fabled 'head' of the Templars which they were supposed to have worshipped. In fact, all the evidence points to this head having been a solid, three-dimensional artefact: a real, probably embalmed, severed head. It is also highly unlikely that the Templars would have worshipped anything connected with Jesus, their reverence being devoted to John the Baptist, with whom the link with severed heads is clear.

13. The so-called '3-D' qualities of the image have always excited the believers, who claim that they mark it out as miraculous as they say that no artist could ever replicate this effect. In fact, as our research has indicated, there is very little 3-D effect at all in the Shroud image. The V-P 8 image, created by John Jackson and Eric Jumper using the alleged '3-D' qualities of the cloth, is always mentioned as 'proving' the uniqueness of the Shroud. Yet, given the fact that there is little that is actually 3-D about the cloth, the V-P 8 image is distinctly suspect. It would seem that the measurements of the man on the Shroud were adjusted to create the V-P 8 image, especially in order to make the shorter face fit the back of the head, and to make the whole image an acceptable height. Jackson's and Jumper's impartial scientific stance may have been prejudiced by their Catholic faith and membership of the Holy Shroud Guild.

14. The anomalies the cloth displays, such as the serene facial expression, are often cited as examples of the special nature of the man whose image it is believed to be. This is the Son of God, the believers claim, and therefore the laws of Nature may well have been altered, speeded up, slowed down, or suspended altogether. While neither of us disagrees with the idea of the miraculous, it must be remembered that these believers are the same people who seize on any scientific or alleged scientific data that may back up their position. Put simply: they cannot have it both ways.

15. Images of Jesus before the 1350 Shroud surfaced are often used to prove that, because they are similar to the image of the man on the Shroud, they must have been taken from it. While it is true that certain aspects of the image are traditional – the marks between the eyebrows for example – it is *not* true that they were always exclusively found in images of Jesus. The 'frown' (or Vignon) marks were found in many saintly icons. While the believers are welcome to their dismissive attitude about the similarities between Leonardo's face and that of the man on the Shroud, it is also true that the alleged match between many early depictions of Jesus and the Shroud image are at least equally subjective. Many of them look nothing like the man on the Shroud. There is also the point that a clever faker could have deliberately included the traditional details in his own 'Jesus' image.

In fact, it was after the Turin Shroud became known – post 1494 – that the general image of what Jesus looked like became standardized. It seems to us that Leonardo achieved more than he intended as it could be argued that his face became that before which generations of the faithful genuflected and prayed.

Since our work became known among the Shroudies, several objections have been raised. The answers to the most common ones are:

1. Believers say that the image on the Shroud matches no medieval school of art. This is true, as we are not dealing with art, but with a photograph.

2. It is said that no medieval or Renaissance faker was clever enough to have produced the Turin Shroud. An oft-repeated line is 'if it is a fake, it is a very clever fake'. Apart from being arrogantly 'epochist', this attitude overlooks the fact that we are almost certainly dealing here with no average dauber or scientific lightweight. Leonardo was intellectually, if not spiritually, light years ahead of, not only his contemporaries, but also most of his modern enthusiasts and detractors put together. (One British art critic revealed his own

exceptionally limited intellect when he accused Leonardo's genius of being greatly exaggerated because he invented things for which the world was not yet ready!)

3. It is often said that Leonardo could not have faked the Shroud because there is no mention of such a thing in his many notebooks. In answer to this it should be noted than one does not commit to paper evidence of faking the burial cloth of the Son of God in the days when simply being a vegetarian could get you burnt at the stake. Also, it is known that many of his notebooks have disappeared over the centuries, some after being bought by the Savoy family, which may or may not be significant. It is also worth pointing out that there is no evidence from his notebooks that he painted the Mona Lisa!

4. The believers say that the fact that the man was genuinely crucified means it is authentic, and that our suggestion that Leonardo crucified someone (either living or already dead) is macabre, and therefore, for some curious reason, inconceivable. Ian Wilson goes to some trouble to reveal his ingenuousness by stating that no medieval faker would dare to do such a thing because it was expressly forbidden by the Church . . . However, we are dealing here not only with uncompromising 'heresy', but with Leonardo, to whom the end always and absolutely justified the means.

When our research first indicated that Leonardo had been involved in faking the Shroud, we set out to establish whether or not he had the means, motive and opportunity to do it. We believe that, in this book, we have set out a convincing case for all three such requirements.

His work on optics and his alchemical pursuits provided him with the means. Certainly, too, he had the opportunity, being in exactly the right place at the right time. Leonardo's heretical and unorthodox beliefs – not least his membership of the Priory of Sion – gave him the necessary motive. One might add to this that his own strength of character and rebellious streak gave him the sheer audacity needed to effect this, the greatest fraud of all.

We now know that the Shroud is not the winding sheet of Jesus, but an astonishingly ingenious piece of work even by Leonardo's standards. Although we do not know how long it took him to complete, we do know how long we have spent on replicating his technique just as far as the face is concerned. As a composite, it must have taken an incredible amount of time and patience, besides enormous secrecy. The risks were astronomical, the consequences of being found out would have been unthinkable. If the laity had discovered Leonardo in the process of forging the Holy Shroud there would have been outcry enough, but what if the Church, who possibly connived in this or even actually commissioned it, found that he was using such a technique with which to create it? Just one generation after Leonardo, Giovanni Battista della Porta was accused of sorcery simply for experimenting with projected images. Given the immense trouble involved, why did Leonardo do it?

One reason may be simple: Giovanni said that Leonardo had been commissioned by the Pope himself to provide another, better, 'Holy Shroud' with which to pull in the crowds. He also said, however, that Leonardo had not been the first choice for this, and that others such as Michelangelo (1475–1564) had turned down this commission. We do not know whether or not this story is true, but tales of Church corruption around that time were commonplace. Other artists may well have rejected the work of faking the next 'Shroud' in a line of fakes for reasons of superstition. Even in the cynical world of the Renaissance, creating the image of the crucified Jesus would have given one pause for thought. Leonardo had no such qualms. If anything, he had good reasons for committing this act of what would have been to many a grave sacrilege.

It seems likely that the idea of putting the image of his face on the cloth was his own. There would not have been the danger that such a confidence trick would carry with it today, when celebrities are so instantly recognizable: in those days, even in his native land, few people knew what the Maestro Leonardo looked like. Besides, the technique itself ensured anonymity, for the likeness is not apparent to the naked eye. It only leaps into focus when seen in photographic negative.

Leonardo worked with optics, lenses and projected images. Serge Bramly wrote of him: '. . . the deductions in his notebooks are dazzling. Whereas men of his age thought that vision was created by particles (*spezie*) projected by the eye, Leonardo understood that the eye did not transmit anything but received rays of light . . . he also perceived that the eye registered a reversed image . . . and envisaged a sort of contact lens . . . He was the first to note the principle of stereoscopic vision – that is, the perception of three-dimensional relief . . . He seems to have invented some kind of telescope a century before Galileo. He writes: "Make glasses to see the Moon enlarged." He assembled lenses . . .'[4]

He also worked on a secret 'machine made of mirrors' in the 1490s, the purpose of which is unknown, but mirrors concentrate light and heat and both are required to produce an image like the Shroud, by the method we have shown.

He was, in all probability, a practising alchemist with a wide range of chemicals at his disposal, most of which can only be guessed at even today. He was also in the right place at the right time and had the opportunity and the means. Surely he did not fake the Shroud simply for the money. What were his true motives for committing this act of high sacrilege?

In all probability he was Grand Master of the Priory of Sion (or another secret order with the same members, aims and hidden agendas, see Chapter 6) for the last nine years of his life, and presumably he had been a high-ranking member before that. We have shown that what may be seen as Priory obsessions are easily traced in his paintings and form part of a tradition among Priory artists, including Botticelli and Jean Cocteau.

We have also shown that there has always been, in Europe, a clique devoted over the centuries to something of which the Shroud is a symptom, a manifestation of their true *raison d'être* and these people have been called 'the Shroud Mafia' by Noel Currer-Briggs. The skulduggery of these people, who included the House of Savoy, involved the Knights Templar, and the Priory of Sion: and it was an agent of the Savoys that sought – then lost – just one notebook of Leonardo's, which might have had particular meaning for them.

If Leonardo can be called a Priory man he was – as far as ordinary Christians were and are concerned – a heretic. He would have believed that Jesus did not die on the cross; that he was married to Mary Magdalene and that they had children; that these children were part of a 'magical' line because they were Mary's descendants. She is revered by the Priory because she embodies the tradition of the Egyptian goddess Isis, the original Black Madonna – and there are schools of thought that would say Mary Magdalene was a High Priestess of Isis (some say Ishtar).[5] Our own research has indicated that this was so, and that she is a key figure in a deeper, darker underground 'heresy'.[6]

The association between the Priory of Sion and Mary Magdalene is well known, but there is another strand to their 'heresy' which has attracted far less attention. Giovanni gave us a clue about this in his most obscure comment during our only meeting, when he asked the rhetorical question 'Why are the Grand Masters always called John?' (His own alias also appeared to refer to this issue.) Although it seemed a pointless throwaway line at the time, we did follow it up and found, to our amazement, that it was far from insignificant.

The authors of The Holy Blood and The Holy Grail draw attention to this question, although they make little of it.[7] Referring to the Priory tradition of its Grand Masters taking the name 'John/Jean' they say: 'This succession was clearly intended to imply an esoteric and Hermetic papacy based on John, in contrast (and perhaps opposition) to the exoteric one based on Peter.' Moreover they note that the first Grand Master, the twelfth-century Norman knight Jean de Gisors, took the name Jean

II and pose the question: 'Who, then, was Jean I?' They offer a few suggestions – John the Baptist, John the Evangelist and John the Divine – before dropping the subject.

But some further clues come from these authors' discussion of the Knights Templar. They refer to the possibility that the Order's infamous head idol was intended to represent the severed head of John the Baptist, noting: 'Certain writers have suggested that the Templars were "infected" with the Johannite or Mandaean heresy – which denounced Jesus as a "false prophet" and acknowledged John as the true Messiah. In the course of their activities in the Middle East the Templars undoubtedly established contact with Iohannite sects . . .'.[8]

Many secret societies over the centuries have revered the Baptist, for example the Freemasons and the Knights of Malta, for reasons that have never been fully understood by outsiders. If the Templars had been Iohannites, this would explain why they were said to have rituals that involved trampling or spitting on the cross. To them, it was a sign that they rejected what they regarded as a false god.

It is also interesting that the key places in this story are dedicated to John: Leonardo's own city of Florence itself, and the cathedral at Turin wherein the Shroud is kept. The only surviving sculpture that involved Leonardo in its making is the statue of John the Baptist in the Baptistry in Florence, on which he collaborated with the utmost secrecy with Giovan Francesco Rustici, a known necromancer and alchemist. And Leonardo's last painting was 'John the Baptist', showing him with the same half-smile as 'The Mona Lisa', and pointing straight upwards with the index finger of his right hand. This in Leonardo's work is a sign always associated with John: in the 'Adoration of the Magi' a person stands by the elevated roots of a carob tree – John's tree, symbol of sacrifical blood – while making this gesture. In his famous cartoon of St Anne the subject also does this, warning an oblivious Virgin. Make of it what you will that the disciple whose face is perhaps accusingly close to Jesus' in 'The Last Supper' is also making this gesture. All these gestures are saying 'remember John'.

But why should any group revere John when he himself admitted that he was only the herald, the forerunner of Jesus? His repetitious and over-humble statements in the New Testament to that effect are familiar. However, it is very likely that those words, 'There is one coming after who is greater than I' were complete fabrications by Jesus' followers.[9] Indeed, there is evidence in the New Testament itself that John was never intended to be merely a spiritual warm-up man. In the Acts of the Apostles[10] Paul arrives as the first Christian missionary in Corinth and in Ephesus, only to discover to his amazement that there seemed to be churches already there. On making enquiries he discovers that they are the Church of John the Baptist. He believed that the Ephesians and Corinthians would, therefore, be delighted to discover that he represented Jesus Christ, the one prophesied to come after John. Not so: they had never heard of such a prophecy.

In recounting that story in his book *Jesus* (1992), A. N. Wilson writes: 'If the John the Baptist religion (and we know there was one) had become the dominant cult of the Mediterranean rather than the Jesus religion, we should probably feel that we knew more than we do about this arresting figure. His cult survived until at least the mid-50s, as the author of Acts is guileless enough to let on . . . In Ephesus, they thought "The Way" (as the religion of these early believers was known) meant following "the Baptism of John" . . . had Paul been a weaker personality . . . or had he never written his epistles, it could easily have been the case that the "Baptism of John" would have been the religion which captured the imagination of the ancient world, rather than the Baptism of Christ . . . The cult might even have developed to the point where present-day Johnites, or Baptists, would have believed that . . . John was Divine . . .

'This accident of history, however, was not to be.'[11]

We found ourselves confronted by uncompromising evidence with such radical implications for our culture that we could no longer ignore it. Because this area of research extends well beyond the main subject of this book, we can touch on it only briefly here.

In fact, John's divinity – or his near-divine role in an ancient line of priests – has always been upheld, and is to this day by several hitherto little-known cults which include the Mandaeans of modern Iraq, whose sacred text is *The Book of John*, and the Hermetic secret societies – among them the Templars, who worshipped a severed head, Freemasonry and of course, the Priory of Sion.

We have seen the the Priory's apparently greatest preoccupation is with the feminine, through its reverence for the Magdalene and, through the cult of the Black Madonna, the Goddess Isis herself. How does this fit with their special devotion to John the Baptist, or was he himself in some way connected with the Isis religion?

It might initially seem extremely unlikely that the Jews would have any links at all with the Egyptian mother Goddess. However, recent research such as that by American anthropologist Karl Luckert[12] has given persuasive evidence to show that the Hebrews were not always the strict monotheists that they later became, nor did they limit their devotions to a male God. There is also evidence that, in the first century, some groups of Jews had not forgotten their ancient roots. There were certainly 'heretical' Jews outside Israel – most notably in Egypt and Ethiopia – who worshipped a goddess alongside Jehovah.[13] Undoubtedly the influence of Egypt's own goddess religion would have made itself felt, especially during the cultural melée of the Roman era.

A question we have never heard asked is 'Who baptised John the Baptist?' – which is more important than one might suppose. Although there were many cleansing rituals involved in Judaic practice, baptism itself was unknown and yet we were to find that it had been practised as such in the temples of Isis in Egypt, just across the border.[14] The New Testament tells us that Jesus and his family fled from Herod's wrath to Egypt and there are non-Biblical traditions that John also went there.

If Mary Magdalene was a priestess of Isis, then this would establish a connection between the cult of Isis and the ministries of both John and Jesus. How far this association went is impossible to prove, but it would explain the reverence given to both John and Mary by goddess-worshipping heretics in Europe, including the Priory of Sion.

The divine priesthood of John the Baptist is, we discovered, one of the most jealously-guarded secrets of that organization, although it is not exclusive to them. It has taken many forms over the centuries, being found, as we have seen, among the Templars and in less well known groups such as the Iohnists of southern France.

In our research, wherever we found any Johannite/Iohnist traditions we also found devotion to the Black Madonna and the Magdalene, even among such unlikely groups as the Knights Templar. Ean Begg's *Cult of the Black Virgin* lists many links between them and the Black Madonna/Magdalene cult.[15]

Mary of Magdala (which means 'place of the Dove') was a rich woman with, so the Church has had it, a background as a prostitute. The Gnostic Gospels stress repeatedly that she was Jesus' 'first disciple' and that he often kissed her on the lips.

The Priory and other ancient traditions, however, say that her so-called whoring was in fact, a deliberate slander. To the Jews any woman with pagan sympathies was as good – or as bad – as a whore (as indeed they are to this day where both fundamentalist Jews and Christians are concerned). If it was known that she was a priestess of a Goddess cult, then this would have gone some way towards the extreme caution with which the Magdalene was, and is, treated by the Church. For although she is a saint in her own right there is still the feeling that there is something 'not quite nice' about her: indeed it is almost impossible to find any statues of her in shops that sell religious images. The very notion of women priest – that is, women as the spiritual equal of men – is regarded with repugnance by millions of Christians even today. It is easy to see how they would regard the idea of women being in some way spiritually superior.

John, Mary and Isis herself share the symbol of the dove – something also found as a Cathar symbol in the same area of France that is ancient Iohnist country: the Languedoc.

It is through the cult of the Magdalene that goddess worship has been maintained in Europe. Wheras she is perceived as a complete woman, the Virgin Mary is desexed and disempowered. There has even been an Underground Church of Mary Magdalene.[16] That is also why there was always in Europe worship of the Black Madonna.

The great Gothic cathedrals were dedicated to her and to the Great Work, the alchemy of the soul, which was such an essential part of the Isian religion. She is 'rosamunda', rose of the world, like Isis herself, a complete woman who comprises Virgin, Mother, Whore and Wise Woman, in the tradition of all true goddesses. When the Church tried to destroy her they set up in her place the sexless goddess of the Virgin Mary, but the Magdalene's power was too great to be overthrown and the people loved her too much; they continued to worship her in the form of the Black Madonna, with Jesus' child at her breast. She is also, like Isis, the *notre dame de lumière* of the Priory and she is the true *Notre Dame* of many an apparently ordinary church the world over, including, as we have seen, Notre Dame de Paris where she reigns over the city of love.

We have come to understand that the Priory and other similar organizations have kept this knowledge – the secret 'underground stream' that ran beneath all mainstream churches – whole and largely untarnished over the centuries. The cult of the Magdalene survived underneath the cult of the Virgin Mary in many places. Yet, in their own tradition, the Priory have ensured that hints are always in the public domain: 'for those with eyes to see, let them see'. In the architecture of the great Gothic cathedrals, in paintings, in poetry, in great plays, and even on one alleged holy relic, the clues are there in abundance.

Inevitably there will be many who dismiss all this as fantasy – and just as many who wish it were – but the fact remains that the clues to this great underground tradition are all around us. In the ridged Gothic arches topped with rosebuds and in the rose windows of the cathedrals, in the Grail stories (one of which has the Holy Grail as a severed head on a platter), in ancient mazes and labyrinths, in legends surrounding the Ark of the Covenant, in Freemasonry, in Cocteau's mural in the church of Notre Dame de France off London's Leicester Square, in the links between *notre dame* and Isis, in the Black Madonnas – and in many secret mysteries which may also, in due course, make themselves known to a wider public. Quite simply, do not take our word for it, go out and look for yourself.

We must not forget that there are clues in Leonardo's least known and most controversial work: the Turin Shroud. Shroudman seems to have a severed head. We hope to have shown that for practical reasons this would have been so, for Leonardo used his own face and someone else's body, so inevitably there would be a visible demarcation line. Yet this obvious dislocation could also be seen as symbolic: Leonardo's visual pun is saying to us across the centuries that the one who was beheaded is 'over' one who was crucified. The blood is incongruously flowing from the wounds as if the man were still alive: here he is saying that Jesus never died on the cross, that he did not redeem anyone, just as Leonardo was careful to omit all but the most token wine from the table of his 'Last Supper'.

Of course there remains a problem. Why should Leonardo, no lover of women, espouse the cause of a Goddess? And a Goddess at that who represents unashamed heterosexuality? Psychologically, however, it is all part of a pattern. We think he may have come to the Priory of Sion through a search for knowledge, being attracted by Hermeticism and by the lure of alchemical secrets, but there was another aspect of his personality that found itself at home with this cult. His mother, Caterina, was a woefully absent parent for most of Leonardo's formative years, and he had been forced to watch his step-siblings enjoy their mother's love while he was alone. Isis is known as 'mother and lover of all': here at last was the archetypal woman in whose love and attention he could bask – and this Goddess was the one woman who would never leave him. Complex, aloof, tormented, Leonardo could find solace in this Lady to end ladies. And, in the tradition of the troubadour, he could also believe himself her slave, enjoying the exquisite pangs of courtly love from a safe distance. In her was his mother and lover, besides the side of himself he found at once so attractive and so forbidden.

As we have seen, his last painting was 'John the Baptist', derided by many art critics as being too dark and the figure as being too effete. Of course this may simply have been because the model – unknown to us now – was a camp young man at court who caught the Maestro's appreciative eye, or it may have been a deliberate attempt to combine male and female in the form of a god. It is also worth noting that although John carries the cross over his shoulder, as was the tradition, it may well not represent the Christian cross at all, for this symbol also belonged to the Egyptian god Osiris many centuries before John and Jesus were born.

Leonardo never wasted a single opportunity in any of his works to imbue it with his own rich and disturbing symbolic meaning and send it down the corridor of time to those who would recognize it.

In October 1993, I (Lynn) was invited by the American art historian

Professor Bill Homer and his wife Christine to a dinner at the National Portrait Gallery in London. As the conversation flowed I was asked by the others at the table – international art collectors and curators of galleries – to expand on our research for this book. Not unnaturally it caused something of a stir, but there were considerably fewer hostile or even critical comments than one might imagine. Interest was great, perhaps because, as one collector said: 'If you are right, then that piece of cloth is not only the world's first photograph, but it's also a self-portrait of da Vinci . . . My God, it is literally the world's most priceless artefact . . .'

We think it is, and for that reason, we urge the Church authorities to look after it well, although they are unlikely to heed our words. It is not just a hitherto undiscovered da Vinci; it is not just the first known photograph; it is considerably more even than that.

Believers have said that the Shroud is a 'timebomb', that it carries a profound spiritual message through the centuries, one that will explode upon a dissolute and irreligious world when its moment has truly come. In that, we are in agreement. But the message is not what they will want to hear, even if thousands of others are already keen to do so. Leonardo himself regarded the Shroud as a magical talisman, an object imbued with the seeds of his own life, thrown like a message in a bottle upon the seas of the future.

For the rest of us, however, the Turin Shroud – the ultimate example of man's creativity – carries within it the seeds of destruction of the old ways of thinking, and the beginnings of a completely new era. It does not herald some magical, mystical or paranormal event, nor some sudden upsurge of New Age mysticism, or a miraculous Second Coming when all the believers will be assembled to be patted on their collective head. If any of the words of the story in this book are ever taken seriously enough to be translated into a 'message' then the implications are enormous. That is all. That is more than enough.

Leonardo's Shroud challenges the very religion it is supposed to exemplify so uniquely (and, ironically, it is kept safe by the priests of the Church he despised so much). The image on that cloth is nothing less than a Iohnist hymn, celebrating the divine priesthood of John the Baptist in the cause of the real founder of the religion of love, the goddess Isis. In doing so, it also challenges the Church's age-old emphasis on male power, the superiority of priests and the submissiveness of women. (Perhaps it is fitting that the Shroud should be a Priory *comedia*, for John eschewed miracles and there would never be a miraculously imprinted cloth associated with him.)

Many armchair critics will no doubt feel justified in being horrified by any or all of this story, or by relegating it to the lunatic fringe. That is their privilege. They may like to take refuge in a blanket denial of the existence of the Priory of Sion and other similar groups. This book is not a comforting tale for those who prefer their history to conform to Biblical certainty: this is not a conformist tale at all. Neither does it suit those whose expertise is implicitly challenged – be it in art history or photography – for they are left wondering why they had no inkling of all of this and tend to dismiss it out of hand. It is worth stating that we have not researched and written this book in order to shock: we, too, have been shocked during its gestation. We, too, have had many of our erstwhile cherished beliefs shaken to the core by our findings, yet few things shook us more than the relative ease with which all of the information in this book could be assembled. It really is a case of the little boy in the story of the Emperor's new clothes: once we started to shed all our preconceptions it all began to fall into place with remarkable rapidity. As Jean Cocteau, himself a recent Grand Master of the Priory of Sion, wrote: 'History is an alliance of reality and lies. The reality of history becomes a lie. The unreality of the fable becomes the truth.'

The implications of this story go far, far beyond the Turin Shroud: the Magdalene has been worshipped – as representative of the Goddess and as the Black Madonna – in the very centres of European Christianity for many centuries: that Johannites did not, as A. N. Wilson believes, die out less than a century after they began – they continued, passing on their message in the 'underground stream'.

If, as we believe, the Church originally commissioned Leonardo to fake a Shroud, then the powers that be in the Vatrican must still know its real nature.

For that reason, perhaps we will find very soon that the Turin Shroud is 'stolen', or that it 'disintegrates' with convenient speed. Whatever the reason, it will no longer be there – physically or metaphorically – to comfort those who seek its power. Even if it is put on display one more time, with all its staggering anomalies and 'heretical' symbolism for all to see, its magic will have taken on a different hue. Yes, it is a miracle, but strictly of man's own making. Leonardo succeeded in soaring above, not only the commonplace minds of his day, but of any day. He mused: 'to be the first, to make the dream a reality . . .' Whatever else one thinks of his Turin Shroud, by creating it he certainly succeeded in making that particular dream a reality.

Generations have puzzled over the Shroud of Turin, and whatever happens to that vexed piece of cloth, it is certainly now, like the Ark of the Covenant, destined for legend and will no doubt, remain just as elusive.

APPENDIX:

LYNN PICKNETT, CLIVE PRINCE AND THE
BRITISH SOCIETY FOR THE TURIN SHROUD

As our research developed, it was natural for us to join the British Society for the Turin Shroud (BSTS), of which Ian Wilson is Vice Chairman, as it would at least put us in touch with useful contacts in the field and give us access to some of the more difficult-to-obtain literature on the subject. Although we realized that the majority of the members would be pro-authenticity – people who dismiss the Shroud as a fake are not likely to be moved to join societies devoted to it – we did hope that some, like us at that stage, were simply fascinated by the mystery and were not part of any particular lobby. After all, the BSTS does declare itself in its Constitution as 'entirely non-denominational and non-aligned' and gives as its primary aim 'the encouragement of, and support for, research into the Turin Shroud'. We were to discover to our cost that although one or two individual members did maintain a balanced approach to the subject, the organization as a whole was firmly in the grip of those who apparently wanted to uphold the belief in the Shroud's authenticity.

We were a little disconcerted at the first meeting we attended, when, some two years after the carbon dating, Chairman Rodney Hoare announced that the society would be keeping 'a low profile' for the time being, because of the test results. To us at least, the Shroud was as much of an enigma as ever, and even more worthy of investigation. It looked as though they were ashamed of it.

In April 1991, I (Lynn) gave a talk in London on our work as it stood at that point, a talk to which a few BSTS members came. It seemed a good opportunity to open up some dialogue and share our findings with those who, after all, were supposed to be this country's experts. Clive wrote an account of the talk for the BSTS Newsletter (edited by Ian Wilson), with the suggestion that I repeat the talk to the BSTS.

The article was published, but together with other material that gave us the first inkling that the 'for' in the society's name gave away its true leaning in its own way, that edition of the Newsletter was a masterpiece of editorial juxtaposition. It was accompanied by a reprint of an article by Isabel Piczek showing that Leonardo could not have painted the Shroud image, an argument with which we were both totally in agreement. Yet, in our view the average BSTS member reading that would have gone away believing that we were both convinced members of the pro-painting lobby. More seriously, however, the Editor appended some of his own comments which declared that our work was based upon mediumistic communications with Leonardo himself!

This was a deliberately garbled version of a conversation Ian had had in happier times with me. It took place on Sunday 22 April 1990 at my north London home. I told him that my occasional attempts at 'automatic writing'[2] had finally resulted in something intelligible, and demonstrated this, but laughed that they were signed 'Leonardo'. 'They would be, wouldn't they,' I said. I added that I had also – quite separately – come into some information that hinted that Leonardo had indeed created the Shroud image.

'When was this supposed to have happened?' asked Ian.

'1492.'

'Yes,' he replied. 'The Shroud did disappear around then . . .' (We later took this to be a clear indication that he was hinting that today's Turin Shroud could have been a substitute for the earlier one. These days he denies that this part of the conversation took place, even writing in the *Fortean Times* that 'this was one of Lynn Picknett's many inventions.')[3]

Then he said, 'But what about the carbon dating?'

I replied that as far as I knew the date of 1492 was totally in keeping with the upper limit, given as 1500, adding that I thought he would be the last person to have used the carbon dating as an argument! (He was also to write to me later: 'When you try to persuade me of the truth . . . that Leonardo created the Shroud there is one part in me that feels fundamentally threatened,'[4] another indication that his own faith in its authenticity was not nearly as certain as many believe.)

My memory of these events is that this brief conversation was the only possible basis for his later accusations of mediumship. He could have been in no doubt at the time that I regard automatic writing as a function of the unconscious mind (see n. 2) and that my scribbles were to be seen as a novelty only. As I recall I also impressed upon him that the conversation was in total confidence and he promised not to tell a soul. There was nothing sinister in this request for secrecy: I was a little embarrassed at demonstrating my 'automatic scribbles', but I felt at the time that he should know about them.

The allegations of mediumship were used as a reason for rejecting the offered lecture, as were the grounds that the BSTS only deals in 'hard, checkable' research.[5] Although we were understandably angry about being so blatantly misrepresented and ridiculed in such a way (there was no doubt about the intention behind their slur), after an unsuccessful attempt to secure an apology, and after a letter from me was included in the next *Newsletter*, the episode blew over. We had better things to do: serious Shroud research called.

However, it became more and more galling to see the *Newsletter* and lectures given over entirely to articles on how the carbon dating could not be trusted and detailing the slenderest 'evidence' that apparently supported authenticity. This trend reached its height at the 1993 AGM, when Rodney Hoare publicly appealed to the members 'for any more ideas on how the carbon dating could be wrong' and Ian Wilson announced that he was going off to Turkey to collect rocks from the vicinity of ancient Edessa in case they proved to be radioactive, the idea being that they might have influenced the carbon dating as the Shroud was allegedly kept there at one point.

However nothing compared with the BSTS' Spring lecture in May 1992 by – in a manner of speaking – Norma Weller. Advertised as 'New Discoveries on the Turin Shroud', Weller's talk promised revelations from a new image-enhancement technique that would reveal some hitherto unseen detail on the Shroud image. An enlarged picture of the face of Shroudman was proudly displayed: what was this incredibly innovative technique of hers? She had coloured the image in.

Norma Weller herself remained invisible, as she had sent her talk to be read *in absentia* by Ian Wilson. This opened with the declaration that the 'speaker' was unwilling to go into details about the enhancement process and did not wish to enter into any debate about it either. When questioned from the floor about the speaker's absence the audience was told that she was 'too reticent' to give her talk in person. Further questions revealed that she is, by profession, a Brighton Polytechnic lecturer. The tiny audience also learned that it was lucky to have the picture to look at that evening, as it had been delivered by car only that afternoon. But for that they would have been treated to a talk by someone who was not there refusing to tell them about something that they could not see.

Norma Weller, despite her reticence, was persuaded to write an article on her method for the next *Newsletter*. It remains a source of complete bafflement to this day, its only real information being that the enhancement was the result of 'the application of three-dimensional colour'. It ends with the declaration: 'My only wish is to authenticate the Shroud.'[6]

The serious side of this farce was that it became apparent from Ian Wilson's introduction that the organizers had had no idea of the content of Norma Weller's talk until it actually took place (or didn't, depending on how you look at it). When compared with the cursory and dismissive vetting of the Leonardo talk, and its rejection on the grounds that it failed to satisfy the BSTS' stringent criteria for scientific research, we felt justifiably annoyed that a double standard seemed to have been used, as it appeared that the BSTS' vetting only leapt into practice where anti-authenticity research was concerned. When, after the fiction about the 'mediumistic' sources, the *Newsletter* gave approving space to an Egyptian medium who channels Jesus (and yes, he confirms that the Shroud is genuine), it really became a bit too much to take.

Clive wrote a letter for publication in the *Newsletter* expressing concern about the direction the society was taking. It was not published, but was answered by the secretary, Dr Michael Clift, in stridently hostile tones, which tagged both of us (in one of its less offensive remarks) as belonging to 'the more scatty side of the so-called occult'.[7] Over the next few months a number of letters were exchanged with the Chairman, Vice Chairman and Secretary. Our complaint against the pro-authenticity and pro-Christian bias of this supposedly 'non-denominational and non-aligned' society, and requests for an explanation about the unequal treatment of those opposed to authenticity were studiously ignored by all three. Also a poem written by me for publication in the *Newsletter* on the subject of the compassion evoked by the wounds of the man on the Shroud was rejected on two grounds by Ian Wilson. First, that the *Newsletter* did not, as a matter of policy, carry poetry: in fact, they had just carried some doggerel verses of a 'Hymn to the Shroud'. Secondly, he thought my poem was at odds with our Leonardo theory! Clearly, the BSTS officers, who had never heard our theory, knew best – or they may not have liked the poem.

In March 1993 writer and theologian A.N. Wilson became interested in our Leonardo theory, and his friend, the reputable Anglican writer Ysenda Maxtone Graham interviewed us, plus BSTS members Michael Clift and Ian Dickinson. As a result, an article entitled 'The Turmoil That is Tearing Apart the Shroud Crowd' appeared in the *London Evening Standard*,[8] a direct result of which was my expulsion from the society. Rodney Hoare wrote to me about: '. . . an article in the *Evening Standard* which I have been told about, bringing the Society into disrepute and mentioning the date of our next meeting. I am sure you realise such behaviour is not acceptable.'9

That meeting took place in April 1993 at St John's Church Hall in west London. Normally around twenty members turn up to BSTS meetings – this one was packed with over forty people, many of whom were clutching copies of the *Standard* piece. Some were heard to ask when I was going to speak, obviously having got the wrong end of the stick entirely.

We arrived and sought to get a proper explanation for my expulsion from Rodney Hoare. Instead, he seized me by the arms and physically ejected me from the hall, saying, 'We do not have to give a reason.'

Later the Committee gloated that 'we got twenty more members that night – something that the writers (sic) of that *Standard* article did not intend'.

Rodney Hoare was also, at the AGM in September 1993, to describe the article as 'libellous' – something that could hardly have been the case, as Ian Wilson had been telephoned two nights before its publication by the Associated Newspapers' lawyers in order to check certain facts.

What Michael Clift thought of it may be gleaned from a note he sent to Ysenda Maxtone Graham, which read in its entirety: 'There is only one possible use for your article, but I do not wish to insult my perineum,' yet apart from interviews with the people listed above, the article was purely a matter of 'hard, checkable,' fact.

I had been told that my expulsion was the result of a 'unanimous vote' (of the Committee). In fact Ian Dickinson had voted against it: shortly afterwards he was also threatened with expulsion, then told by the Chairman that he could stay as long 'as you co-operate'. He wrote back that he 'refused to co-operate with your corruption', and, although virtually ordered to do so, has steadfastly refused to resign ever since. Earlier, Dickinson's criticism of one of the BSTS officers led to his receiving from that individual's wife a thinly-veiled accusation of having used 'occult means' to cause her father-in-law to commit suicide.

After my banishment, Clive was told that, by special dispensation of the Chairman, he could stay in the Society provided he behaved 'like a normal member' (with the hope that he would stay, 'as you might learn something about the Shroud').10 Shortly afterwards Clive was proposed as Treasurer of the Society: he has a background in accountancy. Almost immediately he, too, was expelled. The Chairman's letter informing him of this gave as the reason: 'You have written to me and the other officers and have stood for office.'11 When quizzed about this at the 1993 AGM Hoare's logic was impeccable: 'Normal members don't write letters of complaint, therefore he is not a normal member.'

This AGM (from which we were both barred, although Keith Prince attended and took down verbatim notes of the whole meeting), also witnessed a further attack on my character ('she is clearly an unusual person and we do not want someone like that in our society . . .') and a repetition, as a statement of fact, of the mediumship slur. Clive was also attacked – 'he is even worse – he writes letters'. In all, the character assassination of both of us took up one-and-a-quarter hours out of a two-hour meeting. And, after the Committee's refusals to allow us to share our research with the membership, it also featured a refutation of our theory by Rodney Hoare – a theory to which he has always steadfastly refused to listen and which, in our view, he got hopelessly and ludicrously muddled ('they say that Leonardo painted with his thumbs . . .' etc). He assured the ten members present that 'there is nothing at all to their theory'. Now the membership could get safely back to looking for radioactive rocks and colouring in pictures of the Shroud for talks they would be too 'reticent' to give.

NOTES AND REFERENCES

INTRODUCTION

1   It was difficult to know how to write such an intricate and, in some places, personal, story when there are two people involved. After a lot of experimenting, we decided that the third person throughout would be too impersonal, so we have used the first person, indicating which of us is 'speaking' using the format 'I (Lynn or Clive)' where relevant, then 'we' thereafter.

Anticipating the inevitable accusations of bias, let us state unequivocally that the only reason Ian Wilson and his writings are so frequently referred to in this book is that his are the most widely read works on this subject. We could hardly have ignored them.

1   MORE QUESTIONS THAN ANSWERS

1   At the time of writing – early 1994 – the Shroud (still in the silver reliquary) has been moved from the Royal Chapel into the main body of the cathedral while repairs are made to the chapel. Here it is kept in a modern plate-glass display case, 3.4 metres long by 2 metres high and weighing some three tons. There are, of course, plentiful security devices to guard against attack and fire. Whether this new home turns out to be temporary remains to be seen, as commentators have pointed out that the move places it in Church, rather than state, property.

2   The information in this chapter is drawn from a number of sources, the main ones being Ian Wilson's *The Turin Shroud* (Penguin, 1979) and *The Evidence of the Shroud* (Michael O'Mara, 1986); John Heller's *Report on the Shroud of Turin* (Houghton Mifflin, Boston, 1983); David Sox's *The Image on the Shroud* (Unwin, 1981) and Joe Nickell's *Inquest on the Shroud of Turin* (Prometheus, 1987).

3   Scientists from the 1978 STURP examination found traces of pitch around the edges of the holes, consistent with accidental drips from a torch: L. A. Schwalble and R. N. Rogers, 'Physics and Chemistry of the Shroud of Turin: A Summary of the 1978 Investigation', *Analytica Chimica Acta* 135 (1982).

4   Pia gave his own account of the discovery in 'Memoria sulla riproduzione fotografia della santissima Sindone' which was reprinted in the April 1960 edition of *Sindon*. The full story is also given in Chapter 2 of John Walsh's *The Shroud* (W. H. Allen, 1963).

5   *Sindon*, April 1991.

6   See, for example, the attempts made shortly after Pia's discovery by two Italian artists, Carlo Cussetti and Enrico Reffi, reproduced in Robert K. Wilcox's *Shroud* (Corgi, 1977).

7   There are many other practical reasons why the image could not have been painted. For example, the faintness of the image when seen close up means that the artist would have been unable to see what he was doing. Another objection, pointed out by Joe Nickell in *Inquest on the Shroud of Turin* (p98) is that an artist would have made a preliminary sketch before painting, which would still be visible.

8 Giuseppe Enrie, *La Santa Sindone Rivelata dalla Fotografia* (Turin, 1938). Again, John Walsh gives a full account, in Chapter 10 of *The Shroud*.

9 Paul Vignon, *The Shroud of Christ* (Constable, 1902).

10 Pierre Barbet, *A Doctor at Calvary* (Image Books, New York, 1963).

11 The Commission's report was published in *Rivista Diocesa Torinese*, January 1976. A detailed account of their work and findings is given in Part 2 of Ian Wilson's *The Turin Shroud*.

12 Published by Victor Gollancz shortly before the exposition. A revised edition, updated to include the events of 1978, was published by Penguin in 1979.

13 Produced and directed by David Rolfe. A book of the film, by Peter Brent and David Rolfe, was published by Futura in 1978.

14 Peter Brent and David Rolfe, *The Silent Witness*, p9.

15 STURP's findings were published in a variety of scientific and technical journals. Summaries can be found in Ian Wilson's *The Evidence of the Shroud* and John Heller's *Report on the Shroud of Turin*. Wilson's book also contains a full bibliography of STURP's papers.

16 Sox, *op. cit.*, pp21–2.

17 An account of the carbon dating and the events leading up it appeared in *Fortean Times* no 51, pp4–7.

18 See various reports in the national press, 14 October 1988. The laboratories' full findings were published in *Nature*, 16 February 1989, in a paper signed by all the scientists involved.

19 *The Independent*, 14 October 1988.

20 Quoted in *Fortean Times* 51, p4.

21 Wilson, *The Turin Shroud*, p95.

22 Wilson, *The Evidence of the Shroud*, p136.

23 Ian Wilson, *Holy Faces, Secret Places* (Doubleday, 1991), p255. In the *British Society for the Turin Shroud Newsletter* (no 31, May 1992) Wilson, the newsletter editor, likens the squabbling among Shroudies following the carbon dating to the fight to divide Jesus' clothes at the foot of the Cross, citing Psalm 22:18.

24 Rodney Hoare, *A Piece of Cloth* (Aquarian Press, 1984), p19.

25 Letter, 12 April 1993.

26 *Le Contre-Reforme Catholique au XXe Siècle*, no 238, April 1991.

27 Quoted in Holger Kersten and Elmar Gruber, *The Jesus Conspiracy* (Element Books), 1994, p321.

28 *BSTS Newsletter*, no 35 (September 1993), pp18–20.

29 Robert K. Wilcox *op. cit.*, pp59–173.

30 Max Frei, 'Note a seguito dei primo studi sui prelievi di polvere aderente al lenzuolo della S. Sindone', *Sindon*, April 1976. For an English-language account of his work, see 'Nine Years of Palynological Studies on the Shroud', *Shroud Spectrum International*, no 3 (1982).

31 This great publishing debacle came to a head in 1983 when *Stern* magazine bought the 'Hitler Diaries' for $4 million, after having been assured by three handwriting experts, including Max Frei, that they were genuine. However, almost immediately after extracts were published in *Stern* and in the *Sunday Times*, forensic tests proved that the 'diaries' were in fact crude fakes. Frei had made the mistake of using forged handwriting samples with which to compare the equally forged diaries, despite the easy availability of genuine samples of the Führer's writing. See Robert Harris' *Selling Hitler*, (Faber & Faber, 1986), pp181–182 and 195–196.

32 E. Jumper, A. Adler, J. Jackson, S. Pellicori, J. Heller and J. Druzic, 'A comprehensive examination of the various stains and images on the Shroud of Turin', *ACS Advances in Chemistry No* 205, Archaeological Chemistry III, 1984, pp447–76.

33 Quoted in Sox, *op. cit.*, p45.

34 The VP-8 pictures are reproduced in Wilson's *The Evidence of the Shroud*.

35 It is often stated in the Shroud literature as an established fact that there is no body image underneath the bloodstains. If true, this would be an important argument in favour of authenticity, since it would imply that the cloth was in contact with a body, the image of which was blocked by the blood. No forger would apply the bloodstains first and then paint the image around them. However, the truth is that such claims are erroneous. They derive from a test carried out by STURP scientist Alan Adler when attempting to find out if the blood was genuine. He took a single 'blood'-coated fibril and applied a protease that would dissolve any blood protein. The 'blood' did dissolve – indicating, but not proving, that it *was* blood – and Adler then observed that the remaining fibril showed none of the discolouration found on the body image (Heller and Adler, 'Blood on the Shroud of Turin', *Applied Optics*, vol 19, no 12, June 1980). However, to extrapolate from this test on a single fibre – more than 100 of which make up one linen thread – that there is no image under the blood at all is completely unacceptable. We have already seen that many individual fibres within the image areas are not coloured. STURP's Ray Rogers, in a talk to the BSTS in June 1980, listed the question of whether the image was present under the blood as one of the important, but as yet unanswered, questions of the Shroud.

36 For detailed discussions of the controversy see: Nickell, Chapter 12; Wilson, *The Evidence of the Shroud*, pp91–7; Sox, *The Image on the Shroud*, Chapter 9.

37 Barbet, *op. cit.* Chapter 5.

38 *ibid.*, p112.

39 *ibid.*, Chapter 3.

40 Hoare, *op. cit.* Chapter 6.

41 Barbet, *op. cit.*, p21.

42 Summarized in Wilson, *The Turin Shroud*, pp42–3.

43 A curiously popular practice that mixed blatant masochism with religious fervour. The significance of the presence of flagellants in Renaissance Florence will become apparent later.

44 Hoare, *op. cit.*, p96.

45 See Chapter 7.

46 Francis Filas, *The Dating of the Shroud of Turin from Coins of Pontius Pilate* (Cogan Productions, Arizona, 1982).

47 Sox, *op. cit.*, pp26–7.

2 THE VERDICT OF HISTORY

1 Herbert Thurston, 'The Turin Shroud and the Verdict of History', *The Month*, January/February 1903.

2 See, for example, Chapter 14 of Ian Wilson's *Holy Faces, Secret Places*.

3 The most extensive survey of the Shroud's history is in Ian Wilson, *The Turin Shroud*. Classic studies of the documents relating to the Shroud's history are Ulysses Chevalier, *Étude Critique sur l'origine du Saint Suaire de Lirey-Chambéry-Turin* (A Picard, Paris, 1900) and Herbert Thurston's articles in *The Month* (see Chaptor 2, note 1).

4 The letter is preserved in the Bibliothèque Nationale, Paris (Collection de Champagne, v 154, folio 138). A translation of the full text of D'Arcis' letter, by Rev Herbert Thurston, appeared in *The Month* in 1903, and is reproduced in Wilson's *The Turin Shroud* and Sox's *The Image on the Shroud*.

5 Wilson, *The Turin Shroud*, p100.

6 *ibid.*, The Latin text is as follows:
Et tandem, solerti diligencia precedente et informacione super hoc facta, finaliter reperit fraudem et quomodo pannus ille artificialiter depictus fuerat, et probatum fuit eciam per artificem qui illum depinxerat, ipsum humano ope factum, non miraculose confectum vel concessum.

7 Nickell, *op. cit.*, p15, citing Edward A. Wuenschel, *Self-Portrait of Christ* (Holy Shroud Guild, New York, 1957).

8 In the archives of the department of Aube (rack G822).

9 Even a year later, in 1357, there is no mention of the Shroud in a list of Lirey's relics (Archives of Aube, records of Lirey, 96).

10 Despite this, some believers – for example, in the French Shroud society, CIELT – insist that the earliest date that the Shroud is known to have existed was 1353, since that is when the Lirey church was founded. To them, four or five years is seen as critical.

11 See Wilson, *The Evidence of the Shroud* for a photograph of the medallion.

12 Wilson, *The Turin Shroud*, p241.

13 Christopher Cope, *Phoenix Frustrated* (Constable, 1986), p157.

14 Quoted by Nickell, *Inquest on the Shroud of Turin*, p23.

15 Cope, *op. cit.*, p157.

16 The earliest such theory was advanced by Hippolyte Chopin in 1900 (see Chevalier, *op. cit.*). A more recent version was put forward by Geoffrey Crawley in the *British Journal of Photography*, March 1967.

17 John Tyrer, *BSTS Newsletter*, December 1988. Tyrer was remarkably quick off the mark, as his letter to the *Newsletter* is dated 20 October 1988, just a week after the carbon dating results.

18 John A. T. Robinson, 'The Shroud and the New Testament', in *Face to Face with the Turin Shroud* (Mayhew-McCrimmon/Mowbray, 1978), p69.

19 Although generally believed to be the last of the four Gospels to be written, that of St John is the only one that claims to be derived from an eyewitness – from John himself, 'the disciple who Jesus loved'. Scholars have concluded that, because of its attention to detail and intimate knowledge of the layout and customs of the Jerusalem of Jesus' day, this Gospel is indeed drawn from an eyewitness account of his ministry. See C. H. Dodd, *Historical Tradition in the Fourth Gospel*, (Cambridge University Press, 1963).

20 Robert Eisler, *The Messiah Jesus and John the Baptist*, London, 1931.

21 The most thorough study is that by Maurus Green, 'Enshrouded in Silence', *Ampleforth Journal* 74 (1969).

22 Robert de Clari, *The Conquest of Constantinople* (trans. E. H. McNeal, Columbia University Press, 1936).

23 Geoffrey de Villehardouin, *The Conquest of Constantinople* in M. R. B. Shaw (ed.), *Chronicles of the Crusades* (Penguin, 1963), p92.

24 The theory forms Part 4 of *The Turin Shroud*.

25 Evagrius, *Ecclesiastical History* IV 27, ed Bidez and Parmentier (1898).

26 Translated in *The Anti-Nicene Fathers*, Vol. VIII, ed Roberts and Donaldson (Eerdmans, Michigan, 1951).

27 Averil Cameron's inaugural lecture, 'The Sceptic and the Shroud', given in April 1980, was published as a booklet by King's College, London. Our thanks to Alan Wills for supplying us with a copy.

28 Wilson, *Holy Faces, Secret Places*, p213.

29 Quoted in Wilson, *The Turin Shroud*, p189–90.

30 *ibid.* p169.

31 Philip M.J. McNair, 'The Shroud and History: Fantasy, Fake or Fact?' in *Face to Face with the Turin Shroud*, p37.

32 Brent and Rolfe, *op. cit.*, p67.

33 Joe Nickell (*Inquest on the Shroud of Turin*) quotes micropaleontologist Steven Schafersman ('I find Max Frei's conclusions incredible') and cites Richard Eyde, botanist at the Smithsonian Institute.

34 Schwalbe and Rogers, *op. cit*

35 For an orthodox historical view of the Templars' history, see *The Murdered Magicians* by Peter Partner (Oxford University Press, 1981), which also describes the later

'mythologizing' of the order by occultists. Good historical material – although with very different conclusions as to the Templars' subsequent fate – can be found in *The Sign and the Seal* by Graham Hancock (William Heinemann, 1992), *The Temple and the Lodge* by Michael Baigent and Richard Leigh (Jonathan Cape, 1989) and *Born in Blood* by John J. Robinson (Century, 1990).

36 See *The Trial of the Templars* by M. Barber (Cambridge University Press, 1978).
37 Wilson, *The Turin Shroud*, Chapter 19.
38 Noel Currer-Briggs, *The Shroud and the Grail* (Weidenfeld & Nicolson, 1987).
39 *ibid.*, Chapters 5 and 6.
40 Paul Vignon, *Le Sainte Suaire de Turin devant la science l'archeologie, l'histoire, l'iconographie, la logique* (Masson, Paris, 1939). For more accessible accounts of Vignon's work in this area, see John Walsh, *The Shroud*, pp119–23, and Ian Wilson *The Turin Shroud*, pp116–18.
41 The forehead 'V' mark is also invalid as an argument that it inspired the tradition of Byzantine art, as this is not unique to Jesus in that tradition. A glance through any book of Byzantine icons will show the same feature on the foreheads of saints and even the Virgin Mary.
42 See Wilson, *The Evidence of the Shroud*, pp 107–10.
43 Wilson, *Holy Faces, Secret Places*, Chapter 12.
44 Plate VII in Cope, *op. cit.*
45 Ian Dickinson, 'Recent Discoveries on the Turin Shroud', lecture to the British Society for the Turin Shroud, 27 May 1992.
46 Ian Wilson has made an extensive study of the Veronica in *Holy Faces, Secret Places*.

3 THEORIES

1   Schwalbe and Rogers *op. cit.*
2   Hoare, *op. cit.*, p139.
3   On thoughtography, see Lynn Picknett, *Encyclopaedia of the Paranormal* (Macmillan, 1990), pp 79–80. Interestingly, as, one of the classic examples of this phenomenon involves Leonardo da Vinci's 'Last Supper' – see frontispiece to *Phenomena: A Book of Wonders* by John Michell and Robert J.M. Rickard (Thames & Hudson, 1977).
4   César Tort, 'The Turin Shroud: A Case of Retrocognitive Thoughtography?', *Journal of the Society for Psychical Research*, vol 56 no 818 (January 1990), p71. However Tort has recently retracted his theory, in *Journal of the SPR*, vol 59, no 834 January 1994. Our thanks to Guy Lyon Playfair for bringing Tort's work to our attention.
5   See Wilson, *The Turin Shroud*, Chapter 24. The theory was postulated as long ago as 1931, by P.W. O'Gorman.
6   We would like to thank Keith Prince for his significant contributions to this section.
7   For example, Ian Wilson, *The Turin Shroud*, pp280–81.
8   Vignon, *op. cit.*
9   Hoare, *op. cit.*, Chapter 5.
10 Hoare thinks that the Shroud proves that, because the Resurrection was just a recovery from coma, Jesus was purely human, not divine. Oddly, Hoare does not see this as an obstacle to his Anglicanism, and moreover believes that the Shroud was specially protected to bring this 'message' to the twentieth century, where it will bring about the reconciliation of Christians, Jews and Muslims. (*The Testimony of the Shroud*, p122.)
11 In fact, the similarity of colour and tone between the body and hair images is distinctly suspicious, and will be dealt with later.
12 Ian Wilson, 'Riddle of the Dead Man's Hand', *Observer Magazine*, 31 January 1988; see also *Fortean Times* no 51, p7.
13 Jean Volckringer, *Le Problème des Empreintes devant la Science* (Libraire du Carmel, Paris,

1942). For photographs of Volckringer's images, see p98 of Wilson, *The Evidence of the Shroud*.

14 Allan Mills, 'The Russell Effect', lecture to the British Society for the Turin Shroud, 23 October 1991.

15 W.C. McCrone, 'Authenticity of Medieval Document Tested by Small-Particle Analysis', *Analytical Chemistry* 48 (1976), pp676–9.

16 T.A. Cahill *et al.*, 'The Vinland Map Revisited: New Compositional Evidence on its Inks and Parchment', *Analytical Chemistry* 59 (1987), pp829–33. A good account of the controversy by Michael T. Shoemaker appeared in *Strange Magazine* no 3 (1988), p22, entitled 'Debunking the Debunkers: The Vinland Map'.

17 Quoted in Shoemaker's article (see note 16 above).

18 Sox, *op. cit.*, p22.

19 McCrone's findings were published in a series of three articles, 'Light-Microscopical Study of the Turin "Shroud"', in *The Microscope*, issues 28 and 29 (1980–81). The first two articles were co-authored with C. Skirius. The full text of McCrone's second report to STURP (rejected by them) is given in Appendix B of Sox's *The Image on the Shroud*.

20 Ian Wilson, *The Evidence of the Shroud*, p63. See also our Appendix.

21 Details of this highly technical debate – much of which went on only in private correspondence and the pages of STURP's internal newsletter – are given in Sox, *The Image on the Shroud*.

22 R. A. Morris, L. A. Schwalbe and J. R. London, 'X-Ray Fluorescence Investigation of the Shroud of Turin', *X-Ray Spectrometry*, vol 9, no 2 (1980).

23 J. H. Heller and A. D. Adler, 'A Chemical Investigation of the Shroud of Turin', *Journal of the Canadian Society of Forensic Science*, Vol 14, no 3 1981.

24 J. H. Heller and A. D. Adler, 'Blood on the Shroud of Turin', *Applied Optics*, vol 19, 12 (August 1980).

25 See Sox, *op. cit.*, p35.

26 Published in the first of the *Microscope* articles (see note 19).

27 Sox, *op. cit.*, p39.

28 Wilson, *The Evidence of the Shroud*, pp87–8.

29 Nickell, *op. cit.*, Chapter 9.

30 See Sox, p88, and César Tort, letter in *Journal of the Society for Psychical Research*, vol 56, No 820 (July 1990), p249.

31 Tort, *ibid.*, p250.

32 For example, Ian Wilson in *The Turin Shroud*, pp277–8.

33 Hoare, *op. cit.*, p73.

34 Freeland's work remains unpublished, but is quoted extensively in Sox's *The Image on the Shroud*.

35 Other objections have been raised regarding the scourge wounds. Joe Nickell (*Inquest on the Shroud of Turin*, p60) points out that there is not enough blood from them. Anthony Harris, in *The Sacred Virgin and the Holy Whore* (Sphere, 1988) makes the same point and also notes that the wounds don't overlap, suggesting they were carefully placed for aesthetic reasons.

36 Quoted in Sox, *op. cit.*, p106.

4 CORRESPONDENTS

1 Quoted in Ian Wilson *Holy Faces, Secret Places*, p33.

2 Michael Baigent, Richard Leigh and Henry Lincoln, *The Messianic Legacy* (Jonathan Cape, 1986) p284.

3 Michael Baigent, Richard Leigh and Henry Lincoln, *The Holy Blood and the Holy Grail* (Jonathan Cape, 1982).

4 'The Lost Treasure of Jerusalem' (1972), 'The Priest, the Painter and the Devil' (1974) and 'The Shadow of the Templars' (1979). All three were part of the BBC's *Chronicle* series.

5 The evidence is summarized in *The Holy Blood and the Holy Grail*, pp349–55.

6 Elaine Pagels, *The Gnostic Gospels* (Weidenfeld & Nicolson, 1980), p84.

7 A complete list of the alleged Grand Masters is given in the appendix of *The Holy Blood and the Holy Grail*. On Leonardo's Grand Mastership, see pp449–50.

8 This collection of documents, deposited in the Bibliothèque Nationale in Paris, forms the major source for Baigent, Leigh and Lincoln's insights into the Priory of Sion's history and beliefs. A list can be found on p467–8 of *The Holy Blood and the Holy Grail*.

9 Robert Anton Wilson, 'The Priory of Sion', *Gnosis Magazine*, 1988.

10 Baigent, Leigh and Lincoln, *The Holy Blood and the Holy Grail*, pp179–83.

11 Letter from Ian Wilson to Clive Prince, 5 June 1991.

12 Phone conversation between Lynn Picknett and Ian Dickinson, January 1994.

13 Kersten and Gruber, *The Jesus Conspiracy*, p64.

5 'FAUST'S ITALIAN BROTHER'

1 Quoted in Peter M. Rinaldi, *The Man in the Shroud* (Futura, 1974), p37.

2 Brent and Rolfe, *op. cit.*, p78.

3 Wilson, *The Evidence of the Shroud*, p82.

4 Currer-Briggs, *op. cit.*, p31.

5 Kersten and Gruber, *op. cit.*, p15.

6 See Chapter 5 of Wilson's *The Evidence of the Shroud* for a discussion of Gabrielli's ideas.

7 Anthony Harris, *The Sacred Virgin and the Holy Whore*, Chapter 3.

8 Augusto Marinoni, 'The Bicycle', appendix in Reti (ed.), *The Unknown Leonardo*, (McGraw-Hill, 1974).

9 Martin Quigley Jnr, *Magic Shadows* (Georgetown University Press, 1948), p32.

10 Quoted in Bramly, *Leonardo: the Artist and the Man* (Michael Joseph, 1992), p443.

11 Baigent, Leigh and Lincoln, *op. cit.*, p126.

12 The story of the Rosicrucian Manifestoes, and the subsequent growth of the movement is told in Frances Yates' *The Rosicrucian Englightenment* (Routledge & Kegan Paul, 1972), which also includes translations of the full texts of the manifestoes. Another excellent account of the Rosicrucian movement can be found in Richard Cavendish, *A History of Magic* (Weidenfeld & Nicolson, 1987).

13 The man generally accepted as being the author of the Rosicrucian Manifestoes, Johann Valentin Andrea, was also responsible for setting up the 'Christian Unions', a network of secret societies devoted to preserving knowledge that was threatened by the Inquisition. Some believe that these groups either became, or at least influenced, the lodge system of Freemasonry. Andrea is claimed by the Priory of Sion as their seventeenth Grand Master. See Baigent, Leigh and Lincoln, *op. cit.*, pp144–8.

14 See C. J. S. Thompson, *The Lure and Romance of Alchemy* (Outlet Book Co., 1991), Chapter XXII.

15 Priory sources claim that the organization was using the name 'Ordre de la Rose-Croix Veritas' as far back as the twelfth century – see *The Holy Blood and the Holy Grail*, p124.

16 See illustration. It is reproduced in several books on the Rosicrucians and the Cabala (see for example, Lewis Spence, *Encyclopedia of the Occult*), but appeared originally in 1593 in a work by B. Arius Montanus entitled *Antiquitatum Judacarum Libri IX*. The British Library copy of this work is reported as having been stolen. We are indebted to Gareth Medway for this information.

17 Frances Yates, *Giordano Bruno and the Hermetic Tradition* (Routledge & Kegan Paul, 1964), p435.

18 The theme of the importance of occult thought in the Renaissance runs through much of Frances Yates' works. The most important in this respect are listed in the bibliography.

19 Frances Yates, *The Art of Memory* (Routledge & Kegan Paul, 1966), p224.

20 Frances Yates, *The Occult Philosophy in the Elizabethan Age* (Routledge & Kegan Paul, 1979), pp40–1.

21 See Chapter 17 of Yates' *The Art of Memory* for a discussion of the influence of occult thought on the growth of scientific method.

22 Yates, *The Art of Memory*, op. cit., pp153, 309–11.

23 Yates, *The Occult Philosophy in the Elizabethan Age*, op. cit., pp14–5.

24 See Gershom Scholem, *Major Trends in Jewish Mysticism* (Thames & Hudson, 1955).

25 Apart from Frances Yates' works, see J. L. Blau, *The Christian Interpretation of the Cabala in the Renaissance* (Columbia University Press, New York, 1944).

26 Yates, *The Art of Memory*, pp37–8.

27 This process is most clearly described in *The Occult Philosophy in the Elizabethan Age*, which, despite its title, traces the growth of the Neoplatonic-Hermetic-Cabalist tradition from its origins through to its influence on Elizabeth's England.

28 Frances Yates, *Giordano Bruno and the Hermetic Tradition*, pp76–7.

29 Yates, *The Occult Philosophy in the Elizabethan Age*, p187.

30 See Yates, *Giordano Bruno and the Hermetic Tradition*, chapters IV and V.

31 Judith Hook, *Lorenzo de Medici* (Hamish Hamilton, 1984), p11.

32 *ibid.*, p12.

33 See the bibliography for sources on Leonardo's life and works.

34 Martin Kemp, *Leonardo Da Vinci* (J. M. Dent & Sons, 1981), p63.

35 Leonardo wrote he would not let his body become 'a tomb for other animals, an inn of the dead . . . a container of corruption' (*Codex Atlanticus*, 76) quoted in Bramly, op. cit., p240.

36 Peter de Rosa, in *Vicars of Christ: The Dark Side of the Papacy* (Bantam Press, 1988) cites cases of people being arrested and tortured by the Inquisition because they didn't like pork!

37 Bramly, op. cit., p13.

38 Quoted in Bramly, p12.

39 Apart from his collaboration with Rustici, Leonardo had a long association with the occultist Tomaso Masini (who used the name Zoroastro de Peretola). It was with Masini that he travelled from Florence to the coast of Milan in 1482. In 1493, Masini joined Leonardo's household and was still recorded as assistant during his return to Florence in 1503. Leonardo's protector and patron in Rome during the period 1513 to 1515 was Giuliano de Medici (the son of Lorenzo and brother of Pope Leo X), who was an alchemist.

40 Bramly, op. cit., p357.

41 Peter Friend, *John Dee* (Routledge & Kegan Paul, 1972).

42 Bramly, op. cit., p387.

43 The French historian Michelet, quoted in Bramly, op. cit., p12.

44 Bramly op. cit. p12.

45 The Cathar 'heresy' did in fact survive in northern Italy long after it had been suppressed in France. See Walter Birks and R. A. Gilbert, *The Treasure of Montségur* (Crucible, 1987), pp73–6.

46 Bramly, op. cit., p48.

47 Maurice Rowden, *Leonardo da Vinci* (Weidenfeld & Nicolson, 1975), p28.

48 Some have made much of an isolated note of Leonardo's – 'Talk about the sea to the man from Genoa' – and suggested that Columbus learned much from the Maestro! Although

the two may have met in Pavia in the 1480s, and despite Leonardo's friendship with the young Amerigo Vespucci, it is unlikely that he had any great influence on the discovery of the New World.

49 Vasari, *Lives of the Artists* (Penguin, 1965), pp208–13.
50 *ibid.*, p270.
51 Baigent, Leigh and Lincoln, *The Holy Blood and the Holy Grail*, pp448–49.
52 Leonardo da Vinci, *Codex Atlanticus* (Ambrosiana, Milan), 159.
53 On the previously unseen side of sheets in the *Codex Atlanticus*, until 1965 glued onto pages of the codex.
54 Bramly, *op. cit.*, p121.
55 Lillian Schwartz, 'Leonardo's Mona Lisa', *Art and Antiques*, January 1987, p50.
56 *The Times*, December 1992.
57 See Neil Powell and Stuart Holyroyd, *Mysteries & Magic* (Bloomsbury Books, 1991) p239.
58 *ibid.*, p144.
59 *ibid.*, p143.
60 Fulcanelli: *Le Mystère de Cathédrals* (Neville Spearman, 1971).
61 See illustration on p878 of Kenneth Rayner Johnson, 'The Image of Perfection', *The Unexplained*, no 45.
62 See Graham Hancock, *The Sign and the Seal* (William Heinemann, 1992), plate 13.
63 Grillot de Givry, *Witchcraft, Magic and Alchemy* (Frederick Publications, 1954).
64 Leonardo da Vinci Manuscript in the Royal Collection, Windsor no 19054v, quoted in Richter (ed.) *The Notebooks of Leonardo da Vinci*.
65 *Mysteries & Magic*, p. 162.
66 De Givry, *op. cit.*, p384.
67 C. J. S. Thompson, *op. cit.*, p10.
68 *ibid.*, pp31–35.
69 Ean Begg, *The Cult of the Black Virgin* (Arkana, 1985), p62.
70 *ibid.*, p14.
71 Richard Leigh and Michael Baigent in *The Unexplained*: 'Virgins with a Pagan Past' no 3, p617; 'The Goddess Behind the Mask' no 5, p114; 'Guardians of the Living Earth' no 7, p154.
72 Begg, *op. cit.*, p220.
73 *ibid.*, p25.
74 Hancock, *op. cit.*, pp58–9.
75 Baigent, Leigh and Lincoln, *op. cit.*, p119.
76 Begg, *op. cit.*, pp25–6.
77 Stan Gooch, 'Murder by Moonlight', *The Unexplained*, no 95, p1906.
78 David Wood, *Genisis* (Baton Press, 1985), p218.
79 Baigent, Leigh and Lincoln, *op. cit.*, p163.
80 Bramly, *op. cit.*, p25.
81 Leonardo da Vinci, Royal Collection, Windsor, no 19054v.

6 THE SHROUD MAFIA

1 In his foreword to *Face to Face with the Turin Shroud*, *op. cit.*, p13.
2 The identification with the Lirey/Turin Shroud was made in M. Perret, 'Essai sur l'Histoire du Sainte Suaire du XIVe au XVIe Siècle', *Mèmoires de l'Académie des sciences, belles lettres et arts de Savoie* IV, 1960.
3 See Noel Currer-Briggs, *The Shroud and the Grail*, (Weidenfeld & Nicolson, 1987) for a painting of the Besançon Shroud. Some believers – for example Monseigneur Arthur Stapylton Barnes in the 1930s – have attempted to argue that the Shroud was actually kept in Besançon Cathedral before being acquired by the de Charnys, and that the

Besançon copy was made at this time. There is not a shred of evidence to support this theory, which is simply a conjecture based on the desire to give the Shroud a pre-Lirey provenance. The Besançon Shroud was a sixteenth century copy – see Wilson, *The Shroud of Turin*, p342.

4 Eg Joe Nickell, *Inquest on the Shroud of Turin*, *op. cit.*, p12.

5 Quoted in Thomas Humber, *The Sacred Shroud* (Pocket Books, New York, 1978), p120.

6 Ian Wilson, 'Mystery of the Missing Mandylion', *BSTS Newsletter* no 36, January 1994, pp13–17.

7 Ian Wilson, *The Evidence of the Shroud*, *op. cit.*, p70.

8 See, for example, the chronology in Ian Wilson's *The Turin Shroud*, Appendix A, which lists all the expositions. We have scoured the Shroud literature and historical records for any reference to public or private showings of the Shroud during this period, and have found none.

9 Archives of the department of Côte-d'Or, no B8440.

10 Wilson, *The Turin Shroud*, *op. cit.*, p244.

11 *ibid.*, p299.

12 The document appears in Chevalier's *Étude Critique* (1900). Sixtus' account refers only to the Shroud being 'preserved with great devotion' by the Savoys, with no details as to where or how it is was kept.

13 The following catalogue of papal corruption is taken from several sources, notably Peter de Rosa, *Vicars of Christ* (Bantam Press, 1988) and *The Popes*, ed. Eric John (Burns & Oates, 1964).

14 Quoted in de Rosa, *op. cit.*, p141.

15 Colin Wilson, *A Criminal History of Mankind* (Granada, 1984) p345.

16 Ian Wilson, *The Turin Shroud*, *op. cit.*, p246.

17 Judith Hook, *op. cit.*

18 Maurice Rowden, *Leonardo da Vinci*, p206.

19 *Codex of the Earl of Leicester* (kept at Holkham Hall, Norfolk), 10v, and the *Codex Atlanticus op. cit.*, 87v. See *The Notebooks of Leonardo da Vinci*, *op. cit.*, p333.

20 Ladislao Reti (ed.), *The Unknown Leonardo* (McGraw-Hill, 1974), p59. This suspicious event was also noted by Antony Harris in *The Sacred Virgin and the Holy Whore*.

21 Sox, *op. cit.*, p31.

22 Ian Wilson, *The Evidence of the Shroud*, p70.

23 Frank Smyth, 'Is this the Face of Christ?', *The Unexplained*, no 18.

24 By convention, the Templar Geoffrey's family name is spelt 'Charnay'. For consistency, we have used the 'Charny' spelling throughout this chapter. There is no significance in the different spelling, as there was no convention in fourteenth-century records, and the name appears in many other variations in documents of the period.

25 Wilson, *The Turin Shroud*, pp222–3.

26 *ibid.*, pp200–15.

27 *ibid.*, Chapter 18.

28 See Barber, *op. cit.*, and Chapters 3 and 4 of Peter Partner, *op. cit.*

29 Noel Currer-Briggs, *op. cit.*, pp90–1.

30 Kersten and Gruber, *op. cit.*, p203.

31 The Templecombe panel is pictured in Plate 33 in Wilson, *The Evidence of the Shroud*. Wilson's linking of the panel with the Templars is in *The Turin Shroud*, pp208–9.

32 Noel Currer-Briggs, *op. cit.*, Chapter 1.

33 It is even possible that Jacques de Molay himself (whose ancestry is a matter of dispute among historians) may have been related to the Charny and Vergy families, being the son of Henri de Vergy, the great-grandfather of Geoffrey de Charny's (of Lirey) wife, see Currer-Briggs, *op. cit.*, p111.

34 Currer-Briggs, *op. cit.*, p114.

35 ibid., p150.
36 For an insider's account of the Fourth Crusade, see Geoffrey de Villehardouin, op. cit.
37 See M. R. B. Shaw's introduction to Chronicles of the Crusades, op. cit., pp12–3.
38 Baigent, Leigh and Lincoln, op. cit., pp116–19.
39 The standard historical account of the early days of the Templars is entirely based on William of Tyre's A History of Deeds Done Beyond the Sea, written between 1175 and 1185.
40 Baigent, Leigh and Lincoln, op. cit., p85.
41 Graham Hancock, op. cit., Chapter 5.
42 Baigent, Leigh and Lincoln, op. cit., pp85–6.
43 ibid., p88.
44 ibid., p88.
45 Currer-Briggs, op. cit., p135.
46 ibid., p152.
47 ibid., p176.
48 ibid., p34.
49 Baigent, Leigh and Lincoln, op. cit., p316.
50 Reproduced in genealogical Table 4 in The Holy Blood and the Holy Grail, based on Priory documents published in 1956 in Geneva.
51 The Kingdom of Burgundy covered part of what is now France, Switzerland and northern Italy.
52 Christopher Cope, op. cit., pp35–46.
53 ibid., p103.
54 ibid., pp152–3.
55 Baigent, Leigh and Lincoln, op. cit., pp138–44.
56 ibid., pp141–2.
57 See entry for Innocent VIII, The Popes by Eric John (Burns & Oates, 1964).
58 The Cathars, or Albigensians, were one of the most influential and widespread of all the 'heretical' groups of 12th and 13th centuries. Centred on the south-west of France, they practised sexual equality and vegetarianism and challenged many of the fundamental beliefs and practices of the Church. (They believed in a form of reincarnation, for example.) The Pope declared a crusade against them and all but a handful were wiped out by the year 1244, in what amounted to the first example of genocide in Europe. (See J. Sumption, The Albigensian Crusade (Faber & Faber, 1978) and Walter Birks and R. A. Gilbert, The Treasure of Montségur (Crucible, 1987).
59 Archive Nationale, JJ77, no 395.

7 GETTING THE MEASURE OF SHROUDMAN

1 We also discussed the possibility of computer-matching the images with the help of Lillian Schwartz herself when she visited London in the summer of 1993. Over dinner with Lillian and her husband Jack, and our colleague Tony Pritchett – who used to work with Lillian at the Bell Laboratories in America – we outlined our theory and showed her pictures of the Shroud and portraits of Leonardo. Although captivated by the idea – she is a Leonardophile – she, too, pointed out the near-impossibility of proving the connection given the available portraits.
2 Bramly, op. cit., p17. Aficionados of Rennes-le-Château lore might also be amused by some word-play with the author's name. Taking the most obvious associations (in English) we get blue serge and bramley apple. Non-aficionados won't have the faintest idea what we are talking about . . .
3 Bramly, op. cit., p422, citing Kenneth Clark.
4 Letter to Clive Prince, 12 April 1991.
5 During questions at Lynn Picknett's talk 'Did Leonardo da Vinci Fake the Turin Shroud?',

London Earth Mysteries Circle, 9 April 1991.

6 Isabel Piczek, 'The Turin Shroud: Why It Cannot Be A Painting', lecture to the British Society for the Turin Shroud, 23 November 1992.

7 Quoted in Robert K. Wilcox, *Shroud*, pp30–31.

8 Nickell, *op. cit.*, p109.

9 Thomas Humber, *The Fifth Gospel* (Pocket Books, New York, 1974), p29.

10 Rodney Hoare, *op. cit.*, p75.

11 Peter de Rosa, *op. cit.*, p3.

12 There may in fact be signs that the hands moved during the creation of the photographic image. The disproportionate length of the man's right arm (by that we mean the arm with the hand partially covered by the other hand) has long puzzled the Shroudies. Examining this arm, it can be seen that the apparent elongation is due to the fingers being unnaturally long. Closer study shows that there are traces of the fingers ending where we would expect them to, as if this hand had been 'double-exposed'. As the photographic process used by Leonardo must have needed an exposure of several hours if the arm had moved such an effect would result, especially if the elbow had moved away from the 'camera' rather than out from the body.

13 Nickell, *op. cit.*, p86.

14 Don Devan, John Jackson and Eric Jumper, 'Computer Related Investigations of the Holy Shroud'; John Jackson, Eric Jumper, William Mottern and Kenneth Stevenson, 'The Three-Dimensional Image on Jesus' Burial Cloth; both in *Proceedings of the 1977 United States Conference of Research on the Shroud of Turin*, ed. Kenneth E. Stevenson (Holy Shroud Guild, New York, 1977).

15 Kersten and Gruber, *op. cit.*, p297.

16 The following quotes are from Nickell, *op. cit.*, pp88–92.

17 Wilson, *The Turin Shroud*, p258.

18 Wilson, *The Evidence of the Shroud*, pp47–9.

19 Quoted in David Sox, *The Image on the Shroud*, pp106–7.

20 Leo Vala, *Amateur Photographer*, March 1967. Vala's sculpture – pictured, for example, in Robert K. Wilcox's *Shroud* – vividly illustrates the unnaturalness of the hairline and the foreshortening of the forehead.

8 POSITIVE DEVELOPMENTS

1 Library of the Institut de France (Manuscript A), quoted in Ladislao Reti (ed.), *The Unknown Leonardo* (McGraw-Hill, 1974).

2 *Codex* of the Earl of Leicester, 22, quoted in Bramly, *op. cit.*, p313.

3 See Richter, *op. cit.*, pp107–16.

4 Manuscript C, Library of the Institut de France, cited in Bramly, *op. cit.*, p263.

5 Josef Maria Eder, *History of Photography* (Columbia University Press, 1945).

6 Rowden, *op. cit.*, p105.

7 'The Spirit of the Shroud', *The Times*, 14 October 1988.

8 Brent and Rolfe, *op. cit.*, pp130–4.

9 In a treatise entitled *Perpectiva Communis*.

10 See Eder, *op. cit.*

11 *Codex Atlanticus*, Vol D, folio 8. See Richter, *op. cit.*, p113.

12 Manuscript D, Library of the Institut de France. See Richter, *op. cit.*, p115.

13 See Eder, *op. cit.*

14 Martin Quigley Jr, *Magic Shadows* (Georgetown University Press, Washington DC, 1948).

15 Rowden. *op. cit.*, p117.

16 The following information on early photography is taken from various sources – see bibliography.

17 Letter to Clive Prince, 10 October 1991.

18 Pliny, *Natural History* xxxiii, 55, 3, discussed in Eder's *History of Photography, op. cit.*

19 See Eder, *op. cit.*

20 *ibid.*, p15.

21 C.B. Neblette, *Photography: Its Materials and Processes*, sixth edition (Van Nostrand Reinhold, New York, 1962), p1.

22 Leslie Stroebel and Richard Zakia (eds.), *The Focal Encyclopaedia of Photography* third edition (Focal Press, 1993).

23 Eder, *op. cit.*, p77.

24 *Forster Codex I*, Victoria & Albert Museum, 44v.

25 See Bramly, *op. cit.*, pp386–7.

26 The first patented process exploiting this principle was that of Scot Mungo Ponton in 1839. There were many variations of the basic process – for example, the gum-bichromate process, Artigue's process, and the carbon process. The method led to the development of photo-mechanical printing processes, allowing the reproduction of photographs in print, as it could be used to create printing blocks from photographs.

27 The acacia is sacred to the Priory of Sion.

28 Gelatin reacts to ultraviolet light on its own, without the addition of chemical sensitizers. However (although we have not tried it experimentally), the reaction would certainly be much slower when unsensitized, to the point that exposure times become impractical.

29 *The Kirk-Othmer Encyclopedia of Chemical Terminology*, edited by Martin Gragson (John Wiley & Sons, New York, 1985), p277.

30 *Codex Atlanticus*, 313v. See Serge Bramly, *op. cit.*, p372. Leonardo gives part of the recipe, which consists, significantly, of egg-white, glue and several vegetable dyes.

31 Based on the manufacturer's technical data. Exact calculations are difficult because of the many variables involved, such as the number of lamps used, the distances between lamp and subject and between subject and camera, the reflectivity of the subject etc.

32 This determines the elements present in an object by measuring the wave lengths of a specific sort of energy (light, X-rays etc) reflected from it.

9 CONSPIRACIES AND CONCLUSIONS

1 Manuscript F in the Institut de France, 5v.

2 'Was the Shroud the Tablecloth of the Last Supper?', BSTS *Newsletter* no 35, September 1993, p9.

3 Nickell, *op. cit.*, pp115–16.

4 Bramly, *op. cit.*, pp262–3.

5 Ean Begg, *op. cit.*, pp99–100.

6 *ibid.*, pp145–49.

7 Birgent, Leigh and Lincoln, *The Holy Blood and the Holy Grail*, p64.

8 *ibid.*, p80.

9 For example, Geza Vermes in his classic study *Jesus the Jew* (Collins, 1973), p31: 'The aim of the Gospel writers was . . . to give an impression of friendship and mutual esteem, but their attempts smack of superficiality and . . . suggest that . . . sentiments of rivalry between the two groups were not absent.'

10 Acts 19:1–5.

11 A. N. Wilson, *Jesus* (Sinclair Stevenson, 1992).

12 Karl W. Luckert, *Egypt Light and Hebrew Fire* (State University of New York Press, 1988).

13 See Geoffrey Ashe, *The Virgin* (Arkana, 1976).

14 See entry on 'Isis', *Man, Myth & Magic* (1971).

15 Begg, *op. cit.*, pp106–08.

16 *ibid.*, p145–49.

APPENDIX: LYNN PICKNETT, CLIVE PRINCE AND THE BRITISH SOCIETY FOR THE
TURIN SHROUD

1 BSTS Newsletter, no 28, May 1991.
2 As we have seen, I (Lynn) explained to Ian Wilson that I had experimented with
   automatic writing, and that some of the resulting squiggles were signed 'Leonardo'. I was
   to keep up the experimenting as a novelty only, on an irregular basis, for a few months
   after that conversation took place, eventually transferring the stream-of-consciousness
   technique to my word processor. In the end, however, there seemed no point in
   continuing: I had better things to do with my time.
       Used extensively as a therapeutic tool by orthodox psychologists, 'automatic' writing
   is almost always the product of the unconscious mind. You simply hold a pen or pencil
   lightly against a piece of paper, distract yourself, and wait for the squiggles to appear.
   The result is usually a mixture of repeated single letters, artistic flourishes, names and
   – if one is lucky – a few coherent sentences that obviously reflect preoccupations and
   thoughts.
       Those of a more other-worldly frame of mind frequently ascribe the origins of such
   outpourings to spirits of the dead: a very small proportion of all automatic writing does
   apparently contain information from an unexplained source. As psychical researchers of
   many years' standing, however, we have to say that neither of us has ever come across
   any such scripts that even begin to contain verifiable 'spirit' messages, and the pathetic
   'Leonardo' material was certainly not of that ilk. It was always in colloquial English –
   my own turn of phrase being noticeable in it – and was written in a large, scrawling
   hand not only totally unlike mine, but also poles apart from the energetic Florentinian
   script of Leonardo himself. And it was never in mirror-writing!
       We were, however, momentarily thrown into panic by a very real telephone call from
   one 'Leo Vinci'. However, despite the promising name, this turned out to be the pen
   name of a well-respected writer on occult matters who we had forgotten we had written
   to some months before about background material for this book. Although disappointing
   that our caller was resolutely in the flesh, it was a relief to discover that this was not
   abrupt proof that those allegations of mediumship were right after all.
       Apart from the slurs of the BSTS, the only other legacy from this phase is my nickname
   of 'Lynndear', by which I was always addressed in the scripts, for reasons known only to
   my quirky unconscious mind.
3 Fortean Times, no 71, November 1993, p65.
4 Letter from Ian Wilson to Lynn Picknett, 11 June 1990.
5 Letter from Ian Wilson to Clive Prince, 18 April 1991.
6 Norma Weller, 'Concerning the Meeting on May 27 1992', BSTS Newsletter no 33,
   February 1993.
7 Letter from Michael Clift to Clive Prince, 21 February 1993.
8 Evening Standard, 25 March 1993.
9 Letter from Rodney Hoare to Lynn Picknett, 12 April 1993.
10 Letter from Rodney Hoare to Clive Prince, 29 May 1993.
11 Letter from Rodney Hoare to Clive Prince, 28 June 1993.

SELECT BIBLIOGRAPHY

Baigent, Michael and Richard Leigh, *The Temple and the Lodge* (Jonathan Cape, 1989)

Baigent, Michael, Richard Leigh and Henry Lincoln, *The Holy Blood and the Holy Grail* (Jonathan Cape, 1982); *The Messianic Legacy* (Jonathan Cape, 1986)

Barbet, Pierre, *A Doctor At Calvary*, trans. by the Earl of Wicklow (Image Books, New York, 1963); originally published as *La Passion de N-S Jesus Christ selon le Chirurgien* (Dillen & Cie, France, 1950)

Begg, Ean, *The Cult of the Black Virgin* (Arkana, 1985)

Blau, J. H., *The Christian Interpretation of the Cabala in the Renaissance* (Columbia University Press, 1944)

Boussel, Patrice, *Leonardo da Vinci* (Tiger Books, 1992)

Bramly, Serge, *Leonardo: The Artist and the Man* (Michael Joseph, 1992); originally published as *Leonardo de Vinci* (Editions Jean-Claude Lattés, Paris, 1988)

Brent, Peter and David Rolfe, *The Silent Witness* (Futura, 1978)

Brucker, Gene A., *Renaissance Florence* (John Wiley & Sons, 1969)

Burman, Edward, *The Templars: Knights of God* (Crucible, 1986)

Cameron, Averil, *The Sceptic and the Shroud* (King's College, London, 1980)

Cavendish, Richard, *A History of Magic* (Weidenfeld & Nicolson, 1987)

Chevalier, Ulysses, *Étude Critique Sur L'origine du Sainte Suaire de Lirey-Chambéry-Turin* (A. Picard, Paris, 1900)

Clark, Kenneth, *Leonardo da Vinci* (Cambridge University Press, 1940)

Coe, Brian and Mark Haworth-Booth, *A Guide to Early Photographic Processes* (Victoria and Albert Museum, 1983)

Cope, Christopher, *Phoenix Frustrated: The Lost Kingdom of Burgundy* (Constable, 1986)

Currer-Briggs, Noel, *The Shroud and the Grail* (Weidenfeld & Nicolson, 1987)

De Clari, Robert, *The Conquest of Constantinople*, trans. by E. H. McNeal (Columbia University Press, New York, 1936)

De Joinville, Jean, *The Life of St Louis*, trans. and ed. by M. R. B. Shaw in *Chronicles of the Crusades* (Penguin, 1963.)

de Rosa, Peter, *Vicars of Christ: The Dark Side of the Papacy* (Bantam Press, 1988)

De Villehardouin, Geoffrey, *The Conquest of Constantinople*, trans. and ed. by M. R. B. Shaw in *Chronicles of the Crusades* (Penguin, 1963)

Doerner, Max, *The Materials of the Artist* (Rupert Hart-Davis, 1969)

Eder, Josef Maria, *History of Photography*, trans. by Edward Epstean (Columbia University Press, New York, 1945)

Fulcanelli, *The Mystery of the Cathedrals* (Neville Spearman, 1971)

Haeffner, Mark, *The Dictionary of Alchemy* (Aquarian Press, 1991)

Hancock, Graham, *The Sign and the Seal* (William Heinnemann, 1992)

Harris, Anthony, *The Sacred Virgin and the Holy Whore* (Sphere, 1988)

Harris, Robert, *Selling Hitler* (Faber and Faber Ltd, 1986)

Heller, John, *Report on the Shroud of Turin*, (Houghton Mifflin, Boston, 1983)

Hoare, Rodney, *A Piece of Cloth* (Aquarian Press, 1984); *The Testimony of the Shroud* (Quartet, 1978); *The Turin Shroud Is Genuine* (Souvenir Press, 1994)

Holroyd, Stuart and Neil Powell, *Mysteries of Magic* (Bloomsbury Books 1991)

Hook, Judith, *Lorenzo de Medici* (Hamish Hamilton, 1984)

Howard, Michael, *The Occult Conspiracy* (Rider, 1989)

Howarth, Stephen, *The Knights Templar* (William Collins, 1982)

Humber, Thomas, *The Fifth Gospel* (Pocket Books, New York, 1974)

Jennings, Peter (ed.), *Face to Face with the Turin Shroud* (Mayhew-McCrimmon & A. R. Mowbray, 1978)

John, Eric (ed), *The Popes* (Burns & Oates, 1964)

Katz, Robert, *The Fall of the House of Savoy* (George Allen & Unwin, 1972)

Kemp, Martin, *Leonardo da Vinci* (J. M. Dent & Sons, 1981)

Kersten, Holger and Elmar R. Gruber, *The Jesus Conspiracy* (Element Books, 1994); originally published as *Das Jesus Komplott* (Langen Verlag, Munich, 1992).

Knight, Gareth, *The Rose Cross and the Goddess* (Aquarian Press, 1985)

Kosar, Jaromir, *Light-Sensitive Systems* (John Wiley & Sons, New York, 1965)

Leonardo da Vinci, *The Literary Works of Leonardo da Vinci*, ed. by Jean Paul Richter (Oxford University Press, 1939)

Leonardo da Vinci, *The Notebooks of Leonardo da Vinci*, selected and edited by Irma A. Richter (Oxford University Press, 1952)

Mayer, Hans Edehard, *The Crusades* trans. by John Gillingham (Oxford University Press, 1972)

Neblette, C. B., *Photography: its Materials and Processes*, sixth edition, (Van Nostrand Reinhold, New York, 1962)

Nickell, Joe, *Inquest on the Shroud of Turin* (Prometheus (USA), 1983, revised edition: Prometheus (USA), 1987)

Partner, Peter, *The Murdered Magicians: The Templars and Their Myth*, (Oxford University Press, 1981)

Picknett, Lynn, *The Encyclopaedia of the Paranormal* (Macmillan, 1990)

Quigley Jr, Martin, *Magic Shadows*, (Georgetown University Press, Washington DC, 1948)

Reti, Ladislao (ed.), *The Unknown Leonardo* (McGraw-Hill, 1974)

Rinaldi, Peter M., *The Man In The Shroud* (Futura, 1974)

Robinson, John J., *Born in Blood* (Century, 1990)

Rowden, Maurice, *Leonardo da Vinci* (Weidenfield & Nicolson, 1975)

Seward, Desmond, *Prince of the Renaissance: the Life of François I* (Constable, 1973)

Siren, Osvald, *Leonardo da Vinci: The Artist and the Man* (Oxford University Press, 1916.)

Stevenson, K. and G. Habermas, *Verdict on the Shroud* (Servant, Michigan, 1981)

Stroebel, Leslie and Richard Zakis (eds.), *The Focal Encyclopaedia of Photography* (Focal Press, 1993)

Sox, H. David, *The Image on the Shroud* (Unwin, 1981)

Thompson, C.J.S., *The Lure and Romance of Alchemy* (Bell Publishing Company, New York, 1990)

Treece, Henry, *The Crusaders* (Bodley Head, 1962)

Upton-Ward, J.M., *The Rule of the Templars* (Boydell Press, 1992)

Vasari, Giorgio, *Lives of the Artists*, trans. by George Bull (Penguin Books, 1965)

Vignon, Paul, *La Saint Suaire de Turin devant la Science, L'Archeologie, L'Histoire, L'iconographie, la Logique* (Masson, Paris, 1939); *The Shroud of Christ* (Constable, 1902)

Waite, A.E., *The Brotherhood of the Rosy Cross* (Rider & Co, 1924)

Walsh, John, *The Shroud* (W.H. Allen, 1963)

Wilcox, Robert K., *Shroud* (Corgi, 1977)

Wilson, A.N., *Jesus* (Sinclair-Stevenson, 1992)

Wilson, Ian, *The Evidence of the Shroud* (Michael O'Mara, 1986); *Holy Faces, Secret Places* (Doubleday, 1991); *The Turin Shroud* (Victor Gollancz, 1978, Revised edition: Penguin, 1979)

Yates, Frances, *Giordano Bruno and the Hermetic Tradition* (Routledge & Kegan Paul, 1964); *The Occult Philosophy in the Elizabethan Age* (Routledge & Kegan Paul 1979); *The Rosicrucian Enlightenment* (Routledge & Kegan Paul, 1972); *The Art of Memory* (Routledge & Kegan Paul, 1966)

INDEX